Hell Week is not something a participant remembers clearly; the instructors don't let the trainees sleep. When we were allowed to lie down, a few short minutes later the instructors ran in beating trash-can lids with clubs, blowing whistles, and throwing M-80s, cherry bomb–size explosives. We were kept tired, wet, and cold. We ran everywhere, with sand in our shoes, crotch, and ears and between our buttocks. My head was beaten down into my shoulders, because we carried that damn boat everywhere on the tops of our heads. For me, Hell Week remains a fog, with a few clear snapshotlike memories. . . .

CLASS-29

The Making of U.S. Navy SEALs

John Carl Roat

BALLANTINE BOOKS • NEW YORK

A Ballantine Book
Published by The Ballantine Publishing Group
Copyright © 1998, 2000 by John Carl Roat

All rights reserved under International and Pan-American Copyright Conventions. Published in the United States by The Ballantine Publishing Group, a division of Random House, Inc., New York, and simultaneously in Canada by Random House of Canada Limited, Toronto. Originally published in different form by Janke Humphries Hawes Publishers in 1998.

Ballantine and colophon are registered trademarks of Random House, Inc.

www.randomhouse.com/BB/

Library of Congress Catalog Card Number: 99-91680

ISBN 0-8041-1893-0

Manufactured in the United States of America

First Ballantine Edition: March 2000

10   9   8   7   6   5   4   3   2   1

This book is dedicated to

Frank and Mary Roat,
they traveled through life with grace,
in love with God and one another

**To my classmates
and instructors:
THANK YOU!**

IN MEMORIAM

Our classmates:

Raymond A. Fauls Jr.
Leroy C. Geiger
Clarence T. Risher III
Joseph H. Camp
George E. Leasure Jr.

CONTENTS

FORWARD AND BACKWARD

To quote Rush Limbaugh, "War is about killing people and breaking things." I have done it; war is not a lot of fun, and intellectually there is little to defend the practice. Notice I did not say nothing, I said "little," and it is a damn *big* little.

It is this simple: If they are willing to kill people and break things, and you are not, they win. It is an ugly fact of human nature that if someone will not fight for what is his, he will lose it. This book is about men who choose to be ready to fight. Next to my wife and children, I am more proud of becoming a member of that group of men than of anything else I've done in my life.

Around fourth grade, I saw a movie called *The Frogmen* starring Richard Widmark. When I walked out of that theater, my life's ambition was firmly fixed in every cell of my body. You could have offered me God's job, the presidency, anything—and I would have turned it down; I was going to be a United States Navy Frogman.

This book is about the test to become a Frogman, the men I took it with, and the men who gave it to us. We were tested by the best, and I thank them. Our instructors had all taken the test; they knew the pain and the reasons for all the apparent craziness. In a way, the test was just about finding those who would not take the easy way out. When your back is to the wall, it is easy to fight. The real question is, what do you do when there *is* an easy way out?

People like those described here stand ready to do the bad business of war. To some they may seem sadistic, antiquated warmongers. But think about what you have to *lose*. Now ask yourself this simple question, "When someone wants to break my things and kill me, who do I want watching my back?"

Training is the *test*!

INTRODUCTION

Little Creek Naval Amphibious Base was home to UDT-21, UDT-22, and the East Coast UDT Replacement Training Unit. I was nineteen and standing at the threshold of my life's ambition, being a United States Navy Frogman. I knew the only dangers to my not making it through training were injury or being thrown out. Quitting was not an option; I had never allowed myself to think that if things got too bad, I would quit. The only options I considered were I would complete training, my body would get broken, or the instructors would throw me out.

The only real worry I had was the being-thrown-out thing. I had no history of quitting or broken bones. I had been the kind of child who gave mothers gray hair well before their time. My mom and dad, two very strong, loving people, had found it very difficult to get me to stop doing what I wanted to do. What I did have was a short history of being thrown out of things—the church choir, Boy Scouts, and two California high schools.

True, my being thrown out of the church choir was due to the fact the choir director had a bad head cold the day I tried out for choir. His dropping me from the choir had saved the whole El Segundo Methodist congregation a lot of ear pain on Sunday mornings. Getting thrown out of the Boy Scouts and the two high schools I had accomplished by stubbornly following my own rules. I will note that I was not kicked out of El Segundo High until after water polo season; we were state champs. I was not thrown out of Westchester High until swimming season was complete; I swam breaststroke on the four hundred medley relay. Those negative thoughts had only lightly grazed my teenage brain.

Everything I have written is how I see it now, after years of hindsight. In those days, I didn't think many things out, I just did. When training started, I didn't think at all. I saw, I reacted, and I now believe those that made it through the six months did the same. The instructors wanted men out the backside of that training who *did not quit*, but that wasn't enough. We had to be willing to give any little energy we had managed to hoard to our class-mates. Those two things came from the core; under stress we didn't have time to think them out. They were there, or they were not. Our instructors' whole purpose was to keep that stress applied, day after day, week after week, month after month.

My hope is to describe training accurately. The rest of my life, I have judged myself and others by the standard of those months and the strength of the men involved. Know that I cherish every second of training; it is with me for life. Each of the men who suffered the six months of UDT RT-29* is part of my heart, and I love them all.

I'm going to take the instructors' two-and-a-half-page synopsis of our class and use *each phase section* as a header for what I have to say about *that* phase of training.

*Underwater Demolition Team, Replacement Training (class)-29.

PHASE ONE

Class XXIX convened 2 January and is to graduate 28 June. The class commenced with 134 students; of this total 16 were U.S. naval officers, 5 were foreign officers representing Greece, Belgium, Norway, Pakistan, and the Netherlands. There were 109 U.S. Navy enlisted and 4 Netherlands enlisted men. The first phase of training consisted of two weeks of physical preconditioning. Upon completion of the phase, 18 officers and 76 enlisted men remained to begin actual UDT training.

In truth, it was physical preconditioning; the instructors' objective was to put the body in the condition of *pain*. I had thought I knew a lot about UDT training. I knew most classes started with thirty or fewer. Why was our class so big? Our first formation was a joke; no one knew which end was up. We had been issued used green fatigues that didn't fit and "surveyed" boondockers, that is, worn-out work boots.

When we fell in, there was no military bearing, and Instructor Waddell just loved it. He welcomed us with, "Hit the deck! Start pushing Virginia away!" We had no idea what he was talking about. Waddell quickly taught us a position in which we would spend a good part of the next six months. You start by kicking both feet out behind you, your arms thrown straight out in front of your chest. If you land properly, you have "hit the deck." You are now in a lovely position called the "lean and rest." Your body is parallel to the ground, *no sag,* and you are held up by your extended arms and the tips of your toes—that's the hit-the-deck part. Instructor Waddell gave us our first educational opportunity: "Hit the deck!" and "On your feet!" over and over, until we could do it as a group. When he had us worked into a good sweat, he put us at the lean and rest, then walked through the ranks telling us what low-life scum we were. Waddell was particularly good at degrading officers—but with respect. Whatever he said to them, he always added a respectful, "sir." When he determined that we had mastered the lean and rest, he gave us a class in push Virginia away, which meant lower yourself until your chest is no more than one fist-height from the ground, then raise yourself to the starting position, repeat until ordered to stop or you can't do it any more.

Chief Engineman Bernie Waddell was six foot two or three, with large head, shoulders, and arms. The scariest thing about Waddell was his eyes; you knew he could see through steel. Those eyes said "I will hurt you." Bernie was a rich brown color, a black man of power in the south of the sixties. He handled all that race bullshit the first formation with just the power of his presence. Instructor Waddell let every one of us know that we were inferior beings. He spoke very rudely about the possibility of any of us making it through training. He made us believe he was the mountain between us and the Teams and that he would make us suffer to cross over. Instructor Waddell would more than live up to the first impression he gave us! Capt. Larry Bailey, a trainee from another class, said, "Waddell was the instructor's instructor, and those of us who toiled under him learned to summon up physical and mental reserves previously untapped."

That first day, we ran everywhere, an undisciplined snake dance of spastics. Guys were running over each other, stepping on each other's heels, always in each other's way. The instructors kept everyone off base. I think they were watching the officers to see who would step forward and organize the mess. For me the first officer who stood out of the background was Lt. (jg) Richard "Rick" Shea. The first thing that came to my mind when I heard him was that he should have been a disk jockey; he talked like he was on the radio. I called him Swing and Sway with Rick Shea. Mr. Shea was five foot seven or eight of tightly packed, laid-back energy. The only thing Swing and Sway wanted to organize was a party. He would be one of the three guys who kept me laughing throughout training.

Most of us enlisted men enjoyed seeing the officers get dumped on because usually it was the officers who dumped on us. Instructor Waddell and Ens. David Janke seemed to form an instant bond; Waddell loved to say Mr. Janke's name. He would drag out the word "mister," pronouncing it something like Missster Janke. They had long, one-sided conversations while Ensign Janke pushed Virginia away. David is one of those guys you just have to like, and Waddell did. He liked to give Janke push-ups, squat jumps, eight-count body builders, and the dreaded duckwalk. I suspect I'm not the only one who enjoyed Janke and Waddell's conversations; after all, if Waddell was fucking with Janke, he wasn't fucking with me.

The third officer who came into focus for me was Ens. James M. Hawes. When I saw him, I thought he looked like a college professor. He should have had a pipe in his mouth. Hawes became a big part of the reason I made it through training; he passed energy to me with his voice. I was in his boat crew throughout training. There is no more important thing in training than your boat crew; if you don't learn to work as a team, carry your share of the boat, the rest of the crew will make sure you're gone. Hawes was not an open person. I don't mean that he was sneaky, but like a good poker player, he didn't let you see on his face what was on his mind. He would blend in, almost disappear, then, when needed, *bam!,* he was right there doing whatever needed to be done. Ensign Hawes was an officer in the best sense of the word; he always took care of his men, even when he knew damn well the instructors would make him pay. Hawes could look broken-down, decrepit, dilapidated, extremely dingy, and still project strength with his voice. I had never done well in a group unless I'd had a good leader. In Hawes I had one—tough, demanding, always willing to put his ass where he would put yours.

The first guy I got tight with was Jack Lynch. He had a quick, funny mind and mouth. God bless him; he could make the whole class laugh at our pain. Jack and I started harassing each other from day one, kept it up right through training, and on into the teams. I think Jack needed to be mad every once in a while, deep down pissed off, and I have always been able to piss him off. What are friends for if not to help you through life?

From day one, the instructors started getting us in the condition of pain and introducing us to all their tools. The sand, running in sand. They loved to get us wet, roll us in the sand, then run us up and down, over and over, the biggest sand dune around. The damn thing even had a name, Mount Suribachi. At times, we were required to carry sand up the damn thing and deposit it at the summit; we didn't want it to get smaller, did we? Strange, I had spent a good part of my youth with sand in my shoes and every other uncomfortable place I can think of, but that damn mountain of sand was the worst thing they could do to me. Our first assault on Suribachi was gut-wrenching, but worse was the 134 men who were falling all over each other. Sand was kicked down my throat while I gasped for breath; trainees stepped on each other's feet and hands. If I remember right, that's where the first man quit.

The obstacle course was another of the instructors' tools of pain. So was just getting there. The instructors never took the shortest route anywhere. We might run *past* the obstacle course a couple times before we actually arrived at it. On the third or fourth day of training, I was trying to improve my time on the course when I scared the shit out of myself and came very close to wiping myself out of training. One of the obstacles was a cargo net stretched between two large trees. The top of the net was suspended from a taut cable about fifty feet up. We went up one side, over the top, and down the other. Simple. I had seen one of the faster guys kind of roll over the top. It looked much faster than getting one leg over, then the other. I went up the net. When my chest was level with the cable, I reached across the top, put my chest hard against the cable, pulled and twisted at the same time. As I went over the top, I lost my grip. Oh well. The only thing that saved me was my leg's getting caught in the net about halfway down. I wasn't hurt, but that net had put the fear of God in me; I knew that if I'd fallen all the way to the pit, training would have been over.

Worse was to come, back at the obstacle course that afternoon. I went through the obstacles before the cargo net with no problem. I had a plan. It is amazing how dumb fear can make you. My plan was simple: I would climb the net close to one of the tree trunks, go to the top, but never cross it, just come back down the same side. My stinking thinking had been, there were so many trainees climbing that the instructors would never notice. It worked; I got off the net, stepped around the tree, and finished the rest of the obstacles. Home free! Not quite.

Instructor Tom Blais had me assume the lean and rest and began telling me a long story. At least judging by my arms, it had been very long. It seemed that he had observed my fall early in the day and had a personal interest in helping me overcome my fear of the top of that net.

Damage control CPO Tom Blais looked like he should have been a Viking; Tom would have fit right in with a pointed helmet with horns on his big head, furs hanging down off wide shoulders over his thick chest, one of those big double-edged swords in his hands. He always spoke calmly, as if he were speaking to errant but well-loved children. Tom Blais was a religious man, the only instructor who didn't have a list of profanity to use in describing our shortcomings. He always made the pain he was inflicting sound like the only reasonable course of action. I found out later why my fall halfway down the net had gained so much of Instructor Blais's attention. About a year before, *he* had fallen off the net top all the way to the pit. He had gotten up and finished the course. Then he spent a couple of weeks in the hospital.

All I knew at the time was I had put myself in deep shit, my arms ached trying to hold my body rigid, and Blais was somehow going to make me pay. The rest of the Class-29 had left for the chow hall. I think being alone at the obstacle course with Instructor Blais scared me more than the top of that fucking net. He gave me a special class on going over the top of the net, again and again, time after time. That day, I learned the lesson: Do not cheat. Pain is one of God's teaching tools, and Instructor Tom Blais had used it effectively.

Jack Lynch found Tom McCutchan right away. Jack was always trying to find out what was going on. Well, McCutchan had finished everything but the last two weeks of UDT training, then, with just two weeks to go, broke his leg while getting off a truck. That they had made him start all over was not a pleasant thought. We had just started training, but I was dead sure I didn't want to do one damn day over.

McCutchan was a good guy, but all through training he said things like, "You think this is bad, you should see what is coming next." That drove me nuts; all I wanted to think about was getting past right now. The funny thing was, if McCutchan didn't tell me what was next, I asked. It was like having a harassment factor for the future: as if we didn't have enough to worry about "right now," we could worry about something we couldn't do anything about. In some perverse way, McCutchan loved telling us how tough the future would be. I'm sure his torturing us helped Tom get through training for the second time. Not many guys have done that. Most couldn't even qualify for the training, let alone do it twice. I remember thinking, if he can do it twice, I can do it once.

There were still some 130 guys when the instructors broke us up into ten-man boat crews and gave us our boats. The boats were IBLs, inflatable boats large. After the instructors, they were responsible for more people quitting than any other single factor. One thing you have to understand: the boats were more for carrying than riding in. The men of each crew carried their boat on their heads, and until a crew got its ducks in a row, everyone in it suffered. There was no chance of a boat crew's learning how to work as a team until it got rid of the men who didn't belong in training. Until they were gone, they were just an added harassment factor. Sounds cold, but that's life. The sight of us trying to carry our boats with some semblance of order must have been funny to anyone not trying to carry one. To put it mildly, we were totally fouled up, and the instructors loved it.

They had jammed ten guys under each boat. That was too many and did not leave enough room for us to move. The instructors made damn sure that things were difficult for us. Some boats had guys ranging from six foot five to five foot five, so it was hard for everyone to carry his share of the boat. That was another of the divide-and-conquer techniques our instructors were so good at. There were thirteen boats to start with, and each team was required to move theirs as one. We did not accomplish that until after Hell Week, when we were down to seventeen officers and forty-five enlisted. Until then, we suffered more punishment for not handling our boats in the appropriate manner then anything else.

Keep in mind that we could leave anytime we wanted. Our instructors liked to remind us that we could just take off our red helmets, and they would see we had a *hot* shower, *dry* clothes, and a set of orders to some nice *warm* comfortable duty station.

One ploy Instructor Cook liked to use was to start some form of mild torture, say push-ups in the winter surf of Chesapeake Bay. When we were good and cold, he would tell us we could stop as soon as someone quit. Believe me, if someone I thought was going to quit was near me, I would encourage him, using what seemed solid logic. "If you're going to quit, do it now; if you quit later, I'll kick your ass!" It was strange, but people rarely quit while we were in the middle of something horrible. It was between evolutions, while they thought about what was coming next, that most guys quit.

We were allowed to eat as much food as we could; there was no restriction on volume, just on time. For the first two weeks of training, from the time we fell out, we had thirty minutes to get through the chow line, eat, and be in formation standing by our boats, ready to pick 'em up and move out. The time was cut to fifteen minutes at the start of Hell Week. So we stuffed large volumes of food down our throats "without the benefit of mastication." One of our officers, possibly Janke, had said, "Food without the benefit of mastication is a crime against nature." I'm sure most of us didn't know what the word mastication meant, but just the ring of the phrase caused a bunch of us to bust up laughing. Which, of course, resulted in our pushing Virginia away until the person who instigated the crime of laughter confessed to his guilt.

Our instructors had many ways to punish, but one of the worst was a form of mental and physical torture called the Gig Squad. The infraction could be anything, laughing, not laughing, running too slow, running too fast, etc. After the instructor inflicted whatever punishment he chose on the spot, the trainee would be informed that he had to attend Gig Squad that evening. Gig Squads were held during free time, after chow and before any night evolution we might have. The trainee got to think all day about Gig Squad, what "they" were going to do to him at Gig Squad. The damn things lasted about an hour and consisted of the usual physical tortures: squat jumps, push-ups, duckwalk, etc. I was among a select few who made every Gig Squad held, and my good buddy Jack Lynch was right there with me. On occasion, when a Gig Squad was not held, we felt as if we'd received a gift from God.

Ronald T. Flockton, aka Shorty, was a third class petty officer with four years in the navy when Class-29 started. Shorty was like a mirror for me throughout training; his face always showed what I felt. When things went bad, I would look around for Shorty, check out the look on his face, and feel better. Odd when you think about it what it took to get through each day; one way or another, you gave a lift, and you were given a lift. If you didn't give, you didn't get. By the middle of the second week, we knew who was going to make it, and I could tell the instructors would have to break Shorty's body to get him out of there. I wondered if that determination showed on my face the way it did on Shorty's.

Harry Humphries looked just like his name: big head, shoulders, and chest, with big, extra-long arms. Coal black hair all over, he shaved right up under his eyes. Picture an intellectual caveman, the kind of guy you'd pick to guard your children if you couldn't be there and you knew bad things were going to happen. The talk was that Harry came from wealth and was on the family shit list for being kicked out of one of the Ivy League colleges then joining the navy as an enlisted man. There was always a lot of talk about Harry. I'll tell you the bullshit story the guys passed around, just to give you a sense of how we felt about him. Then I'll tell you the real story; with Harry, all you had to do was ask and you got the truth.

There was a long family history with the college Harry was attending; his grandfather had donated a building to the school, and many members of his family were graduates. It seems Harry had been having a good time chasing the ladies and consuming a large volume of alcohol. He was hanging from the cliff of dismissal by his fingertips. The administration had already disallowed his participation in sports and Harry was at the one-more-thing-and-you're-out level. At that point, Harry, always ready for a challenge, removed one hand from the edge of the cliff and flipped them the finger.

The *big game*, football with the number one rival, always got everyone up. Since Harry wasn't allowed to play, he and some of his fraternity brothers thought up a way to make his presence felt. Wearing an animal skin draped over his large hairy body, at halftime Harry was to jump out of his team's stands, run across the field swinging a big club over his head, and generally make rude gestures and sounds in front of the opposition's stands. Two circumstances escalated the plan well past anything that might have been acceptable: One, it was cold; Harry was sitting in the stands, wrapped in a blanket, consuming firewater with his bros. Two, Harry never wore underwear. When the time came, he threw off the blanket and vaulted over the handrail, but someone grabbed the animal skin while Harry was still in midair; when he hit the ground, Harry was a naked man with a club in his hand. Knowing he was a goner, our boy went out in style; instead of covering himself and getting out of there, he extended his run. Harry took a slow jog around the stadium, swinging his club and waving to the crowd.

Good story. But now for the truth. Another good story.

Harry had not been kicked out of college, he was a member of a naval reserve unit that had been called up over the Berlin Wall crisis in the fall of 1961. He wasn't suited up for the game in question because he was a freshman, and freshman football was over. It *was* the big game with the school's main rival, and Harry was wrapped in an animal skin, drinking with his bros. There had been no plan, and he didn't have a club, but he sure caused a huge brouhaha at halftime.

The opposing team had a guy dressed as a bobcat, their mascot. The guy was really getting into the halftime ceremonies, and for some reason, one even Harry didn't understand, that damn bobcat was pissing him off. The mascot was wearing a big costume football helmet, and Harry decided he was going to take it. He ran across the field, tackled the mascot right in front of the opposition's stands, jerked the helmet off the bobcat's head, and held it up for all the world to see, a captured trophy.

For a few moments of stunned silence, Harry basked in the glory of his deed, then he was running for his life; all those college boys wanted their mascot's helmet back. Harry said it seemed like everyone in the stands moved as one. It was haul-ass time, and Harry did. With the mascot's helmet in hand, he made his escape, the opposition fans down on the field in angry pursuit. Well, both the stories, the BS one and the truth, capture our man Humphries, and thanks to the Berlin Wall crisis, we had Harry, and the Ivy League didn't. He was the one guy who, if removed from the equation of Class-29, everyone would have missed, even the instructors.

On Monday of week two, we were told to have our heads shaved by no later than that Friday. For the paltry sum of twenty-five cents, the instructors would cut our hair, or we could pay the fifty cents at the base barbershop. I didn't care; I'd had a butch haircut most of my life. Well, we had foreign classmates, four officers, Maj. H. A. Qureshi from Pakistan, Lt. E. G. Magnussen from Norway, Ens. A. W. Doumouras from Greece, Lt. A. E. R. Tiel from the Netherlands, and four enlisted Dutch Marines, De Beer, Pauli, Ravensburg, and Hack. The Dutch Marines and their officer, Lieutenant Tiel, went haywire. The air was full of *"godverdomme"*—some Dutch curse—and they were threatening to leave. Their anger was all about haircuts, not pain and suffering. Those guys carried their share of the boat; they didn't speak English, but a grunt, when you're straining, is a grunt in any language. It took two days to get it straight; at one time, our Dutchmen were packing their bags. The consul of the Netherlands intervened to calm them down and get them to submit to haircuts. It seemed that, in the Netherlands, only criminals had their heads shaved.

There were a couple other things I didn't understand until many years later: The big one, four out of five of our Dutchmen were already Royal Dutch Marine Frogmen. Only Pvt. Robertus J. Hack had not been through the Dutch Marine Frogman program; the rest of these guys were already what we were trying to become. They were in a foreign country, spoke little of the language, and, to put it mildly, thought we were all nuts. Last but not least, world over, there is, and has always been, a mild strain between Marines and sailors, and our Dutch colleagues were taking all this shit from sailors. Well, like the rest of us, they would learn what all the craziness was about. One damn thing about training: Somehow the instructors made sure that everyone had some individual little cross to bear.

Jack Lynch figured any idiot could shave a head. He bought a set of hair clippers and went into competition with Instructor Spiegel. I, of course, was dumb enough to be his first client. With about half my head shaved, Jack's entrepreneurial activity came to a screeching halt. We both received some on-the-spot instruction to help us think more clearly, pushing Virginia away. Jack received extra instruction for his monumental stupidity in the dreaded instructors' hut. The last place on earth any trainee wanted to find himself.

I believe that is when Jack became a permanent member of Gig Squad. Our instructors had a whole list of reasons why his one-stool barbershop was illegal, most prominent being that (1) he was not a licensed barber and (2) his enterprise was stealing food from Instructor Spiegel's family. Another small businessman bit the dust.

One of our foreign officers, Ensign Doumouras, was from Greece. The man was a bull among bulls; he could do one-arm push-ups, one-arm chin-ups, and squat jump all day long. The first time he really got my attention was on the obstacle course. One obstacle was called the Sky-scraper. It was a series of platforms four stories high, with no easy way up. We had to jump up, grab the edge of the floor above, and pull ourselves up, floor after floor. When we got to the top, it was down the other side for us. Ensign Doumouras—I always called him Dukie— usually went up and down the Skyscraper fast, but one day he decided to stop at the top floor and get a good look around. While he stood up there taking in the view, two instructors, Blais and Newell, were hollering up at him, trying to get him moving. Now Dukie, like most of our foreign classmates, pretended not to understand English when dealing with the instructors. As Instructor Newell was hollering for him to come down, Dukie looked down at them with a what-are-you-trying-to-tell- me look on his face. Instructor Blais pointed up at Dukie, pointed down at the ground, then did a couple of squat jumps. Dukie got a big smile on his face and started squat jumping on the top floor of the Skyscraper. At that point, Newell lost it and started to swear. Blais was just shaking his head, but Dukie was bouncing up and down like a spring, turning this way and that, getting a good look around.

By the end of the second week, something was hap- pening that took me years to figure out—a network was forming of guys who would complete training. It worked like this: If I fell or got knocked down going up Mount Suribachi, and Lynch was close, he would help me up. I might give Shorty a little push over the top if he was bogged down in the sand. Shorty and Harry might each take an arm and give Pauli a little support if he was hurting on a bad run. By the end of the second week, the guys who didn't give didn't get. Not even a nice word.

There had been no talk about our mutual-aid society that I know of. We still didn't even know everybody's name, but each guy who was putting out knew a couple more who were, and each of them knew a couple more.

Those who cooperated formed an informal safety net, and anyone who wasn't part of the safety net fell through, no matter how strong they happened to be.

Injuries, everyone had at least small ones, and for some guys injuries ended training. The longest-lasting injury I know of was Joe Camp's. Joe was a third class petty officer with a little time in the navy. I'm not sure when I found out what Joe was going through. I think it was around the third month, but I saw the first signs the second week; the rear of his pants was stained. Joe had a bad case of bleeding hemorrhoids throughout training. A case of piles may not sound like much, but we did hundreds of sit-ups every day, not crunches, real sit-ups. The all-the-way-up-and-all-the-way-down kind, where your ass rubs back and forth on the hard ground. Joe never complained, he just kept going. Anybody who thinks Joe Camp wasn't a hell of a man can kiss my ass.

I just wanted Hell Week—the first week of Phase Two—over. I figured most of the nonhackers would be gone and out of my way, plus things had to get easier. Right on the nonhackers, wrong on the easier. Except for the five Dutch Marines, we had started training knowing nothing about each other but that each of us had passed the test to get there. After Hell Week, we would know all we ever had to know about each other, and a good deal more about ourselves.

As I think back, it's clear that the officers had a tougher time, not physically but mentally. Until UDT training, rank had always shielded them from the overt rudeness enlisted men heap on each other as the normal way of going about the day. Well, magnify the normal young sailor verbal bullshit by ten, put a hard edge on it, and that's what our instructors passed out, regardless of rate or rank. Officers are not accustomed to having enlisted men verbally abuse them. Anywhere else in the military, the kind of treatment they received from the instructors would have put the instructors in the brig. The officers pulled together quickly, they were the first strands formed in the net, and of the sixteen U.S. Naval officers to start preconditioning, twelve were left at its end. Hell Week would join all the strands in Class-29's nets.

Lt. (jg) Curt Gibby had two special problems. He was one of our three lieutenants junior grade, the highest-ranking officers in Class-29. In the real navy, being senior was a good deal, not so in the catch-22 world of UDT training! All good was bad, all bad was bad, and it was the senior trainees' fault! Mr. Gibby took life and his responsibilities seriously, but being one of the senior trainees was a no-win situation. Another seemingly insignificant problem was that Mr. Gibby had big feet, just a little bit bigger than the largest boondockers the training department had to offer. Mr. Gibby would happily have purchased civilian shoes that fit, but that wasn't allowed. Over the first four months of training, I think he suffered every foot problem known to man. I know at one time he had lost nine of ten toenails and had an ugly red line running up his leg. *So, you want to be a Frogman?*

PHASE TWO

The next six weeks of training commenced with a memorable week, Hell Week, the roughest and most demanding week of training. The strain of the week showed, as only 12 U.S. naval officers, 5 foreign officers, and 45 enlisted men were left at its completion. Training continued, with emphasis on conditioning, hand-to-hand combat, small-boat training, distance and survival swimming, intelligence collections and dissemination techniques, communication, inland penetration raids, basic electric and non-electric demolition, day and night swimming, lifesaving techniques and first aid. At the end of this phase the class numbered 15 officers and 37 enlisted men.

I *love* the instructors' synopsis, it makes training sound like a reasonable educational experience; it's not, it is a test, a stress test. They weren't looking to educate a group of young men, they were looking for men who didn't take the easy way out. The instructors' job was to apply unreasonable amounts of stress, month after month. According to my *Franklin Language Master Dictionary and Thesaurus*, stress is defined as:

1. pressure or strain that tends to distort a body;
2. relative prominence or importance given to one thing among others;

3. state of physical or mental tension or something induc-
    ing it.

Training was truly about stress, but not to teach us how
to handle it; we and they were learning how much stress
we could take. In that sense, it *was* an educational experience, we and the instructors learned what tools we had in
our box.

The instructors were divided into two teams so they
could apply pressure twenty-four hours a day. Hell Week
is not something a participant remembers clearly; the
instructors don't let the trainees sleep. When we were allowed to lie down, a few short minutes later the instructors ran in beating trash-can lids with clubs, blowing
whistles, and throwing M-80s, cherry bomb–size explosives. We were kept tired, wet, and cold, we ran everywhere, with sand in our shoes, crotch, and ears and
between our buttocks. My head was beaten down into my
shoulders because we carried that damn boat everywhere
on the top of our heads. For me, Hell Week remains a
fog, with a few clear snapshotlike memories.

For the two days preceding Hell Week, both the
instructors and the weather had been a lot nicer, a little
calm before the storm. We had two clear, no rain, sleet,
or snow, sixty-degree-plus days. After the cold, wet, miserable days we'd had from the start of training, the good
weather was a big relief. We had hope in our hearts that
the weather would hold through Hell Week.

The first wake-up of Hell Week is the only one that is
clear in my mind. M-80s exploding, trash-can lids being
struck, whistles being blown. All the instructors and their
alarm clocks started Hell Week. As we scrambled out of
our barracks, we were greeted by a fulfilled promise our
instructors had made, "Snow for Hell Week"; a blanket of
the damn stuff covered everything. Welcome to Hell Week.

Paul T. Smith, known to one and all as P.T. If you had a daughter, and she brought Paul home, you would be happy. If he was your troublemaking son's friend, you would feel hope. P.T. is a nice guy in the best sense of the word. I have a clear memory of P.T., Lynch, and myself at the end of the obstacle course. We are trying to talk a guy out of quitting. He had nothing left, and what we had to give didn't help him at all.

There was one form of torture during Hell Week that was on the funny side, at least to the guys whose ears were all that was being assaulted. For the officers, it was not only their ears that suffered, but whatever dignity they had managed to hold on to. Each of our officers was required to sing his college fight song, solo, for the group. Since none of them could sing, that was not a pleasant thing to hear. Of course, if their singing was not loud enough, or they stumbled over a word, they paid the price for their obvious deficiency.

I remember being at the top of the cargo net and not having enough strength to go over the top; Bob Neidrauer passed me, reached back, and helped me over. I don't think I even knew his name at the time, but the hand he gave me was like a shot of energy. Bob was a small, tightly packed body of muscle with the demeanor of a wolverine. Neidrauer could smile and make it look mean. During the first week of preconditioning, Instructor Benny Sulinski, the big kahuna himself, had taken exception to the way Bob was looking at him. Neidrauer was doing chin-ups, and the chief wanted to know why Bob was giving him dirty looks. Bob's denial naturally fell on deaf ears. Bob was given the same opportunity that I had had, the personal and private attention of Instructor Tom Blais.

While the rest of us went off to other mind-expanding endeavors, Instructor Blais and Neidrauer went over to the log PT area, just the two of them. Bob got a private burn-out PT session, over in the trees, just him and a guy that looked like he might lop off his head any minute. Chief Blais told him, "We are going to keep at this till you quit, so make it easy on yourself!" Bob told me later that when he couldn't do push-ups anymore, Instructor Blais had him doing sit-ups; when he couldn't do those right, he was told to duckwalk, then squat jumps, then eight-count body builders, on and on. Neidrauer told me later, Instructor Blais might have made him cry, but he couldn't make him quit. Instructor Blais had said nothing, but Bob and I had the same feeling after our personal one-on-ones with the big Viking: he knew we would not quit. That's the guy that reached back and gave me a hand at the top of the cargo net.

The around the world cruise for me was like a little break. We spent a good part of the early-morning hours and the rest of the day away from our instructors. They gave us a starting point, a few checkpoints, told us where to end up, then turned us loose on the streams, swamps, and backwaters of Chesapeake Bay. I think that was the first time in training we were given a task and left alone to do it. Of course, it wasn't as if the instructors had been smacking us around; I can't remember even being touched. Those men were *masters* of mental harassment; their job was to keep us off balance, to continually annoy, worry, and impede.

The around-the-world cruise was the longest period of time in three weeks that those assholes weren't telling us what low-life scum we were and offering us some easy way out. Most of that day, it was just the boat crew with a task to accomplish. We were wet and cold most of that day, but the sun shone, and there was no rain or snow. It was funny how a little break from the mental harassment gave me such a large physical boost. We spent the last half of the cruise with our starboard bow inflation tube torn, which allowed a lot of water in the boat, which required continuous bailing. When fully inflated, IBLs were not hard to paddle if the crew worked together, but with half the bow gone and no way to patch it, we couldn't move in a straight line. And, with all the damn water in the boat, we had to paddle twice as hard to cover half the distance. Hawes kept his usual cool and had us swapping positions—bailing or paddling—so that no one got too worn out.

For several reasons, we all knew we would suffer at the end of the cruise. (1) Our boat was damaged, and that was more than enough reason to give us a little extra instruction in the art of duckwalking, squat jumping, or pushing Virginia away. (2) It paid to be a winner and the around the world cruise was a race. The crew that finished first got nothing, everyone else got duckwalks, squat jumps, or push Virginia away. Hawes had done a good job with the map; two other boat crews had become lost, so even with our damaged boat, we didn't come in last.

Shorty Flockton and Harry Humphries were in the same boat crew and they had a bad luck–good luck around the world cruise. I remember seeing their boat up in a yard that fronted one of the lakes we had to traverse. As we passed, I wondered what they were up to. It was obvious that their problem was the same as ours: a punctured inflation tube. They had taken their rubber boat ashore to see if there was any way it could be repaired. Since we were not allowed to carry repair kits, a punctured inflation tube was a big problem. Yet, somehow, without passing us on the water, Flockton and Humphries crew reached the amphib base before we did.

It turned out that the man who owned the house they had stopped at gave each of them something warm to drink, some food, and dry socks. Then, when they couldn't repair the boat, he loaded them and it in his truck and drove them to within a mile of the amphib base. If Shorty, Harry, and the boys had been caught, the shit would have hit the fan. As it was, they got away with it, just one of those little gifts from God. Someone had to have a little extra good luck that day!

They called it bivouac, that's just a fancy word for a camp, and it had nothing at all to do with what went on that night. Before Hell Week started, we had been issued a bunch of gear. A shelter half, so that two of us could put our halves together to make a tent. Canteen, tent pegs and poles, collapsible shovel, etc. Not exactly normal sailor gear.

Sometime after dark on the third night of Hell Week, we ran back to the training area to pick up our "camping gear." After a little of the usual harassment, we were told to fall out, collect our gear, and be back in formation, boats on our heads, in five minutes.

We went straight from the training area to Beach 7 and were told to set up camp for the night. The word was they were giving us the night off, reveille would be at 0500 the next morning. Yeah, right, some of us were so tired that we believed our instructors. By that time in training, you had to be real tired to believe anything they said.

After about twenty minutes, we had a half-ass bivouac set up and were crawling into our tents, when the shit hit the fan. Our instructors came running into the camp, blowing their whistles, throwing Mark-80s, pulling over our tents, and screaming, "The enemy is coming! The enemy is coming! Break camp, collect your gear, and move out!" We looked like some ragtag army running before a superior force. Most of us just grabbed our stuff, wrapped it in a shelter half, and started running with everything in our arms. Tent pegs were falling out, shelter halves were dragging in the sand, we were a mess. The instructors ran us through the same drill over and over till 0500 the next morning.

Years later, P.T. Smith told me that our little overnight camping trip was the only time that he had thought about quitting. He said he had learned a valuable lesson that night, and it had served him well for the rest of training: Do not come to the attention of the instructors. Like me, P.T. had been tired enough to believe that our instructors were going to let us sleep. As soon as he and Major Qureshi had their tent up, off came his boondockers. A few short minutes later, when our benevolent instructors warned us that the enemy was coming, P.T. was a little slower than the rest of us in getting his boondockers back on.

That brought him to the attention of Instructor Fraley, and Mr. Nice Guy, Paul T. Smith, had damn near lost it. Fraley had started giving Paul the usual ration of shit; P.T. had given him a real mean look and started to give it back to Fraley. That was all Instructor Fraley needed; he got between P.T. and the rest of us and started nudging him away from the class. Fraley kept telling Paul over and over, "Go ahead, take a punch, or just give me your helmet and quit."

P.T. said that he knows what it feels like to be a lamb that has been cut from the herd by a wolf. He said he had started asking himself, "Why am I taking all this crap anyway?" The only way he could keep from losing his focus was to look straight ahead and not make eye contact with Fraley. He would just take whatever was handed out and get his young ass back with his class-mates. That night, Paul had made up his mind to come to the attention of the instructors as little as possible. About three weeks after Hell Week, P.T. found out his new strategy was working perfectly. When training had started there'd been three Smiths in the class. At muster one morning, Instructor Hammond was surprised that there was a Smith still in the class; his comment, "I thought we got rid of all the Smiths during Hell Week!"

So Solly Day was the last day of Hell Week. By the time So Solly Day started, the trainees had been going pretty much without sleep for four days and nights. It was a cold, rainy day, a good part of which was spent crawling around in the sand and mud while explosives went off all around us. The instructors had roped off safe areas so spectators could watch and take pictures! There were a lot of controlled explosives going off, and they wanted no one hurt. If the instructors had left it up to me, there would have been a few explosives in the spectators' area. All week, women had been standing around pointing at us and taking pictures. I couldn't understand why they wanted to watch us suffer, but I hated them.

I have just two clear memories of that day. The first is a scene I can pull up in my mind to look at like some cherished old photograph: Joe Camp, Bob Neidrauer, and Ted Risher are crawling out of a mudhole, looking like refugees from some terrible war. Their helmets are all askew; they have on bulky kapok life jackets, the big cumbersome World War II type, and are caked with mud and sand. All three of them have mucus running from their noses, Ted a stream coming from one nostril and a huge bubble from the other. They look pathetic, whipped. In truth, that's exactly what we all were.

The only other thing I remember clearly that day is one of those tasks our instructors gave us that they did their level best to make sure no one accomplished. Down by the beach, on the land slide of the sand dunes, was a large pit, about eighty feet long and forty feet wide, full of dirty water with ice on it. There were large wooden poles about ninety feet apart, one at each end of the pit, with platforms twelve feet off the ground. Two one-inch cables six feet apart ran across the pit between the poles. The objective was pretty straightforward: cross the pit standing on the bottom cable while holding the top cable with the hands. Three moving parts made this damn thing an *infernal* machine: a pulley, a jeep, and explosive charges. The instructors called the hazard the Death Trap.

When we arrived at the pit, our instructors gathered us in a tight group at the bottom of a small depression in the sand dune by the edge of the pit. They then passed out dreaded C rations for lunch. C rations tasted like shit. They were hard to open when our hands were frozen, and the portions were too small to fill a five-year-old, but we were happy to have them.

We were all huddled together, swapping food, opening cans, trying to get a smoke, when charges that had been buried near the top of the depression were set off. The instructors had gotten us again, blowing sand in our open food! We moved over the edge of the pit, down closer to the water, to get the bank of the pit between us and any other explosives. Of course, there's a reason they call it So Solly Day; as soon as we were settled, the no-good rotten fuckers set off an *underwater* charge. Class-29, and its food, was covered with water, mud, and sand. Most of us ate the food, and the crud in it, anyway.

All of us smokers managed to get lit up. Anyone who had an extra dry one passed it on to those who needed one. The hands of Tommy Winter and some of our other smoking classmates were so cold, they could not strike a match. Jessie Hardy went around striking matches for the guys who couldn't; all they had to do was puff. God bless Humphries, he started telling stupid jokes, anything to get our spirits up. Mr. Janke, who didn't smoke, even got one lit up. He sat there with it cupped in his hands, puffing on it like mad to keep the tip hot. It was heat for his frozen hands. I wish I could find film of our class that day; we must have been a pitiful-looking bunch!

After our experience in fine dining, which lasted all of fifteen minutes, the task at hand was explained. We were to cross the Death Trap with no more than three people on the cables at one time. If we fell, we had to climb out of the pit at the far end. Instructor Waddell stressed that exit point in his own special way: "I will not repeat myself; if you fall off the cables, *you will* exit the pit from the far end only. I repeat, if you fall off the cables, *you will* exit the pit from the far side only." When Instructor Waddell used his, "I will not repeat myself" routine, repeating himself, it meant screw up and you will suffer more than you think possible.

What made successfully crossing the pit without falling off the cables damn near impossible was the rigging. The top cable was fixed on the start end. Then it went through a pulley on the exit side and was attached to a jeep. This allowed our beloved instructors to rapidly make the top wire go slack, or tight, as they chose. They just had to move the jeep. I don't remember *anyone*'s making it across. I know I didn't. I was perhaps twenty feet out on the cables with two guys ahead of me. Then a couple of explosive charges went off and the instructors quickly slacked the top cable, and all three of us were swimming for the far end.

As we crawled out of the pit, I looked back just in time to watch somebody put one hell of an effort into staying on. When the instructors slacked the top cable, the trainee wrapped his arms and legs around it and held on. He waited till they made it taut again. Somehow he managed to get his feet back on the lower cable, but the other men who had been on the cable with him were in the cold, icy water I had just crawled out of. He moved about ten more feet down the cables before they slacked the top cable quick. He was ready. Arms and legs wrapped around that cable like he was making love to it. He was still there! When they tightened the top cable again, he got his feet on the lower cable and started moving again.

Everyone near the pit, the guys duckwalking, squat jumping—whatever stage of higher learning we were involved in—started hollering. All of us wanted him to make it. Every time any of us overcame any obstacle the instructors placed in our way, we all became stronger. God bless strong adversaries. The trainee went through the same routine two more times and was most of the way across before they got him when the top cable became fouled in his bulky kapok life jacket. While he was trying to clear that and get his feet back on the bottom cable, he fell. He hit the bottom cable, and as he bounced off, he grabbed it with one hand. Our man did a spastic half spin around the cable, hanging there by one frozen hand. But he still wouldn't quit; he kept trying to pull himself up and get his other hand on the cable. I could almost feel his hand slipping as his weight overcame what was left of his grip and down he went.

My only clear memory of So Solly Day is the Death Trap; by then, we had been nonstop for most of five twenty-four-hour days. All of us who were left somehow still functioned in spite of the fact that we were running on empty. The effort my classmate had made on those damn cables fixed the Death Trap in my mind forever. For me, that man became the poster boy for what it takes to get through training.

Ens. Gerald Yocum, an outgoing straight arrow and general all-around good guy, has only two clear memories of the whole damn week: having to sing his college fight song, and what happened to him and his helmet at the Death Trap. The red helmets we wore every day were really just the liners of the standard military helmets of the day painted red. They are made out of plastic, light, and when used normally, support the heavier metal helmet. The webbing that makes the assemblage fit the head is inside the plastic liner. For So Solly Day, we wore the metal helmet, with liner, to help protect our heads from the explosions that constantly went off all around us.

When Ensign Yocum fell from the cables into the Death Trap, he lost his helmet. Somewhere at the bottom of the scummy pond was his helmet, and he couldn't find it. One of our instructors observed Ensign Yocum's plight. With great compassion, he called Yocum from the pond and gave him another helmet. Of course there was a price to pay, but not of the usual sort. It is hard to believe, but the instructor was actually able to make a man that had had no sleep for five days, was cold and wet, covered in mud, with sand in every crack and crevice, more uncomfortable. So uncomfortable that it's the only clear memory he has of Hell Week.

For the rest of the day, Ensign Yocum wore a steel helmet with no liner. He said his head felt like a BB rolling around in a trash can. Without the liner and webbing, the lip of the helmet came down past his nose. As we crawled around the sand dunes, he couldn't see a thing but the feet of the guy in front of him.

I have no memory of how Hell Week ended, but I've been told that sometime in the midafternoon of So Solly Day, we formed up in ranks on the beach. The instructors were a little quieter than they had been. They got us marching down the beach toward the exit to Beach 7. It should have been obvious that it was over at that point, but we had been screwed so much by then that none of us knew what to expect. The distance from the beach to our barracks was about a mile and a half. By the time we marched off the beach and past the golf course, we began to realize it. When we got near the navy exchange, we were halfway back to the barracks, and we all understood that Hell Week was ending. Someone tried calling out marching cadence but all of us had superficial injuries and many of us were limping so badly that we just couldn't keep in step.

When we got back to the barracks, we were told to clean up and put on fresh uniforms. As we tore off our Hell Week rags, an incredible amount of sand collected on the floor, off of and out of our bodies, buckets of it. We were then told to fall in outside the barracks. With little fanfare and no harassment, we were marched (marched, not run) to the chow hall, where we were able to sit and enjoy a steak dinner.

I woke up eighteen hours after it was over, knowing every man who was left belonged there. Of course, I was under the impression that the rest of training would be a cakewalk.

Our instructors remained split into two groups after Hell Week. For the next three months and one week, we would have both day and night evolutions, and whatever time happened to be left over we could use for sleep. The instructors did teach us some things, but there were easier ways to do that. I believe they had found the guys with what they called "fire in their bellies," and they wanted to see if the bodies that housed that fire could stand up for the long run.

I was surprised by a few of the guys who were still standing after Hell Week. The biggest surprise for me was the survival of Maj. Hakeem A. Qureshi, who was from Pakistan, and old. Well, compared to the rest of us he was old; he had to be around thirty-five. That was the main reason I thought he wouldn't get past Hell Week; he was as old as my dad! There were other things; he spoke little English, was in a foreign country, had nowhere to practice his religion or keep the diet it required. Well, by the end of Hell Week, he had proved his right to continue training, and me wrong. Years later I learned he could have left training without quitting if he'd let his government know that he was being trained with enlisted men. In Pakistan, officers and enlisted men were never trained together. If an officer was belittled by an enlisted instructor, that instructor would be hanged, and I do mean by the neck until dead. I guess old Hakeem had that fire in the belly, big time.

I damn near got myself kicked out of training within a couple of days of completing Hell Week, all over Reese's peanut butter cups. We were at the training area patching our boats, and we had just had a warning order that the night's evolution would be our first night surf penetration. I had a couple minutes and wanted a candy bar, and there was a very nice crew's lounge for the instructors with soft chairs, a pool table, television, and just inside the door, a candy machine. There were only three reasons a trainee was to be in the lounge: to pay an instructor twenty-five cents for a head shave; to occupy the lean and rest position while receiving verbal instruction; or to buy a candy bar from the instructors' machine. The money from the candy machine went into the fund for their lounge.

As I left, Leroy "Gedunk" Geiger asked me to bring him back a peanut butter cup. Leroy deserved his nickname; he loved candy more than any guy I have ever known. He looked like a young Mr. Magoo without glasses. That is, if Magoo had ever been a well-built young buck. Geiger had given me a bite of his peanut butter cup one night during Hell Week. Years later, his mother told me Leroy would share anything he had except his candy. The night he had given me the bite, the peanut butter cup had been squashed and had sand mashed into it. I couldn't believe how good it tasted.

Gedunk tossed me a nickel, and I took off at a run to get our candy. If you were walking, some instructor was going to put you in the lean and rest; the *rule* was *run*. The lounge was warm, so I stood there in front of the candy machine and enjoyed a few seconds of warm peace. My hand was in my pocket, fiddling with my two nickels and Gedunk Geiger's one. It felt nice to be warm and to see all that candy through the glass.

I put the first nickel in and pulled the handle for peanut butter cups; nothing happened. When the machine took my second nickel and still didn't drop a cup I could see through the glass, I wasn't even mad. My only thought was, shit, I'll have to give the one I get with the last nickel to Leroy. Maybe he'll share? In went the last nickel, I gave the machine a few gentle shakes and carefully pulled the handle. I was bent over looking through the glass right at the cup, but the candy never moved. Without a thought, I held the back of the machine with one arm and smashed a forearm into the glass, which broke but not enough. I reached both hands over the top of the machine, and slammed it over on its face. That made a loud noise, and broken glass and coins flew all over the place. I lifted the machine up, took two peanut butter cups, and left.

Strange, but until that evening, I never gave what I had done another thought. Gedunk and I ate our candy, worked on our boats, all seemed well with the world. Right. We had the obstacle course, chow, and the Gig Squad before our surf penetration that night. When our boats were ready, the men in charge of making our life miserable had us leave the boats nicely lined up in front of the instructors' hut while we ran off to the obstacle course. The instructors were not being nice guys by letting us not carry our boats. They just wanted to be able to mess up a couple boats without us seeing. We learned the hard way to guard our equipment.

As we came running into the training area from chow, we saw that all the boats were half flat. The instructors had either opened valves or put holes in our boats. Instructor Waddell was hot, he acted insulted. As soon as we had reached the area, he screamed, "Hit the deck." Waddell was beside himself. "Murder! Today someone in this class committed *murder*, and the whole class will suffer until that individual confesses." Had Waddell said the murder was done today? Of course Waddell repeated himself, he always did when he wanted us to know he took something seriously. It couldn't have anything to do with us; the whole damn class had been together all day. How could anybody have committed a murder? After we'd spent about five minutes at the lean and rest, he started talking about what a mess the murderer had made in the instructors' lounge. A light came on in my head. He was talking about me! If I didn't confess quickly, everyone was going to suffer for a long time. I confessed from the lean and rest. Instructor Waddell had me up, in the instructors' hut, and back in the lean and rest so quick my arms never quit aching. I was in Instructor Sulinski's office; he was a chief gunner's mate and the head enlisted instructor. For the next two hours, they had me just this side of tears. I felt sure they were going to kick me out, that my little loss of self-control was going to cost me big time.

Just being in Chief Benny Sulinski's office was scary. I had never been in the instructors' hut, let alone the office of the guy charged with supplying the Teams with the right people. Most of the guys I had seen go in the instructors' hut were gone. I was more afraid of Benny than I was of Waddell. Maybe because he so rarely spoke to us. He told the other torturers what to do. They all broke starch every day, but Sulinski was always sharp. Every crease in place, spit-shined jump boots without a mar, polished brass, the epitome of military bearing.

For two hours, I had to repeat my confession over and over. The instructors made me confess in front of Lieutenant Griswold and Lieutenant, junior grade Tyrie, the officers in charge of training. They had me duckwalk around the office, push Virginia away, and squat jump. For a break, they had me stand at attention in front of Chief Sulinski's desk. Instructor Blais came in while I was duckwalking around Bennie's desk. He looked down at me, shook his head, and said "Too bad, Roat, I was beginning to think you might make it to the Teams." I was fighting not to break out in tears, when Tom Blais smiled and winked at me. A ray of hope! Maybe they weren't going to shit-can me. The matter ended with my having to pay for repair of the machine, fifty-some dollars, a lot of money in those days. And I was to attend every Gig Squad held until the end of training. One more infraction of any kind, and I would be gone.

I was Gedunk's hero. He even wrote his mom and told her all about me killing the machine because it took our money and wouldn't give me our peanut butter cups. A couple of years later, I learned the instructors knew all along who had killed the machine because instructors Spiegel and Parrish had seen me leaving the lounge, and then discovered the crime. They had just wanted to see how long I would let my classmates suffer.

Class-29 started its hand-to-hand combat classes with much anticipation and, for the most part, no understanding of what we were going to learn. Classes were held in an old barracks that had padded columns, walls, and floors. And all the padding proved to be necessary.

That first class, Instructor Waddell introduced us to a big Marine sergeant, a black belt in *everything*. The sergeant was 100 percent Marine and at least as big and mean looking as Waddell.

The first lesson was learning to bounce well. It is called taking a beat, and if done well, it allows you to be slammed to the floor without being hurt. We spent about half the class that day slamming each other into the well-padded floor. The second half of that class was on a silent-kill tool called the garrote. Basically, you slip up behind a guy and choke him to death with a garrote made from wire, rope, a belt, anything flexible. Instructor Waddell had us sitting on the padded floor, while they told us how to construct and use garrotes. Any questions?

I must have had a secret death wish that day; my hand shot up, and of course, I was called on. "Can the guy being garroted get a shout out before he is dead?" Waddell said, "Well, let's see," and motioned me to stand. Instantly, I knew I had just ka-kaed. Me and my big mouth.

The big Marine stood behind me, with a soft cotton karate gea belt about two inches wide. He told me to holler as soon as I felt the belt on my neck. They wanted to be fair so they let me try five times to get out a holler. Each time, I ended up with the belt around my neck, my lower back over the Marine's hip, my feet about one foot off the floor, and never got a sound out. If he'd been serious any one of those five times, I would have been dead without being able to utter a sound. I know Lynch loved seeing me hang off that Marine's hip, but I sure felt stupid.

We ran, we ran every damn where, and every damn way. As a group, and as individuals, with boats on our heads, and without. We ran the obstacle course for time and had timed mile runs; we ran with each other and against each other. We ran with old, worn-out boondockers on our feet. For the timed mile, the fastest guy in our class was Ens. John P. Hunt. The officers called him Killer Hunt, but I could never figure out how a guy got to be an officer in the world's largest nuclear canoe club and still blush when someone swore in his presence. John was just too nice for words, a truly naive young man. There was not an ounce of malice or quit in Ens. John P. Hunt.

I did better on the long runs, closer to the front-runners, but to this day I believe good runners are born that way. When I watched guys like Ray Fauls or Trailor Lewis, they flowed; they looked like they should be running. I don't mean they didn't hurt. You don't run in wet muddy clothes, in old boondockers full of sand, and not hurt. It's just that guys who are born to run get better results from their pain.

Trailor Lewis was a long, lanky, six foot one or two country boy from outside some little town in South Carolina. He was everything good that you could say about a southern country upbringing. He rarely swore, was always polite, and in those days when bigotry was *big*, he showed not a trace of it. Trailor was one of our fastest distance runners, and only Ray Fauls could beat him at anything over five miles. Troy Vaught might have been able to challenge Fauls if he really busted his butt. Trailor was a pleasure to watch run, because he appeared to just flow across the ground. It is funny, but how things look sure can fool you.

Trailor had been reading about navy Frogmen since he was a small boy, and he joined the navy to become a Frogman. When Trailor had passed his qualification test and had an approved request chit to attend UDT Training, he was stationed onboard the USS *Spiegel Grove*, a landing ship dock (LSD). He later told me all his ship-mates had laughed at the thought of "Mr. Nice Guy" becoming a member of an underwater demolition team. It is nice to know I'm not the only guy whose shipmates were betting against him. Trailor had been granted two weeks' leave before reporting to the training unit. As if training were not hard enough, Lewis would get something while home to make it just a little tougher. Who says bad things don't happen to good people?

Trailor was running ten miles every day while home, but just two days before he was to report for training, he badly sprained his ankle. He reported anyway, keeping his pain to himself. During the second week of preconditioning, Chief Sulinski saw Lewis limping and sent him to have his ankle checked by a doctor. Lewis was sweating big time; a doctor could jerk his ass out of training.

The doctor said Trailor had a bad sprain, but would leave it up to Trailor to decide whether he wanted a medical drop. In Trailor's mind, he had been given a break. But when he reported back to Sulinski, the chief told him he might as well just quit and get it over with; "The whole world hates a gimp." Trailor just said, "Chief Sulinski, I want to continue!"

The chief told Trailor, "You will be one of the first to quit," but he did let him rejoin the rest of the class.

When I saw Lewis on long runs, it was not obvious that he was suffering any pain in his body, let alone a badly sprained ankle. Like his good buddy Joe Camp, and Joe's hemorrhoids, Lewis just kept going till he was numb. I wonder how he would have done on the short runs if his ankle hadn't been sprained. Hell, if Joe hadn't had the piles, he might have been the class sit-up champ, and if Trailor's ankle hadn't been screwed, he might have beaten Ensign Hunt on the timed mile. Oh well, we all had our crosses to bear!

Lewis could do one thing that was truly amazing! When we had been introduced to the obstacle course, Instructor Newell had gone over the Dirty Name obstacle in three strides. Nothing but his feet had touched the obstacle. The first thought that had entered my head was *No fucking way!* Trailor must have had a different thought because he was the only other person I know of who learned to do that.

Most obstacles were given descriptive names or named for some action required to get over them. For the Weaver, we had to go over and under horizontal three-inch pipes about eighteen inches apart, mounted up and down inclined planes. On the Slide for Life, we pulled ourselves down a rope strung from a thirty-foot platform to seven feet off the ground. There were also the Wall, the Skyscraper, etc. Not so the Dirty Name; it had had some official-sounding name in the distant past, but the instructors had heard so many foul words from trainees attempting to get over it that it became known as the Dirty Name. My own particular word was "shit."

No man who ever ran the Teams' obstacle course will have any problem remembering how difficult leaping the Dirty Name is. The working parts of the Dirty Name are three ten-inch horizontal logs, and the trainee. The object is to start on one side of the logs and cross over the top of each. Simple enough. The problem is that the logs are mounted, like uneven stairs for a giant. All three ten-inch logs are about five feet long, they are mounted parallel to each other, at different heights, and about four feet apart. The first log you approach is only about a foot off the ground, the second is five feet higher, and the last is nine feet above the ground.

Most of us hit the first log at a run, using it to launch ourselves high enough to have the second log hit us in the stomach, let us catch ourselves with our arms, hustle over the top of the log, then pull ourselves to a standing position. We then launched ourselves from that log to the last, swung over the top, dropped to the ground, and ran on to the next obstacle. But Instructor Newell and Lewis could *jump* from log to log; three giant, leaping strides and they were dropping off the far log. The worst thing about watching either of them do it was that they made it look so damn easy.

Demolition! There is beauty in a well-done explosion, just the right amount to get the job at hand accomplished. Our first class was on time fuse, Primacord, and blasting caps. The box containing the time fuse lists the burn rate. The instructors taught us not to trust the box, that we were to time the damn stuff ourselves every time we planned to use it. Our first lesson was devoted to pure basics, the little things that would keep us from killing ourselves: *Crimp* a cap, *cut* a fuse. That day, Waddell was heavy into his "I will not repeat myself" then repeating himself routine.

The blasting caps we were using had a two-inch drop test, meaning they *should* be able to survive a drop from the grand height of two inches without exploding. Caps are high-order explosives whose sole purpose is to initiate another, larger quantity of explosive. They were dangerous business, and we were being taught how to use them without being hurt.

That first demolition class, we had our only screwup with caps throughout training. To cut time fuse or crimp a cap onto that fuse, we used a crimping tool that looked like a pair of strange pliers. The crimping tool has special, separate, notches for cutting fuse and for crimping caps. "I will not repeat myself: *Never* cut a cap; you crimp a cap; you only cut time fuse. I repeat, *never* cut a cap." Waddell repeated that mantra several times, because a cap could explode in the hand if it was cut.

Well, a cap was cut that day, a very costly mistake, and the whole class was afforded the opportunity to learn from the mistake. A lot of push-ups, a little duckwalking, for one and all. Of course, the perpetrator earned a wider educational opportunity. He was to attend all meetings of the Gig Squad. He was also given one hundred feet of time fuse, and told to cut it into one-inch sections. Then he was to crimp each one-inch section of time fuse exactly in the middle.

The perpetrator was to become as close to my heart as my brothers. At the time of the crime, I was as pissed at Ted as the rest of the class. Yeah, we got mad at each other. Especially when unnecessary educational experience was brought down on the whole class for a stupid *individual* action. Airman Clarence T. Risher III was just as big a young goofball as I was. The first time I saw Randy Travis, the singer, I thought Ted had been reincarnated. Couldn't be, though; like me, Ted couldn't carry a tune in a bucket.

We became buddies forever when, one night after Gig Squad and before our night evolution, Ted was spending a few minutes of precious time cutting time fuse into one-inch sections. There were no instructors around, so I got my crimpers, went behind his bunk, and started cutting. As far as Ted was concerned, from then on, I could do no wrong. When all twelve hundred one-inch pieces had been cut, we crimped each one in the middle. Ted was one happy camper when he carried the two buckets of cut and crimped time fuse over to the instructors' hut.

Even with my help, it had taken Ted every spare minute of five days to get the job done. The instructors made sure we had very few spare minutes in a day. Risher was back in five minutes, a bucket in each hand, and an "I can't believe this is happening" look on his face: the instructors had looked at his buckets full of one-inch, cut and crimped fuse and told Ted, "Good work, Risher. Now cut them in half and crimp each one in the middle."

This time Lynch and P.T. Smith became part of Ted's cutting and crimping team. Other guys would drop by and cut a few sections. Sort of a social function, an us-against-them thing. Lynch told Ted I should be banned from cutting or crimping. He figured Ted's efforts had been rejected because of my inferior work with the crimping tool. He also said that I had such a piss-poor attitude and personality that the instructors could smell me on the fuse. Jack said they should at least wash the fuse and hide the sections I had cut at the bottom of the buckets. It was nice to be loved.

We were starting to get a lot of water time. Not the jump-in-pool or go-to-the-beach-and-have-a-good-time kind. The work-your-ass-off, cold-and-miserable kind. We had begun with some races at the amphib base Olympic-size pool. The instructors needed to know how strong a swimmer each man was because we were to be paired up as swim buddies. The worst crime in all of training was to leave our swim buddy. We were to be within six feet of him whenever we were in the water. There was one exception, and one only: the timed mile swim; that was a race.

We actually had one man who couldn't swim. How Jessie James Hardy even got to training is beyond me. The first time we were at the pool, Jessie couldn't swim *one* length. But he could hold his breath and crawl on the bottom for *two* lengths of the pool, dragging a bucket full of bricks. Hell, that was one hundred and fifty feet.

I think Jessie James Hardy was loved as much as Harry Humphries. To this day, I have never met anyone else who resembles our man Hardy in any way. Jessie was a walking contradiction. He was a Second Class United States Navy diver but couldn't swim. Jessie drank all the time. I saw him drink aftershave lotion because it had alcohol in it, and our boy was out of booze. Jessie was one of the oldest guys in our class. He had also been partway thought training before. On his earlier run, the instructors had made Jessie wear a cowbell around his neck for some infraction or another. After two weeks of that thing's banging up and down on his hairy chest, Jessie was put in the hospital because he had a bad infection in the roots of his chest hair. His life's ambition was to retire from the navy, and open a used-car lot with blue-and-gold pennants flapping in the breeze. Over it all would be a huge banner that read, JESSIE J. HARDY'S PREMIUM USED CARS.

Two things came of that first pool session that affected me: (1) Instructor Blais took me aside and informed me that if Jessie Hardy could not swim well enough to graduate, I wouldn't either. (2) The fastest swimmer in the class, Ens. Richard A. Hauff, became my swim buddy; I was number two. Dick Hauff had been a college all-American swimmer, and no matter how hard I tried, he stayed number one and I stayed two. Having to help Jessie learn to swim turned out to be no problem. Everybody helped him, and old Jessie was nothing but heart and balls; he was holding his own in the water within a couple weeks.

Due to our instructors' overwhelming concern for our comfort, they gave us a wet- and dry-suit appreciation swim. Wearing nothing but our swim trunks, we were first allowed to swim a quarter mile in the winter-chilled water of Chesapeake Bay. Next we swam the quarter mile wearing wet suits. Then we repeated the swim in a dry suit. By God, they were right; we sure did appreciate those suits after we froze our butts off during that first quarter mile. Our instructors loved to tell us, "It's just mind over matter. We don't mind, and you don't matter."

Another of the instructors' educational tools that was used with some frequency was a small area where we practiced log physical training, commonly known as log PT. The essential tools of log PT were telephone poles, barbed wire stretched a few inches above the ground, and four old World War II–type landing craft sitting on a row of cradles. The deal was that each boat crew, by this time down to six or seven men, got its own telephone pole. The easy part was the log PT, picking the telephone pole up and doing exercise as a group. The tough stuff was crawling around under the wire or getting in and out of the boats with that damn telephone pole. Log PT was saved for rainy, sleety, or snowy days; our benevolent instructors figured we learned a lot more crawling under the barbed wire in the mud.

The log PT that sticks in my mind is the day that Richard Fradenburgh earned his membership in the permanent Gig Squad in a most spectacular way. Fradenburgh was one of our strong silent types. We didn't hear a lot out of him; he was there doing what he had to do and not making a lot of noise about it. That particular cold, gray, crap day, there were little patches of snow and big puddles of mud all around, and we were all groveling around in the mud, moving ourselves and our telephone poles under the barbed wire. The big kahuna, Chief Benny Sulinski—Mr. Spit Shine himself—was observing our efforts from a small mound of dry earth.

Now keep in mind that all we had to do was to take off our red helmets and we could be out of all that silly shit in a heartbeat, no questions asked. We were not allowed outside without that damn red helmet firmly stuck on our heads. If one of us was seen without it, he paid dearly. Our man Fradenburgh would pay dearly for his red helmet being other than on his head that day, but what imprinted the event in my mind was that Chief Benny Sulinski had to pay first.

I had just crawled out the far side of the barbed wire, and as I looked back to the other side, Fradenburgh was in a crouch working with the far end of his boat crew's telephone pole. His red helmet just fell off. Chief Sulinski standing on his little dry mound of dirt called out, *"We have a quitter,"* and bent over to pick up the helmet. Fradenburgh never straightened up, he just dived for his red helmet. Sulinski had it in his hand and was straightening up when Fradenburgh crashed into him and knocked him on his ass in the mud. Fradenburgh grabbed his red helmet and stuffed it back on his head. Everyone stopped at the sight of Benny, our ultimate leader, his spit-shined boots and starched and pressed greens all covered in mud. Chief Blais looked down at Fradenburgh and said, *"You touched an instructor!* Get back to the training area now, stand by outside the instructors' hut."

To most of the guys, it had looked like Fradenburgh had tackled Chief Sulinski. Not so, he had just dived after his red helmet, and Sulinski happened to be in the way. Those minor differences didn't matter; Fradenburgh had been sent to the instructors' hut. Any way we looked at it, very serious business.

Later that day, after we had been to the obstacle course, eaten chow, had a lovely run, and were getting ready for surf penetration, our classmate still had not returned. As it happened, a hole had somehow appeared in my crew's boat while we were running up and down our beloved sand dunes. Since we were not allowed to carry patch kits and pumps with us, I was sent back to the training area, about a three-mile round-trip run, to get what was needed. The rest of my boat crew would be pushing Virginia away, or some such educational activity, until I returned.

As I ran up the road to the training area, I saw Fradenburgh acting like a crazy man in the middle of the road. One of the extra boats was sitting catawampus in the road, about a half a block from the instructors' hut. Our man was running around it, pushing, pulling, and lifting, slowly moving the boat down the road. I couldn't stop because the instructors might see, so I ran in place and asked Fradenburgh what was going on. Well, he'd been told to get the boat down to the beach so he could join the class. Shit, the damn boat even had an anchor in it. I told him I'd be back and hauled ass to the hut, where I paid the usual price for the patches and a pump: some squat jumps.

I had it figured out: I'd help Fradenburgh move the boat far enough down the road that the instructors couldn't see him; out of sight, out of mind. Then I'd get my ass back to my boat crew. Of course it didn't work out that way. As soon as I started to help Fradenburgh, one of the instructors was on us like stink on shit. "What are you doing?" Before I could come up with an answer, the instructor said, "You two get your asses back to the beach and join your class. Roat, you can join Fradenburgh tonight at Gig Squad." Hell, that didn't cost me anything; I was already on the Gig Squad Forever list.

There were only two nice things about being on the permanent Gig Squad: One was when I was told I was such a screwup that I needed to report to Gig Squad. At least twenty more times during training, I was told to show up that evening for extra instruction; being on permanent Gig Squad always made me feel like I had gotten away with something. Like getting two death penalties; how in the hell do they kill you twice? Two, my best buddies, Jack Lynch and Ted Risher, were right there with me, enjoying the benefits of remedial education.

Thinking back, what amazes me most about Jack, Ted,

and me is not all the times we helped each other, but all the extra harassment we dumped on each other. Small stuff mostly, like hiding something the other guy needed in a hurry, his red helmet or one boondocker—anything to put the other guy in a mild panic. Jack was always best at smart-mouthing; his damn mind was so quick. I loved to nail Lynch's bunk; like everywhere else in the military, our beds had to be made properly, otherwise we suffered an instructor's personal attention. The first few times it was easy. I'd just let Jack leave the barracks first, then make a quick tug on his blanket, and Lynch would get a little extra time pushing Virginia away. But Jack quickly snapped to what was going on, then nailing his bunk became a challenge worth the effort.

Deception was what it took. And because Jack had a quick mind, it had to be good. For instance, about ten minutes before we had to fall out for quarters, good old Gedunk Geiger set the hook. Jack was in the head, just finishing brushing his teeth; Gedunk came in and said, "Hey, Lynch, where is Roat? They want him at the instructors' hut *now*."

Jack bit: "Let me tell him the bad news. Maybe they'll give him a bunch of squat jumps." He came to the far end of the barracks where we bunked. I could see him coming and worked hard to keep my face straight. Jack told me the bad news as he walked up. "Hey, John, they want you over to the instructors' hut *now*." I gave the proper-sounding groan, grabbed my helmet, and hauled ass down the barracks and out the doors by the head. As soon as I was through the doors, I turned back, dropped to the ground, and crawled back into the barracks under the first set of bunks inside the door. Everyone was hurrying and paying little attention, so it would be fairly easy to crawl four or five bunks into the barracks and hide there till everyone was gone. When the last guy was out the door, I was out from under the bunk and down to Jack's, quick. A few subtle wrinkles in his blanket, just enough to make Jack look sloppy, and I was out of there, quick. I had to pay a quick twenty-five push-ups for being a couple seconds late, but getting Lynch made my day. Jack would get all red in the face, call me a few nasty names, then go about the business of payback.

Forrest Hedden became a fine example of our catch-22 world. At the start of our second classroom session on demolition, he was brought to the front of the class and placed in the lean and rest position. His crime: Forrest had earned the only perfect score on our first written demolition test. The only thing I could figure, they were punishing him for making the rest of us look bad. Yes sir, it pays to be a winner. Our man Hedden stayed in the position for the whole class. Of course, he was sagging well before the end of our classroom session.

Around that time, Instructor Waddell came up with a question for us that has always stuck in my mind. It was a cold, drizzly evening, and we were standing in for-mation outside the instructors' hut. We could see Wad-dell through a window. He was drinking coffee and watching us. Then he raised the window just enough to stick the end of a loudspeaker out the window and said:

"The sun shines every day in Puerto Rico,
coconuts and bananas on all the trees,
bikini-clad women on all the beaches.
Will you make it to Puerto Rico?"

We had been kept cold and wet for over a month when Waddell planted that little seed in our minds. As far as I was concerned, we couldn't get there soon enough; the grass is always greener, right?

* * *

"Sneak and Peek," how to get from one place to another without being seen, techniques used for intelligence collection and inland penetration raids. Something every young guy I know was learning before he got his first cap gun. Hell, if you couldn't sneak and peek, you'd die of boredom; your mom would never let you do anything if you asked. We spent a lot of time perfecting our abilities to get a job done without being seen, both day and night. Since we were attempting to go from pollywogs to full-fledged United States Navy Frogmen, we spent a lot of time learning to sneak out of the sea. That gets us to scout swimmers and Bubble Butt Jarvi. I'll explain scout swimmers first, then explain how Jarvi and I became so physically intimate.

Scout swimmers are used when a group must penetrate a hostile area from the sea, in our case using IBLs. One man from each boat would generally be assigned as a scout swimmer. Usually two boats went into any one area, and several penetrations would be going on, spread out across a wide area of beach. We were required to navigate our boats to a specific insertion point off the beach, where the two boats would wait outside the surf zone while their swimmers went in and scouted out the beach.

We were looking for enemy patrols, listening posts, anything that might get us caught. A safe way across the beach and a good place to hide the boats had to be located. If an enemy found us crossing the beach or learned where we hid our boats, the operation was compromised; in other words, our world had turned to shit. After signaling the boats to come in, then guiding them across the beach to the hiding place, the scout swimmers generally did not participate in the main operation— recon, demolition, ambush, etc. The scout swimmers removed any signs of the beach crossing, completed hiding the boats, then guarded them till the rest of the crew returned.

Ronald E. Jarvi was a good-size young guy with a big round ass, hence his nickname, Bubble Butt. Ron was one of the best-natured guys around. If asked "Hey, Jarvi, where did you get that big ass?" Ron would pull back his shoulders, throw out his chest, get a dead serious look on his face, and say, "You don't drive a tenpenny nail with a tack hammer." Ron always figured the glass was more than half full, and if it wasn't just then, it would be soon. A good guy to be around when things were miserable.

Ron and I were assigned scout swimmer duties for an inland penetration raid being planned as our night evaluation. During the warning order—the official briefing on our coming mission—we found out that our boat crews would be working together and we would be wearing dry suits for the operation. The dry suits were old style, made of very thin natural rubber, under which we wore one layer of not very good long underwear. That style of dry suit worked all right, *if* it had no holes and we were swimming hard to generate body heat. Two problems: We had to wear the suits for the whole six hours of the operation even though we only had a couple hundred yards to swim; we had to inspect and repair the suits several hours before the operation, then leave them in the care of "the enemy," our instructors.

That night, as we were pulling on the delicate sausage-skin-thin rubber suits, Ron said, "I know they didn't mess with our dry suits while we weren't around. They would never do that, would they?" He had a big grin on his face that somehow made me feel better about what I was sure would come. In the old-style dry suit, all it took to ruin the suit's efficiency was a pinhole. We had made a quick reinspection while we donned our rubber—not that it would have mattered; we didn't have time to do any repairs. Our world was a twenty-four-hour-a-day catch-22; the instructors did their best to make us believe we were wrong just for being there.

Thank God it was a short swim. Hawes had navigated our boat to the assigned offshore insertion point. As soon as we slipped into the water, I felt small rivulets of cold water running down my chest and back. Ron said he was taking water as well, so we were in a hurry to get to the beach. What I didn't realize was how quickly Jarvi was turning into a water balloon.

We were in the water, right up at the edge of the beach, lying very still, looking for sign of our instructors, when Bubble Butt said, "Look at my leg. Let's get out of the water and move across the beach to those bushes." But as Jarvi started to get up, I began to laugh. He looked like he had an advanced case of elephantiasis. The rubber covering his left leg was stretched into a large water balloon that hung down over his foot. There was so much water in the leg of his dry suit that he couldn't walk. Ron had to drag his leg, which made a nice little trench in the sand. Meanwhile, I was running around trying not to make too much noise while laughing and to clear our tracks from the sand. Especially the little ditch that followed the walking water balloon everywhere he went.

We got lucky and found a group of large bushes with a depression underneath them. Then I used a waterproof flashlight to signal the boats to come in as Ron crawled around under the bushes to prepare a hiding spot for the boats. I guided the guys to that spot, then returned to the beach to finish clearing tracks we might have left. When I got back to the hiding place, the guys had departed on the mission. By that time, Ron and I were freezing our asses off.

Every time I glanced at Jarvi, I wanted to laugh; he looked so damn pathetic. We were both shivering and shaking, but Ron had that gross leg. About ten minutes after the boats were hidden, any pretense of our guarding them went out the window. We searched out another small depression under a bush, crawled in it, and pulled leaves, limbs, and sand over us—anything to add a little insulation between us and the cold. The two of us were wrapped around each other tighter than any lover I ever had.

We made so damn much noise shivering and laughing, the instructors had to know where we were; I'm sure they left us alone so we could suffer. Every time I quieted down, Ron would make some remark that got me laughing. "We have to quit meeting like this!" "Will you respect me in the morning?" And on and on until my gut hurt from all the laughter. My best line of the night was, *"I want my mother, and I want her now!"* Bubble Butt damn near choked to death from laughing. For the rest of my life, whenever I have felt the need to whine, I have repeated that line. It's good to have a ridiculous little whine to snap you back to reality. For Ron and me that night, it was just as the instructors said: mind over matter. They didn't mind, and we didn't matter. Thank God, Ron kept us laughing.

As good-natured as Bubble Butt was, Lynch and I were able to find a little irritant to jerk his chain with. The military is big on polished brass and, of course, not having our brass belt buckles highly polished was always worth a few push-ups, squat jumps, or such. Our prank had started innocently enough. We were talking with Jarvi by his bunk. Ron reached into his locker for a can of Brasso and a rag, and started polishing his buckle. As we talked, each of us used Ron's Brasso and rag to shine our brass. No big thing; it was as it should be, classmates sharing. Of course, we then started to take advantage of Ron's good nature; I was out of Brasso, and Jack was low. So we started using Ron's every time we needed to polish our buckles.

Jarvi was good natured, but he wasn't stupid. Soon he was dropping little hints like, "Hey, why don't you cheap bastards buy your own Brasso!" This just gave Jack and me incentive to see how long we could get away with using Ron's Brasso. After a week of that, while Jarvi was standing by his locker, polishing his buckle, he said, "Get your own fucking Brasso!" For punctuation, he put the can of Brasso back into his immaculate locker.

Jack was damn good at this sort of thing, so he started to whine. Of course, I followed suit. When Ron finally relented and retrieved the can from the locker, Jack administered the coup de grace. "To hell with it, Jarvi, we'll use our own Brasso." With that we walked away, Ron calling us a few of the fouler names in his vocabulary.

Of course, we were required to do our laundry. Well, during this phase the washing machines "went down," which gave Lynch and me a golden opportunity. Laundry still had to be done, so Jack and I volunteered. That had nothing to do with our wanting to help out our classmates; it had to do with booze and broads. There are always women at a Laundromat, and we already knew how to get our hands on booze. All that was required was transportation and our overcoming the small obstacle of not being allowed off the base. It was a rare Friday; we had no night evaluation, so after Gig Squad, we were free to run our own little night evaluation. After we promised to get his laundry done, Shorty Flockton loaned us his pickup truck. Jack then used his mind and mouth and bullshitted us right out the gate.

Virginia had stiff liquor laws, state-run package liquor stores with limited hours, *no* over-the-bar hard liquor sales, and we weren't old enough to drink anyway. All that was no hill for a climber, because Virginia's tough laws had made it full of bootleggers who didn't care what time it was or how old the customers were. Fifteen minutes after we were out the gate, we had enough booze to get good and wasted. So we did. Truthfully, that was the only one of our objectives that was fully accomplished; women wanted nothing to do with two loud-mouth drunks. So much for our fantasies. The laundry fared only slightly better; some got done, some got partly done, and some got done not at all.

While we were doing the laundry, a washing machine took our money, filled with water, and refused to wash our clothes. True to my recent history, I nutted up on the machine, and the damn thing ended up on its side, water flowing all over the place. Jack saved the situation by getting us out of there before the cops showed up. I am not and never have been an easy person to control, and no one except Lynch was ever able to do it when I was drunk.

Somehow Jack managed not to lose anyone's clothes, the clean and dry, the clean and wet, and the wet and dirty. But, despite our heroic efforts on their behalf, we were not popular with our classmates; we had not separated the clothes, and everyone who had given us any received at least some soggy, dirty clothes back. In truth, it was all my fault, but Jack received no credit for getting me and everyone's laundry out of there before the cops showed up. He protested loud and clear, but as far as our classmates were concerned, we both were crazy assholes. I tried to ease Jack's mind by saying that no one would ever ask us to do their laundry again, but that seemed to piss him off more than he already was. If I remember correctly, only P.T. Smith, Gedunk, Ted Risher, and Shorty Flockton—who after all had received his truck back unscathed—saw any humor in our failure. As far as I was concerned, Risher summed it up best: "Fuck 'em if they can't take a joke." Somehow, Jack always suffered for being my friend: he was funny; I was just a little over the edge.

By this time, we had become the best *team* I have ever been a part of. It still amazes me how quickly young men with such big egos were forged into a problem-solving machine. We were all stand-alone types, definite individuals who had become strands in a strong net, a team. In the dictionary, "team" is usually defined as something like (1) two or more beasts of burden harnessed together for the purpose of work; (2) a set of workers, or players competing. Keeping the word "beast" in mind, we were all of the above and much more. After all, we were trying to become the best at killing people and breaking things. We were not about sweetness and light. There were big guys, little guys, brash, quiet, all kinds of guys, but no wimps. Every guy still in Class-29 could take what came and fight back.

Our boat crew holds a special place in my heart. Besides Ens. James Hawes, Joe Camp, and myself, there were George E. Leasure, Kenneth T. Winter, Ralph Diebold, and Troy E. Vaught. As diverse a group of Frogman trainees as will ever be found. George was never called George, he was known as "Eddie," "Fast Eddie," "The Chink," or "Skill." He was from Philadelphia and looked to be part Chinese, whence, "The Chink." "Skill" came from the high degree of manual dexterity he demonstrated in anything that required hand-eye coordination. Most of the time, we just called him Eddie, but when asking someone where he was or speaking to him about women or short table pool, both of which he was very good with, he was Fast Eddie. That's a lot of nicknames for one guy named George, but Eddie was just that kind of guy, calm, cool, and collected. Humphries and Eddie were tight and, like Harry, Eddie was a leader without rank or rate, and to top it all off, Fast Eddie was just a fun guy.

Winter and Diebold, Diebold and Winter, I can never think of one without the other, they were both big, strong, serious country boys who didn't do a lot of talking. Touching Ralph Diebold anywhere, from the top of his head to under his little toe, was like touching forged steel. Ralph looked like a block of granite mounted on two telephone poles. He had been raised on a small farm in Missouri and had done nothing in his life but work hard. Ralph once told me that as a child, he got one pair of shoes every two years, and those were for school, when he could go. He had joined the navy to see what was going on in the world he heard about when he could go to school. In the navy, he could have as many pairs of shoes as he wanted. I liked Ralph a lot, but messed with him constantly just to see what would piss him off. It took me a while to find two little buttons I could push to get Ralph mad: Mess with his food or call him fat.

Now, the call-him-fat thing was odd; the guy's skin was stretched tight over big hard muscle. I'd have hurt my hand if I'd been were dumb enough to hit him anywhere. But if I said, "Hey, fatty," Ralph got a "Kill!" look in his eyes and would lunge. The first time I said it, he damn near got his big hands on me. Fortunately, although Ralph could go forever, he was not fast; it took a while for those telephone-pole-size legs to move all that granite. All I had to do was dance away from him for a few seconds, and he would stop, give me a long look, and say in a calm, serious voice, "Roat, one of these days . . ." Ralph could easily have retaliated for my petty harassments. I mean, we were up close and personal all day and a good part of the night. It was soon apparent that he wanted to nail me in the act, like a puppy shitting on the floor, and rub my nose in it.

"One of these days" came at the chow hall, where I had made it a habit, every once in a while, of messing with his food. That, more than anything, pierced Ralph's stoic demeanor. All I had to do when I called him fatty was to maintain a little distance for a short time, and it was over. But if I messed with his food, I had bigger problems. We were in the chow hall for short periods of time, jammed closely together, intent on stuffing food down our gullets. I used the same path to the well one too many times: Get Ralph's attention directed back over his shoulder; reach across the table and snatch his pie plate over to my side of the table; set it on the bench by my leg. Well, it worked that way the first time I did it. He hadn't even noticed his pie was gone till I was up and away from the table. The next time, as soon as my hand reached his pie plate, Ralph spun back toward me and stuck his fork in the top of my hand between the thumb and forefinger. That made his day; Ralph had the biggest "Got you!" grin I had ever seen. *Now don't fuck with my food!*"

Kenneth T. Winter, the other half of our boat crew's dynamic duo, was strong and steady, with a real good, built-in bullshit detector. No one called him Kenneth. I don't know why, but most of the guys called him Tom, and he has always been Tommy to me. Tommy had the same cold eyes Instructor Waddell had. If you could see his eyes, there was no doubt about what he felt, even before he spoke. He was not big on excuses: His attitude was, if you did something, you knew what you were doing; if you didn't know, you were stupid, and that was worse. Suffer the consequences and shut up.

Tommy was quiet, but compared to Ralph, he was a chatterbox. I mean, Tommy might even initiate a conversation. In his blunt style, one day Tommy asked me why I made so much noise. I answered "Because I like to." Tommy just said, "That's what I thought."

I asked, "Why are you so quiet?"

He gave me a long look, smiled that big, rare smile of his, and said, "That's how I am." If I had to pick one word to describe him, it would be forthright. I hope that when I die, I deserve the word "forthright" in my obituary. God bless you, Tommy.

Our crew was topped off with, last but not least, Troy E. Vaught, a hard young stud from somewhere way down in south Texas. Troy had a soft southern drawl that women just loved, and the drawl was coupled with an easy manner that let him fit in wherever he chose. When I think about him, I see a smile on his face and that easy manner, no matter what bullshit they were dumping on our heads. Troy was a lot like Fast Eddie in that he had a natural grace; he knew where all his extremities fit in time and space.

I don't believe we would have ended up with the same boat crew if any of us had done the picking at the start of training. I do know that I wouldn't have replaced one guy; as far as I'm concerned, it was as close to the perfect boat crew as ever went through training! It had nothing to do with who you liked the best; it had to do with melding *hard* young men, most of whom had a strong streak of *get the fuck out of my way, I'm going to get this done,* into a *team*. The best teams are never made up of people with little egos, they are forged in strife from huge egos. Every guy in the class had a big ego; some of the biggest were in our boat crew, mine included.

Our officers were in the odd position of having their authority undercut by the instructors and the circumstances of training itself. There was not the normal strictly enforced separation between *them* and *us*. They did what the enlisted did—bust ass. They ate what we ate, large quantities of crap food. All the power and privileges granted to them by the Congress of the United States with their commissions as officers and gentlemen were just so much bullshit. If they'd wanted the easy life of a naval officer, they could have removed their red helmets and returned to the real world of the United States Navy.

When I started training, I had little respect for most officers. In my mind, chiefs and warrant officers ran things. Commissioned officers were just college boys filling space and trying to look important. As individuals, and as a group, Class-29's officers were men first and officers second. They carried their weight and maintained a little officerlike bearing in the face of having their leadership abilities demeaned at every turn.

Nowhere else in the navy are officers belittled in front of enlisted men; elsewhere respect is maintained at all cost. Navy recruits are taught from the first day at boot camp that they do not have to respect the man, but they'd better respect his commission as an officer. If they don't, they will end up in the brig. In those days, brigs were not very nice jails, generally run by United States Marines. The express purpose of a brig was to make enlisted men *suffer* the consequences of their actions. Bad-mouthing an officer was enough to get your ass locked up.

At the start of training, I loved it when an officer was dumped on. That changed sometime during Hell Week; they were no longer "the" officers, they had become "our" officers. We respected them as men, fuck the commission! They were an odd mix of officers; like us, they ran the gamut of the male condition. Some big, some small, some quiet, some loud, some believers in one All Powerful God, and some who could care less. We all had one thing in common—to become Frogmen we would take anything the instructors passed out. It wasn't "officers and enlisted men" in training; it was "us" against the instructors.

Ens. Thomas L. Gaston, the biggest man in our training class, was bigger than Ralph Diebold and at least as strong, with the personality traits of P.T. Smith, a nice guy. He was nicknamed Bimbo after a famous circus elephant. Several officers swore they had seen him tip over a Volkswagen Beetle by himself. I believe it; I have a clear memory of Bimbo with his big shoulders under the bow of his boat, arms stretching across the bottom, his big hands grasping the rubber handles. There was no one else under the boat. It was hanging down his back, the stern dragging in the sand. Bimbo's treelike legs were driving into the sand, propelling him and the boat toward the finish line. It was one of the myriad races in which the instructors pitted boat crews against one another. I don't remember what had happened to the rest of his crew, but he was still going, determined to cross the finish line with their boat.

In talking about the men of our training class, when I say big, I mean weight, mass, a large object, someone who requires a lot of energy to move. The big guys worked harder to do everything; they had to expend extra energy just to move their mass. When they put us through the obstacle course, had us on the chin-up bars, or on a timed mile run, the big guys never came in first; it was the one-hundred-and-forty to one-hundred-and-fifty pounders who were first through the obstacle course, did the most chin-ups, or came in first on the timed runs. Where the big guys paid off for the rest of us was under the boats; many times they carried more than their share. As much as I hurt throughout training, I was thankful not to be a big guy.

Every guy in our class, big or little, fast or slow, officer or enlisted had *heart*, *guts*, *big brass balls*. Whatever it is you care to call what gets someone through the hard times. Training didn't make us that way. Each guy had brought it with him, the courage to do the hard stuff when there is an easy way out.

One thing made all but one of us whine: *being wet and cold!* One guy, Raymond K. Woodsworth, had been raised in the woods of Maine. He thought the weather in Virginia was just fine. Of course, we called him Woody. He spoke in the special rhythmic way they have in that part of the country. I liked to hear him talk, which he didn't do much; most of the time he just seemed to be amused. When we got to Camp Pickett, Woody would save our collective trainee asses from freezing to death, and the instructors from the consequences of allowing it to happen!

Instructor Spiegel became known as Cool Breeze by Class-29. When he ran with us, he made it look effortless. No matter how fast he ran, he appeared to be taking it easy. Chief Henry Spiegel was one of those guys who made everything look effortless. Spiegel always made it seem like he was sorry we were forcing him to put us through all the unreasonable shit. One day we were twenty seconds late getting to Beach 7 for demolition practical work that Instructor Spiegel was leading. Our punishment was to do sets of twenty push-ups, followed by twenty squat thrusts. Old Cool Breeze had us keep that up for twenty minutes while he leaned on a boat paddle and watched us waste twenty minutes to make up for the loss of twenty seconds. But that's the way Henry was, unemotional, unflappable, and unforgiving.

*   *   *

The separation that is normally kept between enlisted and officers in all branches of the military works well. It is possibly the only way to organize a successful military. Given the nature of the Teams' unconventional missions and the type of enlisted men that get through training, then and now, the only place I know where it would never work is the Teams. Let's speak in plain enlisted language: If an officer can't hack the same damn training program as me, he can stuff being followed. Keep in mind, a Team member as well as a trainee can leave anytime he wants. In those days, most of the black shoe navy had no understanding of what the Teams were about.

Sometime after Hell Week and before Camp Pickett, the black shoe navy struck. It seemed that Little Creek Amphibious Base was about to change commanding officers, and someone figured out that our officers were eating with us at the enlisted chow hall. True enough; they sure weren't going to let a load of enlisted trainees into the officers' dining hall. The problem was, it is uncommon in the military for officers and enlisted men to eat together except in the middle of combat. Then, of course, no one cares. The fleet types thought it was up to them to put an end to this demeaning practice; after all, we weren't at war, were we?

Breakfast, lunch, and dinner, our officers had to return to our barracks and get into dress blue uniforms so they could eat in the officers' dining hall. Considering our officers were in training to be big bad Frogmen, this was no pleasure for them: A normal officers' mess is tight-assed, big on how you are dressed, how you hold your damn fork, and how slow you can eat. Our officers then had to return to the barracks, climb into their dirty greens, and fall back in with us. That was a big pain in the ass for the officers. When they ate with us there was none of the get cleaned up and act like gentlemen crap. We ate as much food as we could, as fast as we could! The instructors felt the new arrangement was interfering with their training program. They were trying to see if we could be team members, and by then, the false barriers of normal military life had been gone from Class-29 for well over a month! More important, by that time we were classmates. It was "us" against "them," no matter who in the hell "them" were!

On paper, the black shoe navy was in charge of the training unit, but they had just pissed off a bunch of Frogman chiefs. The officers of the black shoe navy got their way for a week, then the chiefs won. Once again, our officers got to eat in the enlisted chow hall, stuff as much food in their gullets as they wanted, as fast as they wanted, in the comfort of their dirty greens!

One thing about running in cold weather, it helps you warm up. I never remember shivering on a long run! I do remember some runs that got us pretty hot under the collar. Our beloved instructors would tell us we had a certain distance to run, say five miles. Well, it wasn't long before every man in the class got to the point where he could tell just how far we had run at any given moment. Well, when we'd run past what they told us, the only thing that came to my mind was *shit!* How far? I know we did five-mile runs that were fifteen miles long. The instructors constantly played little head games with pain. After all, we could just leave anytime we wanted!

Late one miserable, cold, rainy afternoon, our head instructor put up a prize for the first man in from a five-mile run. The winner would not have to participate in the surf penetration and sneak and peek planned for that night. It pays to be a winner? All of us had fantasies, and it is hard to believe how much just one night of being warm in a bed while everyone else froze their butts off can mean.

The winner that day was not one of the usual front-runners. Troy Vaught started back there with me, in the middle of the pack, but he won; a guy from the middle of the pack beat the fast guys. Chief Benny Sulinski would use both sides of the double-edged sword of being a winner on our man Troy. Our big kahuna was all smiles; he was happy to let Troy off for that night. Benny was happy because he knew he had flushed a fast runner out of the middle of the pack. Troy would never again be allowed to finish a long run as other than a front-runner. If he did, he paid dearly. A good lesson: *You pay to be a winner!*

Talk about sneak and peek, Joe Camp and I snuck right out of a good part of one of our worst night evolutions. It was just the usual stuff, send in scout swimmers, bring in the boats on signal, then gather information without getting caught. Most nights were cold, many below freezing. That one was below ten degrees Fahrenheit. Joe Camp and I spent the night at the officers' club while the rest of our classmates froze. It was a tough job, but someone had to do it.

There was no plan, it was just one of those luck-outs that come along. We figured the instructors would not be looking for us to run from the beach directly to the sites we had to recon, so we hit each spot quickly, then started looking for a hideout. Someplace to get out of the cold for about three hours. We were behind the officers' club, seeing if we could hide in one of the small outbuildings by the edge of the golf course. As Joe and I skulked around, two black guys came out the back door of the officers' club and entered one of the small buildings.

Joe and I were not a pretty sight: We had on old greens, face camouflage, and ice. A thin sheet of the damn stuff covered us from head to toe. When salt water freezes, you know it is cold. I knocked on the door, and Joe was going to do the talking. As it turned out we didn't have to say a word. The guy who answered the door was the head steward for the officers' club. He had been around for a while, knew who we were, and what we were up to. Before Joe could say anything, he opened the door wide, and said "Get your asses in here." Everyone on the base knew about training, and most of them were pulling for the trainee, not the instructors. We had a foul-weather friend, thank God.

We were in the stewards' lounge, and the place had a big old wood-burning stove. Thank you! Thank you! As Joe and I huddled by the stove, they fixed us hot chocolate. We spent the next three hours relaxing in the stewards' warm lounge while our classmates froze their butts off. The stewards even brought us food from the officers' club. I promise you, neither Joe nor I felt the least bit of guilt.

When leaving time came, we wet down the outside of our clothes with warm water. It would quickly freeze, and we would look just as bad as the rest of the Class-29. Before we reached the rendezvous point, we had a nice little sheet of tinkling ice, from stocking caps to boondockers. At the time, we all thought that was the coldest we would ever be; little did we know! When the class was lit up by the lights of the instructors' truck, everyone sparkled, from head to toe, with little crystals of ice. We looked like not so pleasant pieces of mobile ice sculpture.

Class-29 was close to moving to the fantasy that Instructor Waddell had instilled in all of us. "Puerto Rico, where the sun shines every day, coconuts and bananas on all the trees." We wanted the warm water, warm air, warm rain. Hell, we wanted *warm*, period. We only had a week and a half before we departed for Waddell's Wonderland, Roosevelt Roads, Puerto Rico. Our last week in Virginia would be spent in the mountains at a place called Camp Pickett.

We were to have liberty before departing for Camp Pickett. Some of the guys were going to use the time to go to Camp Pickett and rathole contraband: food, booze, candy, smokes, anything we weren't to have for survival training. Almost everyone was involved in some type of clandestine operation against the instructors and their plan to starve us for a week in the name of survival. If we were caught, of course we'd suffer, but by that time in training, we had become damn good covert operators. After all, that's what they were training us for, and they were the only adversaries we had to test our skills against.

We had the best source of intelligence possible, a trainee who had been there, Tom McCutchan. We were all pumping him, looking for ways to overcome the instructors' inevitable predeparture shakedown. A couple of different cabals were involved in going up to Camp Pickett to stash the contraband. They managed to hide quite a large quantity of contraband within a couple miles of the survival training area. And they had made contact with someone who lived in the woods just off the military reservation. One cabal was headed by two of the officers, Jim Hawes and Bimbo Gaston. The main food item in their stash was canned Dinty Moore Beef Stew, which compared to C rations or going without food was a truly superlative meal. If I remember right, McCutchan was hooked up with a large cabal loosely led by Harry Humphries. I'm sure Harry didn't think of himself as the leader, but he's one of those rare people whom the rest of us follow whether he wants to lead or not.

Ensign Janke managed to get the instructors to carry in two pints of booze for him, probably the slickest move made by any of us. He secured the bottles of Drambuie under a "water buffalo" (freshwater tank on wheels) the instructors were transporting to Camp Pickett. He also managed to get a shitload of Tootsie Rolls in, a great nutritional supplement that any starving man might kill for.

Just before we left for Camp Pickett, there was one small incident of what might be called bathroom humor. Instructor Cook ran the supply room; he was the master of all the crap equipment we were issued to work with. When we checked equipment out, guys would be lined up down the hall, through the instructors' head (bathroom), through the instructors' lounge, and outside. Checking things out was never a fast operation; somebody was always being given "extra instruction." Each instructor felt duty bound to make sure we were late for whatever came next.

That day, Joe Camp and P.T. Smith found themselves last in a very slow line. They were two of the smarter guys in the class; not that day. As their end of the line started to pass through the instructors' head, they both felt the need to take a dump. No sooner had they settled themselves on the instructors' toilet seats, than Instructor Clements walked past the doorless stalls and calmly said, "Instructor Sulinski probably won't like that." Clements had been through the door to the instructors' office all of thirty seconds when the big kahuna, in all his spit-shined majesty, confronted the poopers. There stood the recruiting-poster image of our senior chief petty officer, ranting and raving about their lineage, and all they could do was sit and let nature take its course. It is a good thing I didn't see it; I would have laughed so hard I'd have been in more trouble than our inappropriate poopers.

All of us were ready; just one week in the damn mountains, and we would fly to the land of warm. As far as I was concerned, not soon enough! Of course, the worst two days in training were about to happen, and believe me, that wasn't part of the training plan.

PHASE THREE

The third phase of training was conducted at Camp Pickett, Virginia, for one week. The weather was adverse as seven inches of snow fell during the week of training. Setting up bivouac and training under these conditions was most realistic. At Camp Pickett, the trainees were taught land navigational techniques, day and night patrolling, survival, escape and evasion, combat firing methods, and use of hand grenades. This week of training was highlighted by a twenty-six-mile penetration and demolition raid against a bridge, during which more than three inches of snow fell.

Yeah, right. Three inches of snow, my ass! Try three feet!

The bus trip up to Camp Pickett took close to three hours. In our eight weeks of training, that was the longest period of time we had to just sit and shoot the bull with each other. For a while I talked with Forrest Dearborn Hedden Jr. Forrest was the youngest guy in our class and, judging the book by the cover, did not belong where he was. He looked to be all of a *young* fifteen years old; I, on the other hand, appeared to be at least an old sixteen. Forrest was a Methodist minister's son, a believer who never swore. The first week of training, I had heard him complain to four or five guys about their swearing. At the time, I thought what in the hell is he doing here? That little asshole will never make it. I couldn't have been more wrong; Forrest was rock hard, not an ounce of quit in him. I only heard Forest swear once in all the time I knew him, and it happened over what transpired at Camp Pickett.

We got off the bus in front of a small country store five or six miles from the area we were to train in. Camp Pickett was a large Army Reserve base used mainly for tank training and battalion-size movements. We were going to have a lovely little stroll in the country, something called a forced march, a short one, just a little welcome to the start of Phase Three of training. I came around the back of the bus just as two pint bottles of booze fell out of Jessie J. Hardy's pant leg and broke on the road. With a big tear on his cheek, Jessie just stood looking down, the booze running across the asphalt, repeating, "They broke," over and over. Hell, he was already drunk; he had sucked down a quart on the trip up. I will never forget the look of total loss on his face or how sad Jessie made the words "They broke" sound.

As we formed up for the march, Instructor Waddell was standing in front of the small store. There were two doors, four or five feet apart. The one on the left said WHITE, the one on the right said COLORED. I remember thinking at the time, if Instructor Waddell wanted to go through the WHITE door, who the hell had enough ass to stop him? At the end of the week, he would take us shopping at that little country store.

For the most part, Camp Pickett was a welcome break. No boats on our heads, no obstacle course, no Gig Squads. None of the day-to-day insanity we had been living with for the previous two months. A lot of the guys had never done any camping, so having a tent and sleeping on the ground were new things for them. The way some of them set up their tents, I could tell they didn't have a clue; they raised tents in low spots where water would pool, or on flat ground without digging trenches around them. The first rain, those tents would be full of water. God bless the Boy Scouts. If I learned nothing else from them, I knew how to live on the ground.

There was one huge drawback to being out of our barracks: *no hot showers*. By that time in training, merely being cold was no big thing; it was just part of life. We did have a shower of sorts, a little waterfall in a stream that fed a small lake near the camp. But it was February in the mountains of Virginia, and the water in that stream was damn cold. Until Camp Pickett, showering had been one of our few pleasures.

We did some funny dances under that waterfall. Most of us tried to wash without getting under it. We'd kneel by the stream, naked, and wash with a washrag and soap, then rinse off by cupping water in a hand and pouring it over the soapy area. Of course, if one of our immaculate instructors thought our feeble efforts in the direction of hygiene were lacking, we were ordered under the waterfall. Poor Lieutenant Johnson was ordered to shower one morning around 0600, before the sun was even up. He had to get naked, then break the ice on the stream just so he could walk to the waterfall. In truth, getting under the damn waterfall got the pain over with a lot quicker. That water was so cold that even if you were a stud before your shower, you couldn't find it after.

Besides Woody, we had one other man who knew how to live off the land—Carl Thomas Allen, but everyone called him "Tom." His dad, Ross Allen, was quite famous for being one of the early developers of snakebite serum. Tom had grown up in and around the swamps of Florida, hunting, fishing, catching snakes, alligators, and any other wild creature that struck his fancy. He had even taken a trip up the Amazon with his dad, looking for rare snakes. He was a third class engineman, and one of the few married guys who graduated with our training class. Tom Allen was a big guy who took care of business first. He had a real good sense of how the world fit him.

Most people had no idea how far over the edge he would go. I would later see Tom grab a seven- or eight-foot shark by the snout and dorsal fin, then shake it senseless. With Tom, things like that were not unusual. I think Tom and Woody were the two guys in our class who were the happiest to be out in the wilderness. I do know that if the instructors had dropped either of them in a forest with nothing but a knife, neither would have had any problem surviving on his own.

Our instructors were staying across the valley from us, and *they* were not living in tents. They had a big log cabin with a wood stove and electricity and lots of food. Their cabin was a good quarter mile from us, which made it easy for the men who did nighttime sneak and peeks to retrieve ratholed contraband. We had not been so far from the instructors since our around the world cruise.

For most of the week, being at Camp Pickett was like a minivacation; all of the usual devices of pain that our instructors used to make life miserable were back at Little Creek. Not that they didn't pass around push-ups, squat jumps, and duckwalking, but the harassment took a backseat to our acquiring new talents. Part of the reason for that is that boot camp for sailors is all about ships and how to handle living on them, not the things UDT trainees need to know for land warfare. A lot of the things we were being taught at Pickett would be second nature for any soldier or Marine right out of their boot camp—combat firing methods, how to use a hand grenade, land navigation, and the like.

Throughout training, we had eaten as much as we wanted, but at Pickett, our food intake was cut way back in favor of dreaded "combat rations," better known as C rations, which we were allowed to supplement with any wild thing we might pick or kill. The picking went better than the killing, and the picking wasn't that good.

Our beloved instructors had a load of rabbits brought in so we might learn to kill and skin a small animal. Now these were not wild rabbits; they were cute pet-type bunnies. It was funny to watch a trainee holding his rabbit and stroking it like the family pet. Forrest Hedden said, "I can't kill this cute little rabbit!" and he didn't have to; Jessie J. Hardy made a nice little business of killing rabbits for a portion of their meat. Unlike Forrest, most of Jessie's customers didn't want the rest of us to know.

Jessie J. and Leo Duncan were sharing a tent. Leo was very handsome, on the Elvis level, and he had surprised me already. When we started training, Duncan was in worse shape than many of the trainees who quit during the first two weeks. By the end of Hell Week, Leo was one of the few guys who were physically *stronger*. Most of us had a lot less strength after Hell Week than when training started. What Leo did have was "fire in the belly," and what I like to think of as the "burning in the brain": the need to be a United States Navy Frogman.

Leo and Jessie cooked up a little scheme to get the biggest rabbits. Their plan was simple: They would volunteer to get the rabbits off the truck and pass them out. There was just one problem, each thought the other had ratholed the fat rabbits, so they ended up with the little bunnies. The best-laid plans . . .

Ron Lester and Eddie Leasure were tent buddies and, like all of us, were not happy with the decreased food availability. They hatched a scheme with Jesse and Leo that would increase their calorie intake. Basically, they went on a begging mission. The four of them put their heads together and came up with another simple plan. Since our instructors were not sitting on top of us twenty-four hours a day, the four coconspirators figured the early evening and most of the night were theirs. As soon as it looked like our instructors were stuffing themselves with real food in their cabin, Jessie and Ron would take off on their mission. They would bring back anything that was edible and share it with their tentmates. Eddie and Leo would stay in camp and take care of all the duties of the four of them: clean weapons, stand watch, etc.

Jesse and Ron would sneak out of camp, then beat feet till they found houses where they could beg food. Well, it worked, but they had to bust ass to make it happen. Once they had done their sneak and peek to get out of camp unobserved, they got on the roads and hauled ass. The area surrounding Camp Pickett was boondocks, forest and hills, with little clumps of homes stuck here and there. Our guys didn't score till they had covered most of ten miles, but when they scored, they scored big—sandwiches, Pepsi, one whole strawberry cake(!), and assorted other goodies.

Ron Jarvi and P.T. Smith were also tentmates at Camp Pickett. One evening when we were allowed to have fires, everyone's boondockers were frozen, so P.T., being his good-guy self, tried to show Ron an old camping trick. The idea was to let the campfire burn down, then drive stakes cut from green wood about eighteen inches long into the ground through the bed of coals. Push the coals away from the stake, put a boot, upside down, on each stake, then hit the sack. In the morning, the boots would be thawed, dry, and warm. It worked fine for both of P.T.'s boots and one of Ron's. His other boot fell onto the coals, and by morning there wasn't much left beyond some charred leather and a heel.

Admittedly our boondockers weren't much; the damn things were already worn out when they were issued to us. But when the ground is frozen and worn-out boondockers are all you have, *you love them*. Ron Jarvi was one very unhappy camper. P.T. Smith's walk down to the instructors' hut that morning to grovel and beg for some replacement boondockers for Ron was a most unpleasant walk. He damn well knew our instructors would make him pay. So much for P.T's not coming to the attention of the instructors. Worse than the thought of what he'd have to endure from the instructors was the thought of living in that small pup tent with a one-booted Jarvi. It was odd, but all of us would rather have faced our instructors' wrath than that of our classmates. After that, P.T. kept his hot camper tricks to himself.

The nights were very cold. All my clothes, what I was wearing and any extra—clean or dirty—went into my sleeping bag with me at night. Even my frozen, muddy boondockers were stuffed into the bottom of the bag. We didn't have cold-weather gear, just the same crap surveyed gear we'd had from the start. We were limited as to times we could have fires and how large they could be because we were living a "simulated combat" situation, and fires would give our position away. We took turns standing guard duty, a most important, cold, and very lonely duty. When you're whipped and have to get out of a warm sleeping bag at two in the morning, it is not an easy task to pay attention. What keeps popping into your mind is, I'm cold and tired. It's a very personal struggle to pretend successfully that your shipmates' lives depend on your vigilance. To make yourself do it right becomes a mind battle. But the night before the Kennedy Bridge raid, I had no problem staying awake; I thought there was a bear behind every tree.

Jerky, jerked beef, is one of the truly savory foods on

this earth, and we were being taught how to jerk beef. It was to be our main food source during the twenty-six-mile forced march to blow up Kennedy Bridge. Our instructors had bought an enormous quantity of prime beef, and it amazed me to see what a small amount of jerky came out of that huge pile of bloody meat, wood, and effort. Not only does jerking beef take a lot of meat, but wood and time as well. And the whole time the beef was smoking, the smell was driving us crazy. I had guard duty the night before our forced march, and one of my duties was to keep our smoking fire burning just right. Checking the fire was a pleasure, *warm-warm-warm,* but best, to this day, I can remember the smell of that beef as it smoked. The whole valley was permeated with that wonderful aroma.

There couldn't have been a bear within ten miles, or the damn thing would have been in the middle of our camp. From my experience, smoking that meat was just like what poachers do to attract bears into a kill area. I had seen that done twice: Put a slab of bacon and a can of honey over hot coals and let the wind carry the smell. Both times that had attracted bears. I saw none that night, but every sound in the woods was like a shot of adrenaline. Not me or any of my shipmates was going to be eaten by a bear while *I* was on watch! I took that guard duty damn serious. I had no problem staying awake that night!

The raid on Kennedy Bridge was to be run with as much realism as possible. No live ammunition, and simulated demolition, but the rest of the mission would be according to Hoyle. Our simulated demolitions were very real twenty-five-pound bags of bricks. I would rather have used our imagination. We had a warning order, that is, get ready in general. Then, a couple of hours later, a briefing where everyone was let in on the plan and their part in it. If a briefing is done properly, everyone is given a chance to discuss potential problems and to work out necessary adjustments.

The objective was to reach the area of the bridge in the early-morning hours, while we would still have the cover of darkness, recon the bridge, quietly take out any guards, properly place over a thousand pounds of simulated demolitions, then pretend to blow the damn thing sky-high.

I love explosives. If you know what you are doing, amazing things can be made to happen with small amounts of explosive. For what we had to do, the appropriate amount was critical. We had to carry it every inch of the way. On a forced march through rough terrain, every ounce of weight counts. Our biggest obstacle would be crossing twenty-six miles of wild country. There were dirt roads, but observers would be watching the roads; even if we managed to avoid being seen by them, we'd leave tracks in the dust or mud. Our plan was to stay with the cover of the woods and the rough terrain; we were going to bull our way through. The weather report called for light rain or snow. God had a surprise for all of us, trainees and instructors alike.

It was one of the few times in training that we didn't have instructors right there watching every move we made. When they were around, they were able to rein us in at will. As it turned out, we were pretty successful in our effort not to be seen during the operation. Three hours into the operation, the instructors began trying to call off the raid, but we had no radio contact. Hell, we had no radio! The only reason I can think of that we hadn't been issued a radio was that in World War II the men wouldn't have had them.

We were trying to prove we were tough; we forgot smart. The instructors spent the next fifteen hours running the roads in their vehicles, trying to locate their lost and freezing trainees. The one reason they couldn't find us was that we had the cover of an extremely rare occurrence, a blizzard in the great state of Virginia.

They said we got over three inches of snow during the Kennedy Bridge raid. Yeah that's right, around three feet over three inches. Under the best of conditions, twenty-six miles of rough terrain is not easy to cover in twelve hours. It didn't start off bad, our problem was we didn't know the difference between *quitting* and when stopping was the right thing to do. By this time in training, there was no one left that didn't have a modus operandi of, "Hell, that's no hill for a climber!!!" We kept climbing way too long.

The snow started coming down slowly almost as soon as we left camp. Big wet snowflakes gently floated out of the sky. Three hours into the raid, it was obvious to one and all that the weatherman was a bit off! By then, those big wet snowflakes were coming down hard and fast, and they covered everything. The guy on point was breaking trail through snowdrifts, and all of us were wet and cold, but still heading for the bridge.

Tommy Winter and Ron Lester were rear security. That means they were bringing up the rear. In a combat situation, their job was to keep anyone from slipping up on the column from behind, a very serious job. But during a blizzard, it turned into a serious pain in the frozen ass. The terrain we were moving through was severe up and down, not an easy walk without snow. The men in the rear had nothing to walk on except snow that had been packed down into ice. There was a lot of slipping and sliding going on. The worst of it came from in front of them. The rest of us slipping and sliding downhill and knocking Ron and Tommy on their asses.

For me, it got to the point that all I wanted to do was lie down in the snow and go to sleep. I had been told that's how people freeze to death. They just lie down, go to sleep, and never wake up. I believe it. At some point, we had become lost! Thinking that no one would be out looking for us in the snow anyway, we had decided to get on one of the roads so we could move faster. Well, we couldn't find the road. That's when our situation finally became apparent to all of us: We were in a world of *shit*, very cold shit. Of course, we immediately did the wrong thing. Instead of stopping and building fires, we decided what direction we were to take and continued touring the mountains of Virginia, belly-button-deep in snow. Our persistence could never be challenged, but I must admit, there is some evidence that we weren't too bright.

Class-29 kept slogging around until one of us fell in a creek. I don't remember who it was, but I want to say *thank you*! It was enough to stop our stupidity and get us on the right track. Some of us started gathering wood, and two fires were quickly built. Our man, Raymond K. Woodsworth, aka Woody, then left the fire and went off into the snow-enveloped forest. Thank God for Woody, somebody had to find out where we were.

There are three things I remember clearly about those two big fires: (1) God, they felt good; (2) some of us kept getting too close to the fire and had to be made to move back; (3) some of us hadn't fared too well. There were actually a few boondocker bottoms burnt. And one of our Dutchmen, De Beer, ended up with not only frostbite but burns on his feet as well. As I was sitting on my poncho next to Jessie J. Hardy, we were facing the fire soaking up the heat, and old Jessie had steam rolling off his body when he reached down and took off one of his boon-dockers. I couldn't believe my eyes; a big chunk of ice covered his toes, over the sock and all. I said something real bright, "Shit, Jessie, look at your toes!" I don't know why I said it; he was already looking at his toes. Jessie gave me a funny look and said, "Yeah, well, look at your own toes." With that, I took my own boondockers off. Jessie J. was absolutely right; my socks were frozen to my toes, and each foot had a little clump of ice over the toes, socks and all. Most everyone had the same thing, to one degree or another. The consequences for me were on the mild end of the spectrum, a little extra pain. On the other end, one of our officers, Charley Rand, lost several of his toes and, with them, his opportunity to complete training.

To my way of thinking, Ens. Charles H. Rand was a hell of a man and should have been there with us when we graduated! I believe he had been an English major in college. He spoke very properly and used words that most of us had never heard. Thinking back, it may have been Mr. Rand who said, "Food, without the benefit of mastication, is a crime against nature!" It was him or Mr. Janke, but his use of proper English and his being the tallest guy in our class kept him visible to our instructors. If the instructors could see you, even when you were standing behind everyone, you had a problem. Charles H. Rand was handling everything our instructors dumped on him. In my mind he will always be a graduate of UDT RT Class-29! Our instructors couldn't make him quit; it took an act of God to get him. It wasn't just brass balls and intestinal fortitude that got you through training, it took a large allowance from Lady Luck as well.

Woody is my hero. Like all of us, he had been packing bricks around over snow-covered mountains for eighteen hours. While we sat around our fires, Woody was back out there in the snow, finding out how to get us out of that winter wonderland and back into the arms of our loving instructors. As it turned out, their arms were not so loving. Our instructors were pissed, and as usual, it was catch-22 reasoning. Not to worry, we would receive one more opportunity to suffer as a group before we left Pickett. I mean after all, that's what we were in training for. The instructors had three major complaints: (1) we hadn't stopped soon enough; (2) we didn't accomplish our assigned task; (3) worst of all, our instructors had been running all over the mountains of Virginia trying to locate their lost charges. I didn't think about it at the time, but number 3 was the big one. The instructors had a lot to lose—their careers—if things had gotten any worse. Whether the snowstorm was "an act of God" or not, the navy very well could have stuck the blame for it on our instructors.

The snow had stopped falling while Woody was out trying to find where we were. Then it immediately started to warm up. We would pay for how quickly it warmed up. Well, we would have paid if it didn't warm up; it just would have been a different price. The snow was melting faster than it had come down. Our whole world was about to become melting snow, running water, or nasty-ass mud.

After Woody located Kennedy Bridge and got us there, our oh-so-sensitive instructors came up with a new plan. Knowing that our failure to blow the bridge might scar our fragile psyches, they offered us a way to redeem ourselves. All we had to do was walk back from the bridge to our base camp. There was just one catch, a time limit. Our instructors didn't believe we could cover the distance in the time we were given for the forced march over muddy roads that wandered through the tank training fields at Camp Pickett. We had gone to the bridge through the part of Pickett covered with forest. The way we were coming back had little growth, just a tree here, some brush there. There was a lot of up-and-down and bare ground that had been torn up by years of tanks training for war.

It was gut-check time, not for any individual, but for the class. For many of us, it was the lowest point in training; we were demoralized. Class-29 started the little walk about as down and bedraggled as a group of men can get. I don't remember exactly what it was Harry Humphries said, it was something short, sweet, and not for Mother to hear. What I do remember is watching him go from tired and down, to a "no hill for a climber," in a nanosecond. More important, Harry maintained it every mud-sucking step of the way. No line in our net broke; we worked ourselves from demoralized and bedraggled, to pissed off and bedraggled. We were crazed, and Harry was the head nut. It was just a little trip from here to there. I mean, what was the big deal? We all understood by then, we got shit, win, lose, or draw. So our little walk in the mud was about *Fuck them! Hooray for us!* Nothing more, nothing less.

Hour after hour in slimy, sucking mud, we pushed, pulled, crawled, slid, and at times, we even got to walk. Whatever it took. Sometimes we used the winding muddy roads; other times, it was up and down the muddy hills and across the muddy dales. At one time or another, every one of us had his boondockers sucked off his feet. At times, you were pushing someone and someone was pushing you. Ensign Janke was not his usual easygoing self. He and my boat officer, Jim Hawes, spent most of their time as rear security, making sure no one dropped behind. Janke was passing out tough love; if you were stuck, he and Hawes helped. When Janke thought you were just slacking off, he became *very* chieflike, and piled on heaps of verbal abuse. We didn't have a chief, so somebody had to do the job.

With their smart-ass remarks, Lieutenant Shea and Jack Lynch took me from pissed off to thinking the whole episode was funny. Humphries was all over the place. He wanted us back at the camp early, and was doing whatever he could to make that happen. I had a good laugh when I saw Risher stuck calf-deep in the mud and Harry and Bimbo Gaston each pulling on an arm. It looked like Ted was going to be pulled apart before the mud let him go, and with those two animals pulling on him, dismemberment was a very real possibility.

We were surprised when we finally crested the ridge above our base camp. It was around three in the morning, and we were early. Not just a few minutes early, but a couple of *Fuck them! Hooray for us!* hours early.

Our instructors were all asleep in their nice warm cabin, but we wanted them awake. There would be no doubt in their minds that we had hammered the time frame on their damn mud march. It was a risky move. I figured we were going to end up pushing the mountains of Virginia away. We could have easily come quietly off the ridge and gone to our tents for some well-needed sleep. Not a chance; we were pumped and would happily take the pain just to stick our small victory in their faces.

Each of our instructors had a song he liked us to sing. Not manly military-type songs, but things like "I've Been Working on the Railroad." That one was Instructor Waddell's song, and we were on his operation. Class-29 formed up in a semblance of military order, then came down off that ridge singing "I've Been Working on the Railroad." Class-29 not having choir-type voices, we had never made that song sound good. But that morning we boomed it out in triumph, and *damn* we sounded strong.

Well, Chief Bernie Waddell blew my muddy mind that morning. As we came marching up to the cabin, singing his song, Waddell was standing on the side porch. He had on only long underwear bottoms, his feet were spread, his big hands were on his hips. His large brown muscles were bulging all over the place, an imposing sight. I don't remember who, but someone reported us in. Instructor

Waddell just stood there looking us over, he didn't say anything for at least a minute. When he spoke, I think my mouth fell open. Instructor Waddell praised us, told us he was proud to be our instructor. He then added that he would buy each man two beers at that small store, where the bus would pick us up.

In over two months, we had never been praised. Our instructors had let us know, clearly, that as individuals and as a class, we were the lowest of the low. The worst training class *ever*. It took me a while to get to sleep that morning. My mind was moving a mile a minute. Why had Waddell's little bit of praise made me feel nine feet tall? He gave me another mind picture to think about over the years when he bought our beer at that little country store.

I could taste Puerto Rico, "where the sun shines every day." We just had to break down, force-march all our crap to that little country store, catch the bus, and we were done with Camp Pickett. I think the whole class felt the same: We wanted warm, and we wanted it bad. The pissant little five- or six-mile saunter to our pickup point would take no time at all. Everyone was looking forward to an instructor's buying us beer. But I wanted to see which door Waddell would walk through.

Well, I got to see my first act of civil disobedience. All it did was confirm my suspicion that the human race was full of shit. Chief Waddell walked in the WHITE door. He didn't make a big deal out of it, and no one else seemed to notice. The guy in the store was happy to have the business. But my thought at the time was, if Waddell had been a weak old man, he would have had to suffer for using the wrong door. As far as I was concerned, the human race worked on the schoolyard bully principle; smack the asshole back, and he'll go find some weak fucker to mess with. I have seen nothing since that has changed my mind. The really sad thing is, I think most people choose to be weak! I'm not talking big muscles; all anyone had to do was take a look at my classmates. Most of us were not strapping muscle men. Strength is definitely a mental game. Strong people do one simple thing: Win, lose, or draw, they get back up; they get the fuck back up. But one thing struck me as funny: A lot of us were using the COLORED door, and no one seemed to get pissed about that either.

When we returned from Camp Pickett, we didn't go straight to Puerto Rico, and today it's unclear to me why. It may have had to do with all the cases of frostbite. I have only two clear memories of that week. One was when we were made to sit on tables with our boondockers and socks removed while a navy doctor—a very agitated captain—checked our feet. The doctor was beside himself when he discovered that De Beer had frostbite *and* burns on his feet. It was the only time I ever heard Forrest Dearborn Hedden Jr. swear.

We were being transported to an army base called Fort Story, on the Virginia coast south of Little Creek. There had been a storm, and the surf at Fort Story was coming in big and bad, obviously a good opportunity to practice surf penetration. Most of us were being transported on an old gray navy bus, but a couple of us were with the boats on a stake truck. *Riding* somewhere was rare, so we were enjoying the easy time while going to have large waves pound us into the sand.

I had created a little ditty to the tune of the Mickey Mouse Club song. I used instructors' names to replace Mickey and Donald Duck. Of course, I never intended our esteemed instructors to hear a word of it. Instructors Clements, Hammond, and Waddell were way up at the front of the bus. P.T. Smith, Lynch, Risher, Forrest, Shorty, and I were in the back of the bus. No way the instructors could hear.

A polite person might say that my voice *carries*. Others have said I have a big mouth. Whichever your view, "we" got heard. I think only Lynch, Risher, and myself were singing. The song began:

> Come along and join the club that's
> made for you and me
> F-r-a-l-e-y M-o-u-s-e,
> Fraley Mouse, Sulinski Duck
> Forever let us do our squat jumps high! high! high!

Not the kind of thing any sane trainee would want the instructors to hear us singing. Well, they heard something, and Waddell was going to keep at us till we told him what it was. He couldn't make a lot of guys squat jump or push Virginia away on a bus, so, when we were getting off the bus at Fort Story, Waddell struck. He was standing by the driver's seat telling everyone from the back to hit the deck when we got off the bus. Forrest was right in front of Waddell as I was stepping off the bus. He said something to our instructor that I didn't hear. Whatever it was, it pissed Waddell off bad. I turned to see what was going on. Bernie was blowed up big, towering over our teenage preacher's son. I was looking at them from the side, and Forrest was blowed up, too. They looked like two guys ready to beat the shit out of each other. Forrest, God bless him, opened up first. "Goddamn you! *It's your fault everyone's feet are fucked from frostbite!*" Bernie stopped right then, no push Virginia away, no questions about what we had been singing. We went straight to surf penetration. I think there were big problems for the instructors over our frostbite.

I had never seen anyone stand toe-to-toe with Waddell. I know the thought had never crossed my mind, but what had surprised me even more, Forrest swore. He never swore; at times, he would even make comments about how much foul language the rest of used. The worst word I had ever heard him say was "darn," and he didn't say that much. Thank you, Forrest; I would have had to give myself up about the song. I cannot even imagine having to stand in front of Instructor Sulinski singing that stupid little ditty.

In the name of saving our frostbitten toes, our ever ingenious instructors found a way to make pushing Virginia away more difficult. We had to do our push-ups with our ankles on the flotation tubes of our rubber boats. That raised our legs about a foot and a half off the deck and put more weight on our arms. It was explained that we were doing this to save our toes from additional stress. Oh, thank you! It was so nice to know our instructors cared.

PHASE FOUR

During the next five weeks, training was conducted at Roosevelt Roads, Puerto Rico, where heavy demolition and endurance swimming were emphasized. There the student became proficient at locating and destroying both man-made and natural obstacles of all types. The swimming distances were gradually increased until the students swam a distance of six miles. Day and night reconnaissance exercises were repeated until the student became proficient in every detail of these operations. Numerous inland penetrations and demolition raids were conducted, while rubber boat training proved to be more fun than work in the Caribbean. A final reconnaissance and demolition problem, under simulated combat conditions, was conducted and marked the end of training in Puerto Rico. At that time, fifteen officers and thirty-four enlisted men remained. Major Qureshi of Pakistan and Ensign Doumouras of Greece, after successfully completing the sixteen-week basic UDT course, returned to their home countries.

We stepped off the plane at Roosevelt Roads—commonly known as Rosey Roads Naval Air Station—into bright, warm sunshine; at last we were in the land of warm. Our instructors quickly educated us to one of the drawbacks of heat. We were hungry, so we were taken to our new training area, where we dumped our gear, then took a mile-and-a-half run to the chow hall. It was the same deal there as in Little Creek—we could eat as much food as we wanted. Well, most of us did. And on the short run back to our new training area, in ninety-degree heat with 90 percent humidity, men were puking all over the place. We hadn't had men puking on runs since Hell Week. Nobody wanted the cold back, but it was quickly apparent being warm would take some getting used to.

Our professors of pain had new forms of harassment with which to welcome us—the truck push, and the screaming meemies sacrifice, to name just two. Our areas at Little Creek were all within three miles of each other, so the instructors had time enough to run us everywhere. But in Rosey Roads, our areas of operation were too far apart to run to and have time to get anything done. Some were even on another island. So we had transportation, vehicles whose only purpose was to carry us from one place to another. We had two trucks, a two-and-a-half-ton stake truck and the man hauler, a tractor trailer, with the trailer set up to carry people, rather like cattle on the way to the slaughterhouse. The funny thing about those trucks was that they had to be pushed to start, and the instructors swore they started up easier if we pushed them uphill.

The screaming meemies were tiny mosquitoes that were hard to see but had a painful bite. The "sacrifice" part of the exercise came at the start of Gig Squad. Instructor Fraley liked us to stand at attention in the bushes under the windows of the instructors' living spaces. We would have on only swim trunks so the big-jawed little bastards would have lots of flesh to dine on. It was Instructor Fraley's contention that if he sacrificed us to the screaming meemies, they wouldn't bite our beloved instructors while they slept.

Early on in Puerto Rico, one of the Gig Squads was run by Instructor Spiegel. Until that Gig Squad, Mr. Swartley had accomplished a difficult task, hiding in the middle. He had done his best not to stand out, never last, never first. Never come to the attention of the instructors as an individual. That evening, all his effort went for naught when Instructor Spiegel asked the question, "Mr. Swartley, where have you been?" From that moment on, Cool Breeze became Ensign Swartley's personal instructor. The only thing worse than having an instructor take a personal interest in you was having two instructors taking a personal interest.

In Puerto Rico, keeping our helmets on became an odd little annoyance; in the cold the helmet helped keep the head warm. But in the heat and humidity of Puerto Rico, we didn't want our heads kept warm. We were not required to wear the damn thing inside any building, but we had better not come out the door uncovered. If it wasn't jammed down on the head, we suffered. I screwed up so many times that at one point, I was required to wear my helmet for three days, twenty-four hours a day, inside and out, showering, in my bed, and taking a dump.

Our boats were no longer a major harassment factor because they had become one of our basic working tools and, at times, a lot of fun. One of the major insertion and extraction methods used by UDT was called cast and recovery. It leans heavily on the use of the rubber boat and, if done right, is more fun than Disneyland. The insertion part was fairly easy: A rubber boat would be secured alongside a low-silhouette, high-speed boat, called a steel-hulled PL. PL was short for LCPL, or Landing Craft, Personnel, Large. The PL would move rapidly, on a wavy course, parallel to the enemy shoreline so that enemy gunners couldn't get a good shot at the boat. To shield from view men going in or being snatched from the water, we were cast and recovered from the side of the boat away from the beach. Everyone would be huddled belowdecks with explosives, weapons, survey gear, etc.—whatever equipment the mission called for. When the word was given to go, one by one, we came out of the cabin low and fast, dragging our gear with us, then we rolled over the gunnel of the steel-hulled PL, dropped into the rubber boat, then rolled into the water. That is the cast part; the fun came when we returned from the mission, the recovery.

The boat coxswain and the snare man, now there's two guys you had better have a lot of faith in! The recovery begins with everyone's having swum back out to a pre-arranged area at sea and spread themselves out in a recovery line. The steel-hulled PL, guided by the trusty coxswain, comes barreling down at the first man in line. Of course, it's done at sea; with wind, waves, and chop, the boat is not a stable platform at all. The coxswain wants to miss splitting the swimmer's head with the keel of his boat by about six or seven feet, and he is not going to slow down so the swimmer can get in. The snare man is going to jerk his ass out of the water and into that rubber boat tied alongside the PL.

The best snare men have two important qualities. First and foremost, they know their exact relationship to their surroundings, to space, and to time, no matter how fast and hard they are being slammed around in that rubber boat. Second, and damn near as important as the first, the more upper body strength and mass, the better. He has one tool, his snare—a hard-rubber loop with a good rope core. He is going to place that snare over the swimmer's outstretched left arm as the boat goes flying by. The man being plucked from the water is not to reach for the snare; that would screw things up, and he could be missed or, possibly, get picked up by the neck. Once the swimmer is in the pickup line, there are only two things for him to do. When the bow of the pickup boat gets even with his shoulder, he thrusts his left arm, fist closed, into the air, keeping his head over to the right, away from the left arm. Meanwhile, his legs kick his big duckfoot fins as hard as possible, because the more his body sticks out of the water, the better. At that point, he's a good target for the snare man. When he sticks that snare over the swimmer's left arm, the swimmer quickly grabs his left wrist with his right hand and pulls it to his chest, then just holds on. If he's done it right, the snare is lodged in the crook behind the elbow of his left arm, and he is jerked out of the water, into the rubber boat. Then he scrambles to get the hell out of the way because there's another man about to be jerked into the boat. It's back over the gunnel of the PL, and low profile down into the cabin.

Cast-and-recovery was developed during World War II as a technique to get the Frogmen to one of their prime work sites, a fortified enemy-held beachhead. Before the UDT came along, many thousands of soldiers and Marines had been lost when landing craft struck natural or man-made obstacles. Those who didn't drown were easily picked off by enemy gunners. Nothing makes a good general sicker than having his men dead, their bodies floating all over some beachhead, when the poor bastards didn't even have a chance to fight.

Their answer, find some men who, armed only with a knife, will volunteer to:

1. Swim into an enemy-held beachhead to locate and chart obstacles, natural and man-made, that might rip out the bottom of a landing craft, then gather all pertinent back-shore information, for example, enemy emplacements, the location of beach exits, how much weight can be run through them without bogging down, etc.

2. Swim back in with explosive, *skin*-dive down—that

means holding their breath, no high-tech there—and place the explosives on the obstacles to be removed, tie in the field so all charges will go off as one, pull the fuses, and get the hell out of there before going sky-high with the obstacles.

3. When the troops land, act as lifeguard, for combat troops are carrying fifty to eighty pounds of weapons, ammunition, radios, and assorted gear to break things and kill people. It's extremely rare that troops get a dry landing; they usually have a couple hundred feet of water two to three feet deep to wade through. All it takes is a small hole, or just a trip and, with all that weight on the back, even the strongest grunt can die quickly, sucking water into his lungs. I know from experience that Marines and sailors are always hassling each other. But pull a face-down Marine out of one of those holes, and he will think the sun rises and sets on your sailor ass. And it just feels damn good to do it!

Underwater Demolition Teams were born out of a need to get the troops on the beach alive. We were being trained in the basics of the trade, the thing that made those badasses from World War II and Korea so damn successful. It boils down to finding people who will go balls to the wall to get their part of the job done, then look around and see if anyone needs help. We trained with nothing high-tech. We couldn't even *say* the word scuba, or we would be squat jumping or duckwalking while the instructor explained what inferior beings we truly were.

Our boats, no longer being the harassment factor they had been, left a void that needed to be filled, and our duckfeet more than filled that void. For a Frogman, the classic web-footed warrior, fins are the basic form of propulsion. In the land of warm, we damn near propulsed our feet off. Having UDT-model duckfeet on was like having foot-and-a-half-long boards tied to the feet with very rough one-inch rope around the ankles. Given enough leg to punch them, duckfeet will lift half the body out of the water. But after thirty minutes, our feet felt like they were going to fall off.

Puerto Rico was for water work, and we did just that; many days, more than half the day was spent in the water, then we would get some more that night. Soon, we had fin burns to go with the blisters and frostbite sores. Everyone was walking wounded to some degree, but we could taste victory; nobody was going to let fin burns and a little duckfoot pain stop him.

As in Little Creek, Gig Squad was after dinner and before the night evaluation, and usually run by Instructor Fraley. He was not the trainee's friend! He had let me know he loved having me at Gig Squad, and hoped I didn't quit. Fraley told me it would give him great pleasure to see that I was given a rare administrative drop the last day of training. I don't know if that had ever been done, but he made me believe he would do it, if he could. I don't think he hated me, it was more like an intense personal dislike, and to be fair, I had felt the same way about him since the first day of training.

Fraley's conception of extracurricular studies was special. All Gig Squads hurt, but when he ran them, there was always a little extra pain. His technique was simple: Repeat an exercise for an hour. For example, "Hit the deck! On your feet!" That means drop to the lean and rest position, then jump back to attention, all within four or five seconds. Do that for an hour! You'll get the picture! On the rare occasion when someone passed out, the men on each side of him picked him up, then carried him to the porch where the instructor and the resuscitator were. One man stayed with the downed man and the instructor, the other man returned to the fun and games. As soon as

the downed man came around, the man who'd stayed
returned to the fun. With the downed man, of course. I
remember only one time when the man that passed out
did not have to return to the fun and games.

I'm not sure, but I think it was Neil Dow. Neil was
around six feet tall and nineteen or twenty years old, and
real quiet, like Ralph Diebold. It's funny when I think
about all the things we *didn't* know about each other;
they just didn't matter. One thing mattered, we were still
there, if not standing, either in the process of being
knocked down or, more important, getting back up.

Neil was not a perpetual member of our little fraternity
of extra pain. Like most guys, he got nailed once in a
while, but he did his best to stay clear. Nobody volunteered, or even watched; some smart-ass instructor might
make him join in on the fun.

We had our screaming meemies sacrifice that night,
then went right to "Hit the deck! On your feet!" We were
on the grass, spread out so we didn't kick each other's
teeth out. Instructor Fraley was sitting on the steps. Neil
was between me and the porch. God knows how long we
had been going when Neil fell, but I had never seen anything like it before. I had seen lots of people fall down,
and a few pass out, but Neil went down like a big tree.

When we came up from the lean and rest, we were
to be at attention, back straight, feet together, hands at
our sides, and looking straight ahead. When the command "Hit the deck" was given, we kicked our feet out,
keeping the body straight, and fell toward the ground,
bringing our arms out and catching ourselves in the
lean and rest, on toes and palms, arms extended, body
straight. I'm sure Neil wasn't already passed out when
Fraley gave the hit the deck command; Neil kicked out
his feet, in the approved way. I know he was when he hit
the deck, because his hands were still at his sides.

Straight as a tree, he landed on his toes and nose, in that order.

It scared the shit out of Instructor Fraley; there was blood all over the place from Neil's nose and mouth. When they got Neil back around, after some oxygen, he tried to get up and rejoin us, but Fraley was having no part of that. He had someone take Neil down to sick bay, so the pecker checker could make sure there was nothing permanently wrong with him. I was more pissed at Fraley for sending him to sick bay than anything; none of us wanted those medical people getting too close a look at us. Neil had no more desire than any of us to get a medical drop, then have to repeat the course. Well, Instructor Fraley and I were even; he was sure I was an asshole, and in my mind, he was a natural asshole, born that way. With just a bloody nose, a split lip, and some loose teeth, Neil was lucky. Nothing to knock him out of training, but I think he had to do a makeup for missing part of the Gig Squad.

Swing and Sway Rick Shea had one of the strangest reactions to a Gig Squad I ever heard of. One evening, we had given ourselves to the meemies and went straight to jumping jacks. Our beloved instructor, again Fraley, had informed us that we were going for a record. Of course he was the only one who knew what the record was. Somewhere around eight hundred jumping jacks, Lieutenant, junior grade Shea started acting strange, like someone who was having *fun*. Shea told me later that he had gone into some kind of twilight zone and had felt like he could do jumping jacks forever. Lieutenant, junior grade Shea wanted the *record* and he wanted it bad. He started counting louder and calling on us to pick up the pace. At just over a thousand jumping jacks, Instructor Fraley stopped Rick Shea and dismissed him from Gig Squad. Now a normal human would have been happy to get the hell out of there; not Shea. He was big-time pissed; Fraley, that no-good blankety-blank, had robbed him of being part of the Gig Squad jumping jack record.

We learned some pretty nasty but necessary habits in training, some of which could cause an untimely demise if the student wasn't lucky. For example, we learned to "blow" our sinuses, a misnomer as we were really imploding them. In the harbor, about thirty feet down, a bunch of lines were secured between pier legs. We had to skin down and tie the knots that were used for securing explosives to an obstacle and join all the demolition into one net. We didn't get do that once and receive a passing grade; we did it almost every day. The *test* would come near the end of basic training, when we would use blacked-out face masks to make it a no-visibility situation. Most of the time, everyone mastered the task with little problem. The dive only got nasty if a trainee couldn't equalize his sinuses.

Thirty feet is just shy of two atmospheres, or double the pressure at sea level. When a man's sinuses won't equalize, his face feels like it is in the grip of a very pissed off giant. And it is very natural to head back to the surface, because the pain is intense, and going back up relieves it. I don't remember who got to be the example, but it was the first time we tied knots at the pier. Our overly compassionate instructors heaped ridicule on the first failure to reach the lines—squat jumps, all the usual. Two things the instructors said stuck in my mind, the first absolutely true, the second close but no banana: (1) if you failed to get down and place your charge, Marines might die on that obstacle; (2) when you take the pain long enough for the sinuses to rupture, it feels as good as the best orgasm you will ever have.

Some of the guys went through it several times, anything to keep the instructors off your ass; I only needed to do it once, thank God. By the time my sinuses blew, the pain was so intense I couldn't think; it was like having thumbs smashed into my forehead and down around my eyes. But when they burst, two things happened: All pain was instantly gone, and my face mask half filled with snot and blood. I did not give a shit about the snot and blood; there was not a trace of pain! It was gone, and I couldn't believe how good normal felt.

Now, a couple of sinuses have only membranes separating them from the brain cavity; if the sinus ruptures into the brain cavity, *that's* where the mucus and blood go. At a minimum, the trainee will have a brain infection, which is very hard to treat; on the maximum side, a slow unpleasant death. In truth, our instructors were teaching us a moral certitude: If we wanted to wear the name, take the fucking pain. Our job was to clear the way so grunts didn't die on the way to work. The rule was do it or get out.

At sixty feet, the instructors also had a weighted bucket at the end of a rope. All we had to do was skin down, take a rock from the bucket, and bring it to the surface. Sixty feet was the deepest we were required to free dive. Ens. James C. Walker was doing all right with tying the knots at thirty feet, but the sixty-foot bucket was giving him fits. But no rock, no graduate.

Mr. Walker was a tall, lanky, dark-haired young officer with a bent toward the serious side. I know how seriously he took graduating into the Teams; he broke both eardrums and blew his sinuses to get that rock! Almost all of us blew our sinuses, one time or another, and that is damn intense pain. Rupturing the eardrum is at least an order of magnitude of pain higher. Like someone's pounding a spike in your ear. I think we will have to agree, James C. Walker had the fire in the belly and the burning in the brain.

If the truth had been known about Ensign Walker's ears, he wouldn't have been allowed into training. After college, Jim had signed up for OCS, officer candidate school. Many members of his family had served in the military, and he thought he would do his part. The navy sounded good, that is, until halfway through OCS, when they took his class of future young naval officers on their first cruise. Jim Walker's only thought about that first cruise was, "What the hell have I done?" The cruise had been in rough seas on a destroyer, a very small ship, and to top it all off, he'd been assigned to the engine room. Destroyers are nicknamed tin cans, mainly because they have relatively thin armor, are small, and bounce all over the place in rough seas. Engine rooms, particularly on those old-style tin cans, were unbelievably hot and noisy places. Jim Walker found himself very badly seasick and with a splitting headache. To top it all off, the young ensign who ran the engine room screamed over the noise, "If you're lucky, you can get a job like mine."

Jim Walker didn't want that kind of luck. He started doing a little investigating. What the hell did the navy do that sounded interesting and would keep him from becoming a fleet officer? Sea duty was definitely not the thing for him. Underwater demolition team? Now that sounded interesting, plus if he signed up to try out for training, he got out of study hall. Well, that's what he did.

Everything was going great guns; Jim liked everything he heard, and the heavy emphasis placed on physical training suited him fine. That was where he wanted to go. Then Jim received word to report to the decompression chamber to take a test. Somehow that day, Mr. Walker was running late. He arrived at the chamber just as they were closing the hatch on the last group of guys to be tested that day. He was told to get his shoes off, remove any flammables from his person—lighters, matches, etc.—and get his ass in the chamber. The young Mr. Walker did not have a clue what the test was about, but he was willing to take it anyway.

As they pressured up the chamber, his ears started to hurt, but none of the other guys were saying anything. He thought, maybe it's a test to see how much pain we can take. Walker looked around, and everyone else seemed fairly at ease. He thought, this is a tough group of bastards! Jim didn't say anything till both eardrums ruptured and he had blood running out of his ears and nose. At that point a young naval doctor, in the chamber to run the test, brought everything to a stop.

The doctor was chewing him up one side and down the other, the whole time it took to get Mr. Walker out of the decompression chamber and examine his ears. The thrust of the doctor's verbal abuse was: Jim was stupid, tough, but stupid, and because he had ruptured his ears, he could not go to training. Now Walker may have been young and naive, he certainly didn't know a thing about diving and the effects of pressure on the body, but stupid? No. Jim reminded the doctor that he was in charge of the test and had not briefed Jim on what to expect and how to handle any problems. Now Walker might not get orders to training, but the doctor would certainly have a little problem on his fitness report. The young doctor, recognizing that what Jim said was correct, said something like: "Fuck it, you belong in that crazy outfit!" They both kept their mouths shut, and Jim got his orders.

Our shortest distance swims in Puerto Rico were the timed-mile swims held once a week. We would do several at each distance, building up to six miles. Our swims were measured as the crow flies, a straight line. Of course it's impossible to swim in the open ocean in a straight line. If the swim was said to be four miles, only God knows how far we really swam to finish it. The wind, waves, and current added to our instructors' plans.

The professors of pain loved our distance swims; for them it was a combination boat ride, picnic, and fishing trip. They were out there as lifeguards, sailing around making sure none of us drowned. I never worried about drowning. I don't think anyone did. My big worry was more a personal thing that each of us went through. I kept thinking my feet might fall off!

By that point in training, I couldn't remember what my feet felt like without pain, and mine were some of the healthier feet in the class. Just pulling on our duck-feet added to whatever level of pain our feet were at. For me, the pain peaked after an hour to an hour and a half of pushing my fins, then blessed numbness arrived! The funny part came at the end of any long swim; when we took our duckfeet off, our feet went from numb to an intense pain that slowly eased off to the level of merely constant pain. For a while after every long swim, we walked around like a bunch of escapees from a rehab ward.

It paid to be a winner on long swims. Each swim pair was placed in one of three groups: fast, medium, or slow, and the breakdown came from the timed-mile swim. So those who didn't bust their butts on the timed mile would find themselves in a slower group. On the long swims, we not only had to stay with our swim buddy, but we had to stay with our group; each group could be no faster than its slowest pair.

If there was any downtime in training, it was after the first group of swimmers had finished its swim. They had more time to get their feet back to normal after hours of working those duckfeet than the last group in. By the time the last group hit the beach, the fast group's feet were back to normal pain levels. It paid to be a winner, and the poor bastards in the last group got no downtime for their feet.

On any swim except the timed mile, the *cardinal sin* was leaving your swim buddy. In our world, leaving a swim buddy meant being more than six feet away from him. The punishment for that dastardly crime was swimming the next swim with a three-inch hawser—a rope used for mooring ships—between the errant swim buddies. The line weighed nothing—hell, it floated!—it was the drag it created that made it such an effective punishment. I think it was the only punishment the instructors passed out that I didn't receive. But on one of the four- or five-mile swims, Ensign Hawes and his swim buddy got to drag that three-inch mooring line along for the swim. Better my boat officer than me.

A common call we might hear on any long swim came from Ron Jarvi's Dutch swim buddy, Cpl. Coenraad Pauli. "Yarvi, Yarvi, where are you, Yarvi?" It seemed they had a small problem staying close, and Pauli didn't want to suffer the consequences. His call brought a lot of smiles to many a tired swim pair.

Explosives are like magic, and the whole damn class loved our demolition problems. We used small amounts, say, a quarter pound of C-4. And we used large amounts, five thousand pounds plus, of assorted explosive: C-3, C-4, PETN, and HBX. Explosives are one hell of a tool when used properly. But try to break God's laws of physics, and you damn well may pay with your life.

The military does not use dynamite, those red sticks with a fuse coming out of one end. Old Alfred Nobel got rich off that invention, a method to stabilize nitroglycerin just enough so the demo man could sneeze without killing himself. Blasting caps were the only truly sensitive explosive devices we used. C-3 and C-4 can be thrown around like a football; they can even be burned without exploding. The type of explosive we needed had to be very stable because the way we were required to operate, it was going to have the crap knocked out of it.

The day we made that five-thousand-pound shot was the most pleasant day of training. Seven miles off the coast of Roosevelt Roads is the Island of Vieques, a military reservation used for training Marines in amphibious landings with battalion-size forces practicing for war. They wanted a new LST slot through the reef on the lee side of the island. The LSTs could only cross the reef at high tide, but the desired channel would give them access around the clock. An LST is a ship with a shallow draft and a bow that opens to discharge tanks, trucks, jeeps, or any other large vehicle needed to do battle. Our instructors volunteered us for the job. Nothing like a little practical experience for learning.

It was a full day of busting ass, with no harassment, just pure on-the-job learning. We started out early in the morning loading 160 twenty-five-pound packs of C-4 and fifty-six sections of Mark 8 hose. Each section of Mark 8 was twenty-five feet long and housed twenty-five pounds of PETN and HBX explosive. The shot that day totaled 5,650 pounds, more than two tons of explosives. We hand-loaded everything from the magazines to a truck, from the truck to a boat, and off the boat onto the beach at Vieques. After more than three months of around-the-clock harassment, one day of just working hard, with real work to accomplish, was pure pleasure.

Many factors come into play when figuring how much explosive to use on any job. Blasting through a reef requires a surprising amount. The channel would be one hundred feet long, twenty-four feet wide, and six to seven feet deep. At low tide, the reef had four feet of water over it, so if we did the shot right, we would end up with a channel ten to eleven feet at low tide. A reef is like a huge sponge made of millions of tiny compartments that absorb and disperse the shock of an explosion. Up to that time, the biggest shot we had set off was about two hundred pounds. So none of us trainees had a clue what we would see when setting off 5,650 pounds.

What a workplace! A tropical beach! We had the sun and the coconuts, but Instructor Waddell had lied about the bananas and the bikini-clad women. As it turned out, we had enough problems with the coconuts; God knows what would have happened to us if we'd had the bikini-clad women. I have to give our instructors their due; they warned us not to drink too much coconut milk and to make sure the coconuts we did drink from weren't green. Many of us suffered for not heeding that warning. Let me just say, I would rather have Instructor Fraley at Gig Squad than malfunctioning *bowels*.

The central part of the charge was to be constructed on the beach, then floated out and placed in position on the reef. We joined the sections of Mark 8 hose by their couplers into one-hundred-foot sections, then tied them into three bundles, one with six hundred-foot sections and two with four hundred-foot sections each. Those were then laid across the reef, the bundle of six in the center with a bundle of four on each side. The bundles of four were placed six feet from the central bundle. We then stacked twenty-five-pound haversacks of C-3 and C-4, four high, five feet apart, six feet outside the bundles of four. All those diverse explosives were then joined into one charge with Primacord, a clotheslinelike cord with an explosive core. Tying in the charges was critical, but no problem because we had been practicing that daily in much deeper water. We ran trunk lines of Primacord from each side of the shot to the beach.

All of us were ready; we wanted to hear, "Fire in the

hole!" the traditional warning shouted just prior to setting off any noncombat shot. The instructors had moved us well back from the water, under a line of coconut palms on the shore side of the beach. "Fire in the hole!" There was no loud explosion, but the beach and the palms shook with a deep rumbling sound, and the ocean over the charge blasted straight up, over two hundred feet into God's sky. It seemed to climb forever. A hundred feet in all directions from the shot the ocean boiled, and a dirty brown foam seemed to appear instantly. The water was still climbing when the first big pieces of reef started to rain back down. It took over two minutes for the big pieces, the little pieces, and the water to fall out of the sky.

As I stood with my mouth hanging open, little spots and squiggly lines appeared, running every which way in the foam over the reef. Tom Allen was standing next to me; I said, "Tom, what in the hell is moving all over that foam?"

"Eels."

There were thousands of them, big and small, running on the surface, crazed from the blast impact. Those that weren't killed in the blast seemed to be trying to climb out of the water. But nothing that had been killed would go to waste; the sharks were already gathering, and what they didn't eat, the crabs and small reef fish would.

All we had to do then was to inspect the channel, run a search pattern for misfired explosive, and clean up the beach. As the end to an almost perfect day, our instructors held an impromptu one-bottle auction of hot Coca-Cola. Now, what kind of dumbasses would bid on one hot bottle of Coke? Well, I'm going to clear only one guy of bidding, me, and I'll give up one guy for bidding, Leroy "Gedunk" Geiger. He was the highest bidder and can be forgiven because he was a known candy and soda abuser. He wasn't called Gedunk for nothing. To this day, I wonder how they got so many guys even to bid. To make it worse, the men weren't even bidding money; they were bidding the dreaded squat jump, an exercise so foul that it has been banned in the military for the last twenty years. Nevertheless, Gedunk Geiger won with a bid of three hundred squat jumps, fifty that day and fifty a day until the debt was paid. Needless to say, Leroy didn't share his Coke with anyone.

We all learned something from Tom Allen on the way back from Vieques that evening—how to manhandle a two-hundred-pound sea turtle. Tom wasn't the fastest swimmer, but to my mind, he was the best all-around waterman in the class. He was an accomplished skin diver (hold your breath) and could spear fish at depths in excess of one hundred feet. He was a civilian-qualified scuba diver, a rare thing in the early sixties. He had even wrestled alligators!

As we headed back to Rosey Roads, maybe a half mile off the coast of Vieques, we came upon a big old sea turtle that was just swimming along, minding its own business. Most of us had never seen one, so the boat was pulled close, and a bunch of us jumped in the water to get a better look. Of course, we couldn't leave well enough alone; someone said, "Let's catch it!" Well, believe me, we were giving it a good try, but that turtle was kicking our asses. A couple of guys got smacked by its big flippers, then someone got a hold on it and was taken for a dive. Let's say the turtle had him. Anyway, the turtle took him deep enough that he was forced to let go. We gave up and got back on the boat, but as soon as we were on the boat, that damn turtle surfaced. That time, Tom Allen jumped in, swam over, and grabbed that big old turtle by the shell, one hand behind the head and one just over the tail. Once he had hold of it, Tom quit kicking his fins and let the turtle do the work.

His method was surprisingly simple: If he wanted to go down, he pushed down on the shell behind the head, and pulled up on the shell over the tail. Down they went. When he wanted to come up, Tom pushed down over the tail and pulled up behind the head. The turtle swam to the surface, bringing Tom with him. Lean to the right, the turtle went to the right. Et cetera. All Tom had to do was stay out of the way of those flippers; the turtle was his. There was some conversation about taking the turtle, but in the end, we left it. Our easy day was over.

By then, we were down to our last couple of weeks in Puerto Rico, the end of the four months of *basic* UDT training. There'd be one more week of the usual day-to-day nonstop physical and mental harassment, then came the big ones: eighteen-mile run; six-mile swim; final physical exercise test; the last timed-mile swim; and our all-important final demolition problem. A written test was the only thing we had coming that most of us worried about.

When we had started training, I thought I knew everything there was to know about Underwater Demolition Teams; I had wanted to be a navy Frogman since age eleven. Things had changed, one of the changes being that successful trainees no longer graduated into the Teams after the four months of basic UDT training. Our beloved "harassment factors," the instructors, had been telling us that from the start of training, but I'd thought it was just more of their harassment bullshit, trying to psych us out with comments like, "Will you make it through army jump school? Will your parachute fail?"

Personally, I could see no reason to jump out of a perfectly good airplane. At the ripe old age of eleven, I was educated as to just what a Frogman did by Hollywood and Richard Widmark, and there had been not one damn thing in the movie *The Frogmen* about jumping out of airplanes. What I wanted was the locking out of submarines, sneaking behind enemy lines, and blowing things up stuff. Well, if I wanted in the Teams, I'd jump; if I didn't do it, no Teams for me. After army jump school at Fort Benning, Georgia, we had five weeks at underwater swim school in Key West, Florida. We wouldn't find out why so many men had started Class-29 or what the two extra schools were about until graduation day.

About that time in training, our instructors tried to reinsert a little of the normal separation between us and our officers. Their main tool? If an enlisted man screwed up, an officer would pay. Not a bad deal for us enlisted, but our officers were not enjoying it. To tell the truth, it is one of the few objectives the instructors failed at; our officers just took it as part of our catch-22 world. After our plane touched down at Fort Benning, it would take an army sergeant major about five minutes to accomplish the task.

Our long swims in the open ocean were nothing but *pain* and *drudgery*, the very essence of training. When you think of one of our swims, don't think of arms coming out of the water, pulling us along, and feet kicking a large wake. We were required to use "nonrecovery" type strokes, i.e., no splash, no wake. What that meant was sidestroke, with fins. There were a couple of very good reasons: We wanted to make it as difficult as possible for an enemy to spot us swimming in; we had to drag whatever equipment we were to use on the job, explosives, weapons, survey gear, etc., along for the swim; and there was always the real possibility of having to drag an injured teammate back as well, because no SEAL Frogman would ever abandon a teammate, injured or dead. Every man wore an inflatable life vest, which was a real pain in the ass because, no matter how well the air had been sucked out of it, the damn thing was still a lot of drag, like having on a big piece of clothing. But we never went into the water without it, because it would be needed if someone had to drag us back.

One thing some of us towed along on a swim looked damn strange: a line with rubbers (condoms) tied to it, a candy bar in each one. The condoms made for waterproof lunch boxes, safeguarding a little snack for quick energy and to get the saltwater taste out of the mouth. As part of waterproof firing assemblies, we had rubbers available by the gross, so we had enough to waterproof a few candy bars. We just didn't have the time to use them for their original intent.

Our ever-ingenious instructors knew how to read tide tables, so all our swims were planned so we would get the worst currents and tides. In addition to the harassment factor, there was a very good reason to do that, because troop landings are planned for the best time to get the *combat troops* on the beach alive, not for the people clearing the way. Our instructors allowed God's tides and currents to teach us the hard way the tricks of swimming against fast-moving water. The most important trick is *do not stop swimming*!

Every man among us knew the sinking feeling of losing hard-won distance while he stopped to tend severe leg cramps and the current pushed him back. If you want to feel useless, swim for an hour watching the same spot on shore without getting any closer. Everything in training is about swimming against the tide; a Frog must be willing to win one inch at a time.

Nothing but bad luck could have stopped any of us by then. We could feel, smell, taste, and see success. Even Mr. Gibby and Ted Risher, whose feet were so bad they should have been in the hospital, limped and gimped with a new strength. It's amazing how being close to the end of a painful effort eases some of the pain.

* * *

Just before our last week in the land of warm, we got a rare weekend liberty. Most of Class-29 headed for San Juan, in those days a wild and woolly liberty port. Most of us hit the usual sailor haunts, just letting it all hang out. A lot of young-guy shit.

On Sunday, I took Lynch and Neidrauer to a nice little place I knew called Papa Doc's. Its normal trade was upscale locals and tourists. Just a nice little restaurant with a bar. We were having dinner and boasting about our powers with women and booze. Just then there was no way to outdo each other with women; at Papa Doc's, booze was another matter.

As it turned out, my classmates had never tasted 151 proof rum. On the other hand, I had acquired a taste for drinking the poison, straight up and on fire. Since I didn't want to frighten them off, I said nothing about its burning like kerosene. I just bought three double shots of 151, and bet Jack and Bob they couldn't drink them straight down. I figured they would both puke. To my surprise, they downed their grog and held down their food. Jack was gasping for breath, but Bob was stunned; he could not talk, not a word. Well, I lost the bet, but it was worth it to witness Neidrauer's reaction. The three of us returned to training with nasty hangovers, as if our instructors didn't pass out enough pain.

Everyone hated their damn inflatable life jacket! I guess if one of us had been drowning, we would have quickly loved the damn thing. They caused a lot of drag in the water and chafed our necks heavily. Leo Duncan's chafing sprouted several nasty boils, and like all of us, Leo had no desire to see a doctor. Just the thought of "doing a McCutchan"—being medically dropped and starting all over—was enough to keep us clear of doctors.

Well, old Jesse James Hardy reached down into his vast knowledge of folk medicine and operated on Leo. Dr. Hardy cleaned up the nasty-looking things, put cold towels over them, and with a hot knife, made a small cut in each one. Jesse then placed the open end of a Coke bottle over the small cut and heated the bottle bottom. Out popped the crap, core and all.

One funny thing about Jesse's vast knowledge of folk medicine, it didn't extend to Alka-Seltzer. That was particularly odd, because the rest of us hard-core drinkers knew well its benefits in relieving hangovers. But it wasn't until one of our rare Friday night liberties in Puerto Rico that Dr. Hardy received an education on the proper use of Alka-Seltzer.

Jesse, Mr. Janke, Mr. Swartley, and Harry Humphries were all drinking at a small local bar, four or five miles off the base. For some reason—could they have been drunk?—they decided to walk back to the training area. But when they finally reached it, they were a mess because they had left the road to take a shortcut through a cane field. Class-29's intrepid explorers got lost wandering around in uncut and cut-and-burned cane fields for an hour or two before finding the way back. After cleaning off ash from burnt cane, Harry reached into his locker and pulled out some Alka-Seltzer.

Jesse asked, "What is that for?" Harry said that he didn't like waking up with a hangover. When he was drinking hard, Harry took two before he went to sleep and woke up hangover free. That was good enough for Dr. Hardy; he wanted some. Harry handed Jesse two Alka-Seltzer and walked off to get some water. Jesse thought the pills were a little large, but he popped them in his mouth and ate them anyway. When Harry returned, Jesse was holding his throat, with a screwed-up look on his face.

Some of the Alka-Seltzer had stuck in Dr. Hardy's

throat, and he could feel it popping and fizzing. When he told Harry, Harry laughed, handed Jesse his water, and told him to drink. Well, that flushed the popping and fizzing from Jesse's throat, but his belly started to swell alarmingly. Jesse James Hardy was not having a good experience with his first Alka-Seltzer.

Ensign Hauff and I were swim buddies throughout training. That was unusual, because swim-buddy pairs were determined from the times we got on our weekly timed-mile swims. Once a week, since the start of training, I had set myself the goal of kicking Hauff's ass. If I'd beaten him, that would not have changed a thing; we would have still been swim buddies. I just wanted to beat him. My last chance was our final timed mile in Puerto Rico.

In high school I been on the swim team and played water polo. Our coach, Ural Sarri, was one tough guy: Anyone who wanted to be on the team had to swim a mile every morning before school. It didn't matter how good the swimmer was, if he didn't swim the morning miles, he wasn't part of the team. Coach didn't care what stroke was used, to him the practice was all about building endurance and making young boys work hard to be part of a team. I swam those miles backstroke or breaststroke, my races on the swim team.

In the Teams, breaststroke was termed a "nonrecovery" stroke; no splash, no wake. I was dead sure that I could beat Hauff if I could just swim that mile breaststroke, without fins, face mask, or life jacket. I had been after the instructors to let me try for a couple months. Well, they finally gave me the chance. Of course I didn't get everything my way—I had to wear my lifejacket. Instructor Blais told me that if I didn't win he would squat jump me till I dropped. Instructors Blais and Waddell had a bet, Blais took me, Waddell took Hauff.

Well, my swim buddy had his own ideas. Each time I had improved, so had he. Just enough to beat my ass. Ens. Richard Hauff again prevailed. I did beat his previous best time, but so did he, and by just a little more than I did. I was not Instructor Blais's hero.

To my mind, our final demolition problem was what we had come to training for; it was Frogmen work. Under the cover of darkness, we did a standard UDT cast. Then we swam in and made an initial reconnaissance of the designated landing site. We couldn't just say, "Yeah, there's a big fucking piece of metal down there!" We had to be able to place each obstacle on a chart, each in relationship to the others and known fixed points on the beach; the type of obstacle, e.g., steel tetrahedron; thickness of the steel, five-eighths of an inch; depth of water; etc.; etc. All the harassment we had taken had a purpose, making it possible for us to work together under tough conditions, *as a team*. Each of us recorded, on plastic swimmer slates about nine inches long and four inches wide, what was found in his area of the recon. We made little marks, drawings, and brief notes that helped us remember what we had found.

Recovery, the fun part, went off without a hitch. We all swam back out and assumed our positions in a perfect recovery line. That big steel-hulled PL bore down on us, right on time. *Bam, bam, bam,* our snare man jerked us out of the water, one right after the other, without a miss.

At debrief time, each man's information had to be collected, interpreted, and placed on a chart showing what lay just under the water ready to rip the bottom out of the landing craft. The rest of the planning was derived from that chart, how much explosive to use on each obstacle, and whose responsibility each one would be. The whole operation had to be carried out on a tight time schedule.

In a combat situation, the landing craft full of Marines might well be on its way in as the shot went off. At times like that, we'd have one chance to do it right.

Our instructors didn't tell us anything. This operation was ours to pass or fail as Class-29. Everything else in training was in one way or another focused on bringing a bunch of egocentric young bucks together as a *team*. In truth, it was more a test of how well the instructors had done their job than anything else. How fast one of us swam the mile, ran an obstacle course, how deep and long we could free dive, or how many nasty exercises we could do, didn't mean a thing. What counted in the end was *team*, each guy doing his part, and whatever else it took to accomplish the *mission*.

Another cast, and this time we were dragging C-4 explosive, Primacord, caps, and waterproof firing assemblies. Each obstacle would get the necessary amount of C-4 to blow it to hell, plus a little extra we called a "Jesus factor," just to make sure. After the charges were set, each was tied into a net, with Primacord, that allowed every obstacle in the field to be shot as one. Each end of the field had its own waterproof firing assembly. One assembly would do the trick, but if there was a misfire on one end, two made sure. Just another Jesus factor; it always pays to back yourself up.

The last two guys to leave the obstacle field pulled the fuse initiators, then swam like hell to catch up. The last place any of us wanted to be when the shot went off was in the water. I know I had never been more interested in doing a perfect recovery. Again, the swimmer line was perfect, the coxswain and snare man gave each of us a quick trip out of the water and into the boat. We then had one of the longest short waits of my life.

I have no idea what would have happened if the shot had not gone off. What would the instructors have done?

Failed the whole class? Of course, at the time and given everything we'd been through, that seemed a very real possibility. Besides, Jessie James Hardy had been in a previous class that graduated *no one*. That class had started with ten or twelve guys and was shut down shortly after Jessie was sent to the hospital. Hell, McCutchan had broken his leg with just a couple weeks to go, and they hadn't let him graduate.

Thank God, we never found out! The whole damn field of obstacles went up as one! It was nothing like our reef shot because we'd used less explosive and spread it over a wider area of the bottom. But a ten- to twelve-foot geyser of water shot up over each obstacle. That was quickly followed by the concussion, which slammed into the bottom of the boat. Most important! We had proved we knew the basic business of being navy Frogmen. A bunch of hairy-ass young guys who could overcome their egos and work as a *team*.

That last week of basic UDT training was odd. We had all our longest runs, the swim, the final PT test—all the biggies. Then all our equipment had to be repaired and stored for the next training class. What was gone was the hard-edged harassment we had been living with for damn near four months. I know the first time Instructor Fraley smiled at me and had something nice to say, that was a shock. More surprising was how quickly my dislike for him disappeared. I guess that was our true graduation: being accepted by our instructors. I know it meant more to me than any piece of paper that said I was a graduate.

PHASE FIVE

The fifth phase of training consisted of three weeks of airborne training at Fort Benning, Georgia. Lieutenant Tiel and the four enlisted men from the Netherlands spent these three weeks at the naval amphibious base at Little Creek participating in on-the-job training. Lieutenant Magnussen, Norwegian Navy, was the only foreign student to attend airborne training. This phase of training included progressive training, from parachute landing falls (PLFs) to practice body position and airplane exits from a thirty-four-foot tower to a captive jump from a two-hundred-and-fifty-foot tower. During the last week, "jump week," five qualifying jumps are made from jump aircraft; a simulated combat jump with full combat gear and a mass jump made up the last two of the five qualifying jumps. Upon completing the five qualifying jumps the students were presented their silver jump wings.

Our C-130 landed at Fort Benning full of not-so-squared-away sailors; most of us, including our officers, were drunk. We were reporting in for duty, but reporting in drunk was a big no-no, and drinking on a military aircraft was another big no-no. As we were off-loading the plane, a very agitated sergeant major wanted to know who the hell was in charge of us. We found out later that

114

he was no run-of-the-mill sergeant major (I soon learned there are *no* run-of-the-mill sergeants major). He was one of the senior enlisted men in the United States Army. More important, that man wore a set of jump wings with five little stars on the wings. Each of those little stars stood for one combat jump. Five times he had jumped out of a perfectly good aircraft while people on the ground tried to kill him. If I recall correctly, at the time he was one of only three men in all branches of the military who had survived five combat jumps.

Well, that sergeant major got all our officers in one little group and gave them a curt lecture on their lack of leadership. He reminded them we were guests of the United States *Army* Airborne, and the army was not going to put up with a bunch of nonsense from "leg swabbies." Combat troops called sailors "swabbies," meaning they were safe on a ship mopping the deck. The term "leg" was used to describe anyone not jump qualified. I think that lecture was just what our officers needed to hear; they had been acting like a bunch of enlisted men. They quickly figured out how to keep that sergeant major happy without screwing up a good time for all of us. The army Airborne was in for a dose of United States Navy hairy-ass Frogmen action.

I think an old joke will best describe the different attitudes displayed by the officers and enlisted men in the army, Marines, and United States Navy. It seems there was a big joint-service exercise involving the army, Marines, and navy. All operations went off without a hitch, and it had been the best exercise in years. At the end of the operation, the officers had a party to tell themselves what a great job they had done. Toward the end of the party, when the officers and gentlemen were soundly shit-faced, the senior army and Marine generals had a heated debate over whose troops had the biggest balls.

The admiral in charge told both of them to put up or shut up. The army general said, "All right, Admiral, you and the general each get your best man and meet me out front by the flagpole in thirty minutes."

When they all met by the flagpole, both generals had a tough-looking corporal in tow, but there was no one with the admiral. One of the generals asked if he needed more time to find a tough sailor. The admiral just laughed, and said, "Any swabby that comes along will do just fine." Lo and behold, along comes a skinny, young, cocky seaman, with a very unmilitary appearance and demeanor. The admiral called him over, the young sailor gave him a sloppy salute and said, "What can I do for you, Admiral?"

"Sailor, just stand by here and watch; I'm sure you will know what to do when the time comes."

The two generals took one look at the skinny unmilitary sailor and laughed. The army general called his corporal to attention and told him to climb the flagpole. The corporal gave a snappy salute and shinnied up the pole. When he reached the top, the general hollered up, "Jump, Corporal!" The soldier saluted, hollered, "Airborne, General!" and jumped.

The Marine general smirked, called his corporal to attention, and ordered him to climb the flagpole with one hand behind his back. The Marine gave him a sharp salute, and started climbing with one hand behind him. When he reached the top, his general hollered up, *"Marine,* jump head-first!" The marine saluted, screamed *"Recon!"* and jumped headfirst.

The Marine general said, "Top that!" The admiral called the sailor to attention and said, "Climb that flagpole, sailor!" The swabby gave a sloppy salute and said, "Fuck you, Admiral." With that, the admiral turned to the generals and said, "Now that takes *balls*, gentlemen!"

It's a joke, but it has a large grain of truth in how the different services viewed and treated their enlisted men. Our officers had been hit with a big problem within minutes of our stumbling off the plane. We were sailors at an army school; if anything went wrong, it would look bad for the navy. Our officers were all tough guys, but none of them had any experience in interservice operations. There was no instructor with us, and worse yet, the officers had not one chief, first-class, or second-class petty officer to help them get control of their situation. And every navy officer there knew he was part of a group that was perfectly capable of causing more trouble than God would believe.

About 250 young solders fresh out of boot camp and advanced infantry training were going through jump school with us. They were good guys, but a couple of things set us apart. First and foremost, the physical demands that the army placed on trainees at jump school made for an easy day for us; the same demands hammered most of the army guys. We had just completed four months of the toughest training any branch of the service offered, so our stamina was boundless. Second, in the early sixties, the army's officer corps had a very bad attitude. There needs to be some separation between troops and their officers, but those guys were ridiculous; they acted like enlisted men were inferior humans.

The example that stuck in my mind was the water-bag incident. Spread all over the Fort Benning training area were wooden frame structures without walls, just a roof, with six big canvas water bags hanging from the support beams. At each location, there were two structures about thirty feet apart: one for the officers, one for the enlisted. Whenever we took a water break, the army officers couldn't get away from the enlisted men fast enough.

Trainees run *everywhere* at jump school, doing what they call the Airborne shuffle, running in step with the left foot slamming down. All those left jump boots slamming the deck as one makes for a haunting beat. Sometime during the first week, while we were running, one of the soldiers started to get heat prostration. The corporal in charge sent him up the hill to the break area. He was told to get some water and sit in the shade. We ran around the track for another fifteen minutes, then headed to the break area.

Well, guess what? The officers' bags had water, and the enlisted men's didn't, and that soldier had sat there and not drunk from the officers' water. The army officers didn't give a damn whether we mere enlisted scum had water or not. Ensign Janke had some not so friendly words with the army officers. Then he and a couple other of our officers took the sick soldier to the officers' water and had him drink.

In stark contrast to their officers, the army instructors were all sergeants, and about the only thing the United States Army of the 1960s had going for it. They knew how to lead men into scary shit and get them out the other side. Not only were those men good, they looked it. The army called it "strac": It means everything from your weapon to the crease in your pants is ready, and where it should be. Those guys broke starch every day, and if they got dirty, they did it again. We could see our faces in the shine of their jump boots. It's like that in all the services, young officers come and go, but senior enlisted men are there for the long haul. Some of those sergeants had seen combat in World War II and Korea. They knew the tools needed to do the dirty business of war, and they did their best to give them to us.

Jump school gave me a new appreciation of our officers, who shined in comparison to what the army called officers and gentlemen in the early sixties. No, that's not right; there was *no* comparison, our officers just shined. Sixteen United States Naval officers started our UDT training class. Eleven of them were going to graduate. It

damn well should have been twelve, but Ens. Charley
Rand lost those toes to frostbite! That is an unheard-of
attrition rate. Whole graduating classes hadn't had eleven
people, let alone eleven officers. Our officers were as
diverse a group of humans as could be found. They ran
the gamut from Lt. (jg) Rick Shea, who could make a
joke out of anything, to Lt. (jg) Richard G. Johnson, who
was quiet and took everything as serious as a heartbeat.
Before Hell Week, that diverse group of officers had
somehow come together as the first line in the net of
Class-29. The oddest thing was, the natural leader of our
class was Harry Humphries. But none of the officers
seemed to feel threatened by his ability. Our officers gave
a damn about their men; the army officers we saw just
seemed to care about being officers. Anyway, the incident
with the water, coupled with our demeanor when we
landed at Fort Benning and a little rebellion we staged at
the chow hall, put our officers in the spotlight.

The instructors told us there would be no passes—that's
liberty to a sailor—during Airborne training till just before
jump week. The army of the sixties was an odd place. Fort
Benning was what they called an "open post," meaning
there was no gate. The main highway ran straight through
the middle of the military reservation, and people could
drive on or off the base without being stopped. For the next
three weeks, Class-29 put its sneak and peek talents to good
use—liberty! Some nights our barracks was damn near
empty; we were all the places we weren't supposed to be.
Hell, one night I hitchhiked from the middle of Fort Benning to downtown Columbus, Georgia. Had a date with a
nice librarian lady—God bless librarians—then rode the
bus back to the base. Harry Humphries even crashed the
officers' club and got away with it. Some of the guys were
renting cars and parking them right behind our barracks.

We had the only barracks with a name, the Frog Farm. Of course, we named it. We even made up a sign. The army had one previous experience with a whole UDT training class coming to jump school. Before that, the teams had sent down just a few men at a time. The class before ours had infected the army's enlisted men with what I can only call hairy-ass Frogman disease. One of the major manifestations of this rare disease is disregard for stupid rules and the willingness to suffer the consequences of that action. With our class, the army decided that if they broke us up during the training day and kept us all together at night, there was less chance of their troops becoming infected.

The best thing about Jump School was good boots on my feet. We all had new jump boots. If the army knew anything, it was troops move on their feet, give them good boots. One of the guys talked me into filling my new boots full of hot water and then wearing them till they were dry. Now, this might sound dumb, but it was the best and quickest way I'd ever broken in a pair of boots. It amazed me how quickly my feet quit hurting. After the first week of jump school, I was pain free from the top of my head to the bottom of my feet.

Odd to think about jump school as a break, a place to let our pulled muscles and sore body parts heal, but that's just what it was. For Class-29, the daily physical demands had been more than cut in half. And there were no more night evaluations, Gig Squad, long swims, burnout PTs, and harassment just to see what we could take. Our idea of maximum effort and that of our army classmates had no similarity. Physically, our three weeks at Fort Benning was a cakewalk. As far as food went, well, let's just say . . .

The army had broken us up into different platoons, a few here, a few there. They did have all of Class-29's enlisted men living in one barracks. Their thinking was, keep those navy animals from leading our young soldiers astray. That was good thinking: case in point, the chow hall rebellion.

From the beginning, all of us were pissed off about the food quality and, mostly, the quantity. Our first meal in an army chow hall was a shock. All through training, the navy fed us as much as we could stuff down our throats. The army gave us a measly portion of things like powdered eggs, canned meat, powdered potatoes, canned vegetables, and garbage like that. No wonder the army troopers got tired so easily. The army didn't give them enough fuel to run their damn machine. To add insult to the whole process of starvation, each company that ate had to provide its own servers. That meant these guys had to pass out the miserly portions to their own classmates. When a company arrived at the chow hall, each platoon took a turn supplying servers. Their job was to stand behind the food line and pass out just the amount of food the cook told them to. No one liked to serve because their classmates were after the servers to give them more food and the cooks stood right behind them to make sure they didn't.

Ronald W. Lester (Interior Communications Electrician Third Class) was the leader of this particular action. Ron was not usually a shit stirrer. He was medium high with wide shoulders and a thick chest. Lester held the class record on the obstacle course. He was not only a fast runner, he had a lot of upper-body strength and was extremely well coordinated. Ron could stand flat-footed, jump straight up, flip, and land in the same spot.

I think it was the same morning as the water-bag incident, Ron said, "Let's volunteer, we'll show 'em how to serve." Lester had no trouble getting his classmates to go for his little rebellion, and every man serving was from Class-29. As soon Ron threw the idea out, I wanted to be on the toast tray. The cooks cut each slice of toast in *half*, a full piece of toast was counted as *two*! What a racket.

We had that fat-assed cook and his two assistants going nuts for a little while. If they were busy chewing me out for giving three triangles of toast, Ron Lester was giving out extra bacon. While they were chewing out Lester, Lynch would be passing out extra eggs. We were having a ball. It felt good to screw with the cooks and pass out extra food. They sure didn't let it last long.

Maybe ten guys had gotten through the line when the straw (toast) that broke the camel's back fell. The fat cook had finished chewing Jack Lynch out for giving out too big a scoop of powered eggs. Then he waddled down the line to jump on Lester for giving more than two pieces of bacon. Of course, I started passing out too much toast while he was at the other end of the line. I had just placed six wedges—three whole pieces of bread—on a guy's tray when the cook started screaming, "Stop the line, stop the line!" He ran back to our end, leaned across the line, stuck his fat belly in the powdered eggs, grabbed the six wedges of toast, and threw them back on the line. After throwing the toast, he threw us off the serving line. The real heartbreaker was, we were never allowed to serve again. Not only could these guys not cook, they couldn't think either.*

Add this to the manner of our arrival and the water-

---

*A little aside on what was going on with the army and food. About three years after we got out of jump school, the army had a huge financial scandal. It seems the supply sergeants had been pocketing money meant to feed the troops. They had a lot of little tricks, like calling one piece of bread two. If five thousand men eat three times a day, and each man is allowed two pieces of bread per meal, that's thirty thousand slices of bread per day. At two cents per slice, that's six hundred bucks a day. If an army cook can make one slice of bread into two, he's magic, and he can pocket three hundred dollars a day. Of course, similar "savings" were being made on *each* of the items offered at mealtimes.

bag incident, and the army didn't think much of the way we were fitting in. Our officers were given a little talking to by a senior army officer. It boiled down to "straighten up and fly right." Fat chance. Their biggest complaint was that the navy enlisted men did not show the proper respect to the army officers in the class. They were right. If those guys were good officers, I was a Girl Scout. A good officer's first concern is his men! I'm not just talking morals here; his men are the tools he has to accomplish his mission. Those guys wanted to wear the name, but still didn't understand the game. They wanted form, not fact, and that's what we gave them. They got the image of the four-O squared-away sailor. It was yes sir; no sir; spit-shined jump boots; break starch every day; be the best troops at jump school—but do things *our* way after hours.

The first thing we had to learn was a PLF, or parachute landing fall. We learned by leaping from wooden platforms, about three feet high, set around pits full of sawdust. Over and over, we jumped off the platforms into the pit. Easy enough, but the PLF had to be done just so. In real life, if we didn't do it just right during a jump and broke a leg, we would be of no use as combat troops. Truth be known, I needed all the practice I could get.

Feet together, legs slightly bent at the knee, arms stretched above the head, hands tightly gripping a set of make-believe parachute risers, chin tucked tightly onto the chest. When hitting the ground, the feet were to strike it flat, the legs acting as springs, absorbing the shock, slightly twisting the upper body and falling on the side. As soon as we were down, we were to jump up and collapse our make-believe parachutes. Getting up quickly and collapsing the chute could prevent a soldier's being dragged all over the drop zone. A proper PLF would prevent a broken leg or other damage. The army instructors did a good job on driving the basics home.

All the training at jump school was important, but had nothing to do with the two things that concerned me. How was a parachute packed and why did it work? I mean hell, who was the guy stuffing all that canopy in that little backpack? For all I knew, he could have been the brother of the fat cook who stuck his belly in the eggs.

Beside the PLF pits, there were three main training mock-ups: aircraft cargo bay; the 34-foot tower; and the best carnival ride in the country, the 250-foot tower. The cargo-bay mock-up was used to teach what was required of us in the aircraft—most important, how to leave it. It boiled down to being able to march. I'm not making light of that stage of training. If everyone didn't take the same step, in unison, they would never get a hundred jumpers out the door over the drop zone. The consequences of not leaving that aircraft asshole-to-belly-button could be dire. The whole objective was to get a *lot* of combat troops in a *small* area on the ground, ready to fight. If anyone gets out of step, the whole operation can turn to shit in less than a heartbeat, with troops strung out all over the countryside.

The army's style of instruction was the *do-it-over-and-over* method. I have a special place in my heart for this method; it's the only way I can learn. To make the school of repetition work, failure to perform properly was rewarded with public physical pain and ridicule. At jump school, that meant push-ups or extra running.

We went through the mock-up again and again, getting the steps down to near automatic. We put on our parachutes before we loaded the dummy aircraft. Each of us was assigned a spot in what is called a "stick." A stick is just the order of jump for the troops; they want you to end up as close as you can be on the ground. The guys in the stick check each other's parachutes and harnesses out, then each man is checked by an assistant jump master. The troops load, sit, and jump in stick order. Everything is done on the jump master's command, in most cases by hand signals. In the cargo bay the jump master is king; rank and rate mean nothing. The jump master has final say on when and if the jump will be made. If a general is in a stick, he takes the jump master's orders like everyone else. With the command "Stand up," everyone stands up and faces the jump masters. At "Hook up," each jumper hooks up his static line to a cable running the length of the cargo bay. When we were hooked up, safety pin installed, we gave the static line a few jerks. Each jumper checks the parachute of the man in front of him. At "Stand in the door," the whole stick shuffles forward, and the first man stands in the door.

Most of the guys in Class-29 would have happily made their five jumps the first day at jump school; *I* wanted every bit of training they were passing out. I figured the more I practiced, the less chance I might freeze in the door. For me, making my first jump had focused down to the aircraft door. It was like the bull riders tell me, "It don't take balls to ride a bull. What takes balls is getting off the fence onto that big bastard's back; after that you just hang on." That's just how I felt about jumping: If I could get out the door, the rest would take care of itself.

The thirty-four-foot towers were fun. They were just rooms, about fifteen by twenty feet, with three doors perched thirty-four feet off the ground on pilings that looked like telephone poles. The back door was the entrance, and a set of wide stairs led up to it. The two front doors were the exits. Neither had stairs, but from each a set of cables ran for a hundred or so yards. The cables sloped down to, and were mounted on, a telephone-pole frame about fifteen feet off the ground. A twelve-foot-high earth berm ran under the cables on the frame end.

The object of that tower was to accustom us to jumping out of safe places into nothing.

I must not have been the only one worried about freezing in the door! Most of the guys who weren't going to make it wiped out at the thirty-four-foot towers. It was the only place we had to stand in the door, then jump of our own free will.

Each of us wore a working parachute harness with a dummy parachute attached. We started out at the bottom of the stairs leading to the thirty-four-foot tower. We shuffled up the stairs in two lines, one for each exit door. When my turn came, I was hooked to a small trolley that rode on the cables. Time to jump! Again, the army had a very specific way they wanted us to do that. Some of the guys did it right. From the start. Not me. That first time, I just leaped, like someone committing suicide.

Big surprise! It was fun, but I had done nothing right. I had dived out the door as close to headfirst as the harness would allow, my body parts in all the wrong places, nothing tucked in tight. That caused me to be jerked around and come sliding down the cables, my arms and legs flailing all over the place. Of course, my not-so-perfect effort was observed by all the army instructors. I paid the price with push-ups and a little ridicule from every instructor in sight. They loved it when one of us leg swabbies didn't do something right.

It was fun, but I had to concentrate and get the procedure right. All I had to do when I stood in the door was to have the palm of one hand on the outside of each door edge. My feet should have been slightly apart, one foot a little behind the other, legs bent a few degrees. My eyes should have been looking straight out the door. When the jump master said "Go!" I should have jumped up and out, then brought my arms hard to my sides, hands gripping my reserve chute, feet together, chin tucked hard on my chest.

The thing that nailed us on the thirty-four-foot tower was similar to the opening shock of a parachute: We received a good jerk when our risers took up the weight of our falling bodies. Even if we didn't have a tight body position and we jerked all over the place, it was still a fun ride. Like the PLF, the thirty-four-foot tower was an over-and-over-again operation. It was fun, not as much fun as cast and recovery, but something young, dumb, and full of *it* guys could enjoy. What we didn't get was prop wash, a 120-mile-an-hour wind just outside the aircraft door. That tower couldn't fly!

The army Airborne is justifiably a proud outfit with a long history. We, of course, wanted them to know that Underwater Demolition Teams were a prouder outfit. We played a little fast and loose with a couple of their verbal traditions. We were to reply to any direction from an instructor with a hearty "Airborne, Sergeant!" Being good sailors, the members of Class-29 always replied to our army instructors with, *"Airborne Frogman, Sergeant!"* Our reply generally got us some extra push-ups or such. My personal favorite "or such" was to have to run *around* the group. It was fairly simple, the instructors would have us run around the rest of the platoon while the platoon ran wherever it was bound.

Running around the platoon was a break from the boredom of the airborne shuffle; we just sped up on one side, ran across the front, and coasted down the other side. If we really wanted to hassle the instructor, we just hollered, "Airborne Frogman!" every time we ran past. That was sure to get us some extra push-ups when the platoon stopped running.

Everything at Fort Benning was in the shadows of the 250-foot towers, immense steel structures that stood in the middle of a huge grassy field. There were two, each with four arms sticking out from the top. The arms were about a hundred feet long. On the end of each arm was a large, odd-looking, round contraption, that could be raised or lowered as needed. When the odd-looking contraption was lowered to the ground, crew riggers would attach a special unpacked parachute in its dome. The dome held the parachute in an open position with mechanical hooks that could be released on command. When the chute was rigged, its risers were hooked to a trainee's harness, and the fun began. The dome was raised to the end of its arm, 250 feet straight up as the trainee dangled under it, slowly being lifted over the state of Georgia. In the sixties, there wasn't a carnival ride anywhere in the nation that could touch them. The towers would be our last training device before jump week.

On the 250-foot tower, there was no door to stand in; hell, the parachute was already open. The instructors' monitored the wind conditions closely, and if a man was lucky, he might get to hang up there and enjoy the view. I saw two men who hung up there, just checking out Georgia, for over thirty minutes before they were slowly lowered to the ground, because the wind was wrong. From the top, the whole base was laid out below my feet, and I felt like I could see half of Georgia—the Chattahoochee River wandering past the base and off through Columbus, Georgia, and all the little towns, roads, farms, and the huge drop zones we would use for our first jumps.

Only two things could get us hurt on the towers: an unplanned gust of wind and a bad PLF. The army instructors were very careful about the wind. They carried loudspeakers so that we could hear their commands while hanging at the end of one of the tower's arms, waiting to drop. We had to do our own PLF. Each trainee must have performed at least two hundred practice PLFs by the time he started the 250-foot towers. But none of the practice seemed to take for some of us. On our first tower jump, a lot of us hit the ground like large sacks of sand. Which made our army instructors feel needed. They could point out our weaknesses to one and all, apply some push-up study techniques, and send us to the PLF pits.

It amazed me how quickly the first two weeks passed. It seemed to me we'd hardly stepped off that C-130, and it was the weekend before jump week. Everyone was given what the army calls passes, and what the navy calls liberty, for the weekend. A lot of the guys from Class-29 were from the south, so some of them went home for the weekend. For the army guys, the pass was a big deal. None of them had been off the base in two weeks. We, of course, had been taking our own liberty since we arrived. *During* jump training, we were the best troops there. *After hours,* fuck the army; we went and did what we wanted.

The only other guy I'm sure felt the same way I did about jumping out of a perfectly good airplane was Jessie James Hardy. One night toward the end of tower week, I got back to the base about two o'clock in the morning. Old Jessie was standing by the trunk of a car someone had rented, drinking beer. The trunk was open, and the better half of a case was just sitting right there in the middle of it. We stood by the trunk of that car, drinking beer for a couple hours, just talking guy BS.

Jesse was a stone alcoholic, he knew it, and so did everyone else. But Jessie was one up on me; I was an alcoholic and didn't know yet. Over the years, I have had my struggle with booze and witnessed a lot of people with the same problem. Never have I seen anyone like Jessie James Hardy. How anyone could go through the four months we had just completed yet be drunk a good part of the time was beyond me. The class wasn't carrying him. Jessie James Hardy was a reach-down-in-your-gut-and-pull-it-out hard guy!

As we sucked the suds, I told old Jessie how I felt about jumping out of a perfectly good airplane. The same two things were still bothering me: I wanted to know exactly how and why a parachute worked, and who the hell was packing my chute. Jessie felt pretty much the way I did, but he commented that if we wanted to be Frogmen, we didn't seem to have much choice in the matter. After talking with Jessie I didn't sweat my two questions so much. I don't know why; he hadn't told me anything I didn't already know.

On jump day, all of us were introduced to a very good reason to jump. It was called a C-119, the Flying Boxcar. Those damn things had been around since World War II, and they rattled and creaked just sitting on the ground without the engines running! The skin of the planes was dented and rippled as if someone had been beating on them with a big hammer. Just the look of the C-119 was reason enough to jump. Hell, if those things got off the ground, no telling how long before a wing or something might fall off. To put it mildly, the Flying Boxcars did not inspire thoughts of soaring with the eagles. All questions had been removed from my mind. I didn't like landing in aircraft anyway. Taking off and flying were okay, but landing was too much like a controlled crash for my taste. Given an opportunity, I would happily leap out of a C-119.

The C-119 could be jumped from the back if the two clamshell doors at the rear of the aircraft were removed. We used the other method, side door. There was one on each side of the aircraft, just ahead of the clamshell doors. The two side doors had been removed before our flight. Everything in the door frames that might hang up a jumper was covered with aircraft tape, extra-heavy duct tape.

When we loaded onto the Boxcars and the pilot fired

up the engines, the noise was unbelievable. Every piece of metal in the aircraft shook and rattled. By that time, we had been standing around with our parachutes on in the Georgia heat and humidity for over an hour. Then we were sitting in that vibrating noise bucket, sweating our asses off. To my mind, there was no question whatsoever: If that thing made it into the air, I'd jump out of it!

All morning, I could look around and see the fear on a lot of faces. I'm sure there were guys from Class-29 besides me who felt fear that day. None of them were showing it. I had made up my mind I wasn't going to let those army dudes see fear on my face either. My sphincter muscle might be tight, but I was going to show cool. There were guys doing their Rosary, others reading from small Bibles. Some guys looked stunned, their eyes bulging, mouths hanging open, sweat running down their faces. Screw 'em! I might feel that way, but they weren't going to see it. So I thought.

Our Flying Boxcar got off the ground and actually sounded better. Most of the rinky-tink rattling was gone, replaced by a strong, deep, straining throb. At least it sounded strong, maybe the C-119 wouldn't fall out of the sky. Another nice surprise: The interior cooled down quickly. For me, one of the biggest surprises was how long it took to fly the couple miles to the drop zone. We must have flown around the state of Georgia for an hour.

Our jump master that day was a sergeant. And the blackest man I have ever seen. He was as big as Instructor Waddell and all business. He had been at ground check, helping the assistant jump master go through the checks on us. I had watched him inspect the aircraft inside and out, and the sergeant's professional bearing had made me feel a little better about the piece of flying junk we were vibrating through the sky in. He must have felt my eyes on him all morning, because just before our jump, he singled me out and caused me to lose my Mr. Cool cover.

My place in the jump order was number six in my stick, jumping from the right door. Five men were sitting tightly packed together between me and that *door*. Our jump master was standing in the middle of the aircraft, just to the stern of the two side doors. He had his big legs spread for balance. I sat, with my eyes glued on him. He pulled a piece of eight-by-eleven paper out of his pocket, unfolded it, and started to read. After a few seconds, he looked up, straight into my eyes, one of those serious-as-a-heartbeat looks on his face. He just barely nodded his head a couple times. His eyes never left mine. We went through this little routine three or four times. The sergeant was trying to communicate something to me. What the hell it was, I couldn't figure out. While he was looking me straight in the eye, he held the paper chest high. His big hands started wadding the paper into a ball. That heartbeat look never left his face, his eyes never left mine. He held the wadded piece of paper between two fingers in front of his chest. He opened his fingers and let the wadded paper fall. It landed between his spread, spit-shined jump boots.

I had almost forgotten where we were and what we were about to do; our jump master had me right where he wanted me. He was going to remind me in a way I would never forget. Two or three times he looked down at the wadded paper, then up at me. The last time he looked down, he slowly lifted his right jump boot, and set it down so the wadded paper was between his right boot and the right door. His spit shine was so good, I could see the wadded paper reflected in the toe of his jump boot. Now, that damn piece of paper was at least seven feet from the door.

The jump master nudged the paper with the toe of his

boot. It moved slowly about six inches, then was gone, just gone! It happened so quick, I had no idea what had taken place. I must have looked around for the paper for at least thirty seconds, before it dawned on me what had just transpired. When I looked up, the jump master had an ear-to-ear grin on his face and was shaking his head up and down. My Mr. Cool image was gone. All I wanted was my cherry jump over. What had made that wadded-up piece of paper disappear was the one thing we couldn't practice: the hurricanelike wind rushing past that door. That wind had sucked the paper out. Just to make sure I got the point, he did it again, minus all the theatrics. That time I saw it go out the door. It was still fast, but I knew what I was looking for. Oh well, if I wanted to be a Frogman, I had to be a jumper!

It was a relief when we got the stand-up signal. We stood and faced the rear of the aircraft. We hooked our static lines to the cable and inserted the safety pins, two long lines of young bucks with very tight sphincters. One line on each side of the aircraft. We checked each other out. I have no idea how long we stood, but it seemed like a long time. Our jump master was standing in the door and the wind was moving the flesh around the side of his face. He stepped back, and gave the signal: Stand in the door! Both lines of jumpers shuffled forward, first man in the door.

I remember the first guy going and the line shuffling ahead. The next thing I knew, I was looking at the spit shine of my boots, and Georgia was laid out twelve hundred feet below me. Even if the fat cook's brother packed my chute, he'd done a good job. That beautiful canopy of nylon was floating me to the ground. My plan had been to holler, "Airborne Frogman!" as I stood in the door. No idea if that was accomplished. My memory went from shuffling ahead to hanging under that parachute. No door, no blast, no opening shock; I remembered none of it. I was a jumper. Well, in my mind I was a jumper. The army figured I had four more jumps to make it so.

It's odd having no memory of that door. Freezing in it had been the biggest fear I had throughout training. I never feared it again. In truth, those leaps of faith became a time when there was nothing between God and me. I kept the doubts about the fat cook's brother and my parachute for another year. Then, to my way of thinking, I became the fat cook's brother, one of the team's riggers—that is, I packed the parachutes.

Class-29 did well, everyone jumped, no one broke any bones. We had not graduated into the Teams, but were already exhibiting strong Frogman tendencies. Bust ass and party hardy. Jump week was easy on the bust ass but heavy on the party hardy. Our main mission that week was five jumps. Getting more than two hundred men through five jumps requires a lot of standing around, and waiting. There was little time for runs or physical training, but we had all night to party. Party we did!

The Frog Farm, our barracks, had more beer in it than the enlisted men's club. On base, the army did not allow anyone under the rank of E-5 to drink anything but "near-beer," a disgusting low-alcohol brew. The noncommissioned officers' club, for pay grades E-5 and above, and the officers' club had all the booze a man could want. Unfortunately, all the enlisted men in Class-29 were below the rank of E-5. Since we were not allowed in town, at the noncommissioned officers' club, or the officers' club, we couldn't drink. *Right!* The Frog Farm was the starting point for whatever illegal activity we were about that night. My personal favorite was downtown Columbus, Georgia, but several of the guys were hitting the NCO club, which took a lot of balls as that's where our army instructors did their drinking.

They had to have known what we had been up to from the start; young guys partying are not very stealthy. Sneaking into the officers' club, the NCO club, or leaving the base without authorization could earn us the brig. Let us not forget all that beer in the barracks and the rent-a-cars some of my classmates had. To the military's way of thinking, those were more infractions against good order and discipline. There was only one reason we got away with all that shit at Fort Benning. The sergeants liked us.

In a strange way, the military is run by those men in the middle. The chiefs in the navy, and the sergeants in the rest of the forces. They are the keepers of the faith. The guys who hold the grunts together in the good times, peace. Those army instructors saw things in Class-29 they knew were needed when things got bad. First and foremost, we had officers who would hang their asses out in the wind for their enlisted men. The eleven officers in our little group gave a damn about their men. Fort Benning was a big place, with a lot of different training commands. There were at least a thousand junior-grade army officers running around that base. If they were lucky, they had eleven army officers on that whole damn base who cared as much about their men. Second, and very difficult without the first, we had that military favorite, "unit cohesion."

Unit cohesion is one of those terms that everyone thinks they understand. In truth, most people don't have a clue. It is definitely not about everybody liking each other or being nice. It means you have a pride in the ability of your group to function at a higher level than possible for the individual. The unit doesn't shine because you're a member, you shine because you're good enough to be a member. It doesn't matter if the discussion is about front-line troops or rear-echelon supply people. If the military has enough little units competing to be the best at their job, it's ready to fight. Class-29 had unit cohesion, a rare thing in the military of the sixties. We were allowed to get away with a lot because of it.

Graduation day at jump school was a madhouse. Class-29 was packing its gear, running all over Fort Benning to get paperwork done, to pick up our pay records, etc., all the administrative bull the military is so fond of. We couldn't do all that crap in one place; that would have been too simple. So it was spread all over the base.

Sitting on the tarmac outside the hangar where graduation was being held, the navy had a C-130 ready to fly us to Key West as soon as the graduation ceremonies were over. To tell the truth, many of us were hungover, and just wanted to get on the plane and have a little rest. To hell with the graduation.

The military generally tries to put on a nice graduation ceremony from any of its schools. There are bands, moms and dads, the whole nine yards. Because of our tight outprocessing deadline, Class-29 showed up well after the ceremonies had started, and tried to slip in without causing much commotion. That's when our army classmates and instructors blew our jump boots off and made us feel a little humble: They stood en masse and gave us an ovation. It was one of those things we'll carry with us for life.

PHASE SIX

Lieutenant Tiel and the four Netherlands enlisted men rejoined the class at the naval base, Key West, Florida. During the following five weeks, the students were trained in the use and maintenance of all types of navy SCUBA (Self-Contained Underwater Breathing Apparatus) equipment. They learned diving medicine and physiology, underwater search procedures, underwater communication and navigation, and submarine escape hatch lock-in and lock-out procedures.

The last week at jump school, I kept thinking of Key West and finally becoming a diver. I figured we would learn how to put the gear on and do a lot of diving. Well, that was true as far as it went, but the world of academia was about to rear its ugly head. Until jump school, we'd had an excellent intelligence source in Tom McCutchan. Since Mac had done the first part before, he was more than happy to let us know what was going to hit us next. Of course, it wasn't too hard to figure out what jump school would be like. If we were surprised about anything at Fort Benning, it was that jump school was easier than we had thought. Not so with underwater swimmers school!

We were greeted as we stepped off the C-130 by an old (maybe thirty-five) Frogman, a first class petty officer, known far and wide as Shorty Lyons. Shorty was on the cover of *Life* magazine around 1966 or 1967. Not only was Shorty a Frogman, but he was one of those strange men who figure they are smarter than the guys who build the bombs. It's called EOD, explosive ordnance disposal. To my way of thinking, anybody who takes apart *bombs* is being told things by God that I don't hear, or has a *big fucking screw loose*.

During one of Shorty Lyons's tours of duty in Vietnam, he had helped a doctor remove a live mortar round from a Vietnamese soldier's chest cavity. Well, all three of them lived through the experience, and Shorty made the cover of *Life*. That's the hard old bull they placed in charge of Class-29.

He was our class proctor, which meant that, besides teaching some of the classes, he was to take care of any problems the class might have. God bless Shorty! I wouldn't change that choice for anything, but I'll bet most anything he would. Besides Shorty, three other men from Underwater Demolition Teams were instructing at the school: the executive officer, Lieutenant Schaible, and two first class petty officers, Cahill and Durks.

Navy-wide, an executive officer is simply known as the XO. To my way of thinking, it is a bad job; the XO does all the scut work that the commanding officer is too busy for. It is also a job that if not well done will end a naval officer's career. To the navy way of thinking, "well done" means not only does it work, but it has a fresh coat of haze-gray paint, *it looks good*. Of course, that's the problem with the peacetime navy—how it *looks* counts more. Class-29 was about to threaten the XO's advancement. We worked great; it was just that at times we didn't look too good.

Lyons struck fast, with push-ups as soon as we stepped off the plane. The plane was late, and since the C-130 couldn't pay the price of being tardy, we would. To top off our welcome to underwater swim school, as soon as we dumped our gear, Lyons took us on a little tour of Key West. Of course, we ran; our proctor rode. He had a sick-green Cushman motor scooter, and he loved to have us run while he *putt*ed along. He was particularly fond of hearing our left feet collectively slam the pavement. All our runs with Shorty were accompanied by the soft steady *putt* of the Cushman and the hard *slam* of our left feet echoing through the streets of Key West.

The Key West of the early sixties was a beautiful small town. Even the naval base had an old-style laid-back charm. One thing was the same then as now. Key West had a lot of people of a different stroke. Class-29 fit right in; we were full of different strokes.

The shock came for a lot of us when we found out just what it was we were supposed to learn there. We actually had scholastic standards to meet, written tests and all. Not only that, but there were physics and diving medicine, serious subjects. In those days, the military did not require a high school diploma for enlistment. Many of us enlisted men were not academic giants. In high school, I had done nothing more than was required of me to stay eligible for sports. Hell, Ralph Diebold had only been allowed to go to school when there was no work to do on the farm. We were in some serious shit.

On the lighter side, the main drag and the bars were two short blocks out the gate. The gates on the base were manned by United States Marines, for whom we stopped, showed identification, and stated our business. Unlike the situation at Fort Benning, we needed liberty cards to get off the base. But for the first time in almost five months, we were allowed liberty every night we didn't have duty—if we kept up our grades and stayed out of trouble. It turned out that keeping up the grades was easier than staying out of trouble.

A few things should be kept in mind: Every man in Class-29 was well past what might be called normal. By "normal," I mean restrained by fear. I don't mean we didn't have guys who didn't maintain themselves in a proper manner, we did. Robert J. Young, Ralph Coligan, James H. Cook, John Kopetski, Trailor Lewis, Forrest Dearborn Hedden, were all nice quiet guys who would fit in anywhere and never upset the balance of nature. That is unless someone made the mistake of fucking with them. Not one bully in our class, and not a guy who would roll over for a bully. No one who couldn't carry his own weight and some of yours, too. Not one phony with a pocket full of three-dollar bills. I know now how rare a privilege it is to be part of such a group. Thank you, God.

We hadn't walked to meals in over four months; it had always been run to, run back! In Key West, we didn't even have to go to chow if we didn't want to. Strolling over to the chow hall while talking with a couple friends was a pleasure. I have one mental snapshot: We're walking to lunch. Up in front are Leo Duncan, Jessie James Hardy, and Harry Humphries. They're just strolling three abreast, talking. Right in front of Risher and me are Shorty Flockton, Jack Lynch, and P.T. Smith. When that snapshot pops into my mind, it feels like walking to lunch with well-loved brothers. None of us thought at the time that in just five weeks we would graduate into the Teams. Some of us would never see each other again.

They broke the class, and the day, into two parts. One group had classroom in the morning, and the water in the afternoon. The other had the reverse. A few times we had night dive/swims, but most nights belonged to the pursuit of a good time. Well, let's qualify that, the kind of a good time only young, dumb guys go after. Key West was a different form of stress test for most of us, a little self-abuse.

The test went like this. Work all day; in the early evening, start slamming back large quantities of whatever booze tickled the fancy. Keep it up all night if possible, or at least till the bars closed. With little or no sleep carry out your daily duties. Now, do the same damn thing again. My rest periods came when I was out of money and none of my classmates had any to lend. For a bunch of young hard-chargers, Key West was the icing on a hard-to-bake cake.

We learned to dive with two kinds of scuba gear, one is called "open circuit"—standard scuba gear. The other was secret shit, the Emerson rebreather, the latest thing in sneak-attack diving gear. No bubbles, nothing to give away the swimmer's presence to anyone watching the surface of the water. Diving has its inherent dangers, but the rebreathers of the early sixties had an extra-special one: They were pure-oxygen rigs. Use them incorrectly and a man could shake himself to death, each cell in his body consuming itself with the oxygen toxicity. The job we all wanted to do required us to use the rig, right up to its limits.

The instructors never tried to hide the risks of the things our job would require us to do. On the contrary, they had spent a lot of time and money finding men who would run full tilt to the edge of the cliff without going over. My class was full of guys like Ens. John "The Killer" Hunt, a mother's worst nightmare. John was a nice polite Christian kid, but as far as moms are concerned, he had one huge flaw. John had to climb the highest cliff around, jump off the loftiest spot on the bridge, and sit in the top of the tallest tree. Mothers have bad dreams about that kind of thing. What most moms don't understand, but our instructors did, was that we were not interested in *failing* at dangerous things.

Our water time started in the pool with basic scuba.

Just getting comfortable with the gear. All the same routines offered in a well-run civilian course today. Ditching and donning, taking the gear all off, laying it on the bottom of the pool, ten feet deep. After coming to the surface, we took a breath, skinned down, and put the gear back on. Buddy breathing, two guys breathing one rig. Treading water with the gear, etc. The only differences between today's civilian course and our basic course back then was that our instructors didn't have to play nice with their charges; they were not trying to sell us gear, they wanted us to stay alive. When we did something less than perfectly, they would talk very rudely to us and give us some remedial instruction such as push-ups with a set of twin nineties on our backs. Nineties were the biggest and heaviest scuba bottles around at the time. A set weighed around sixty pounds. The instructors would be in the pool with us, pulling off face masks, jerking out mouthpieces, shutting off air. Just keeping the stress test up.

The class work was heavy on physiology and diving medicine. To put it in the simplest terms, the instructors wanted us to understand how people die from little things like holding their breath, not knowing what time it is, not knowing exactly where they are. If a diver holds his breath while rising, all the little alveoli in his lungs rip apart, and frothy blood and mucus bubble out his mouth. Believe me, it is not a pretty sight. Being late: You plan a dive, dive your plan. If you stay too long, it is going to be at least painful because of the dreaded bends. Not knowing where you are again relates to the bends, and depth and time are critical factors. Worse than the bends, 100 percent oxygen rebreathers are extremely depth sensitive. Well, that's not quite right; the rig will function at most any depth. With pure oxygen the *human body* is depth sensitive. Humping a pure-oxygen rebreather deeper than thirty feet for any length of time will end in a very unpleasant death. By humping, I mean swimming hard against a current, dragging along whatever weapons or explosives are needed for the mission. If a diver kills himself on the way in, the mission does not get accomplished.

We were out of the pool within a couple days and into the beautiful Gulf Stream, a huge river of warm, deep-blue water, that runs out of the Caribbean, up the East Coast of the United States. One of the practical tests we had to pass was called the blow and go. I loved that one! An open-bottom diving bell hung off the back of a boat at eighty feet. We left the boat with standard scuba gear and swam down to the bell. The water was clear, and we could see the bell all the way down. When we reached the bell and looked back up, we could see the boat and the safety swimmers waiting in the water.

The test was simple: Stand inside the bubble of the bell and remove the scuba bottles. Easy enough; the bubble was full of trapped air. When given the signal, the swimmer was to step out of the bubble, holding firmly on to the lip, look up at the bottom of the boat, and expel every drop of air he can force out of his lungs. On signal from the instructor, he would start swimming for the surface.

Doesn't sound too bright, does it? In fact, the diver had better be exhaling all the way up because air is a gas, and compressible. All of us breathe compressed air. At sea level, just the weight of all that air stacked over our heads exerts 14.7 pounds of pressure per square inch on everything. It turns out that a one-square-inch column of sea water, thirty-three feet long, weighs 14.7 pounds. So every thirty-three feet of sea water exerts one atmosphere. To keep it simple, but stupid: If a man were standing at sea level holding his breath and were suddenly whisked to the edge of space, his lungs would be ripped apart by the expansion of the air he was holding in because the volume of air would have doubled. The laws of physics that God has established for this life are hard and fast. If you want to be a diver and live, you had better know the rules and follow them. *Rule #1: Do not hold your breath coming up.*

The blow and go drill was beautiful. We swam up at the same rate of travel as our bubbles. As the bubbles traveled up around us, they expanded and broke apart into more bubbles. All the time, we continued to exhale, putting more bubbles of air in the water surrounding us. The bright sunlight flashed beautifully off all those bubbles traveling through the clear blue Gulf Stream. It is a strange experience to exhale for a minute and a half.

The problems between Lieutenant Schaible, the XO of underwater swim school, and Class-29 began after a beach party the school put on for us. The naval base had two excellent white-sand beaches, one being the enlisted men's beach, the other being the officers' beach, which was right in front of officers' housing where most of the officers with families lived. All the fun was at the enlisted beach.

The party was great, there were large quantities of two things that most divers love, beer and lobster. Most of us had never eaten lobster of any kind. What was provided at the party was to become my favorite, *langosta,* a lobster with no claws that flourishes in warm waters all over the world. The party started early Friday afternoon. The married instructors brought their families; some of the single guys had lady friends. So, most of the females attending our little tropical beach party were spoken for. One of the exceptions was the XO's lovely young daughter, the source of problem number one later that evening. Of course, all of us single young bucks were strolling around with our chests puffed out, doing our best to attract her attention. Well, at least our boat crew won out; she had eyes for our smooth Texas boy, Troy Vaught.

It was just a nice party, everybody laid back in the south Florida sun, eating good food, sucking suds, and flapping jaws. I don't know which of our officers started the "our guy can beat your guy" thing, but they were all in on it. The first I heard was, Roat can beat the chief. The chief in question was the chief master at arms of underwater swim school. The bet had to do with who was the fastest swimmer. Now, a swimming race should have been no problem at all. First, being a young cocky guy, I figured I could whip that old man's ass. Hell, he had to be at least thirty-five years old, maybe forty. Second, we were encouraged to compete and to foster that, the instructors were always letting us know who was the best at what. The problem with our little swim competition was how and where.

The problems all started when the party was over, well after sunset. Most everyone was heading back to the school to get ready for a weekend of liberty in Key West. Troy Vaught was headed for the XO's house in the back of the Schaibles' pickup truck. They had no problem with Troy and their daughter liking each other; the XO had started out as an enlisted Frogman himself. They were just going to make sure that no horny young Frogman got at her when they weren't around. Troy would have to visit her at their house.

The chief and I rode Shorty Lyons's sick-green Cushman motor scooter down to the officers' beach, and parked it at the top of the beach, one block south of married officers' housing. There was no moon, so we were far enough from the houses that no one would see us get naked. At least, that was the thought. Our plan was for the chief and me to swim out around the half-mile buoy, and back. First one back to Shorty's scooter was the winner.

Both of us would have been legally drunk in a court of law. If there were such a charge as drunken swimming. The truth is, we would have done the same thing without the booze. It was just a little competition between two guys for bragging rights. This was a no-fins, no–inflatable life jacket, no–swim trunks race. Two naked men against each other and one mile of Atlantic Ocean.

I didn't see the chief after the first hundred yards. It's not like swimming a mile in a pool; in the ocean you have to figure current. No matter how fast a swimmer is, if he figures the current wrong, the slower man will win. Key West is just a little piece of land stuck out in the Gulf Stream, a huge river afloat in the ocean. The buoy was one-half mile due east of officers' beach; the Gulf Stream runs from south to north. We were cutting the current all the way.

Well, as they were always telling us, it pays to be a winner. I hit the beach a little less then a quarter mile north of Shorty's motor scooter. The base housing for married officers was at the top of the beach. I stayed down close to the water and ran like hell for Shorty's Cushman. I was one happy camper when I got there and there was no chief. I had just enough time to let a tiny worry wander across my brain: I hoped the chief hadn't drowned.

Bam! Bright light bathed my naked self. There I stood, a lot bigger and a whole lot less adorable than the day I was born. The lights went off almost as quickly as they had come on. It was the damn base police, I was in *deep* ka-ka! The navy was not going to be happy with a naked enlisted man standing on the edge of married officers' housing. Every little synapse in my brain was firing at full warp speed.

I could hit the water and swim away. But what if the

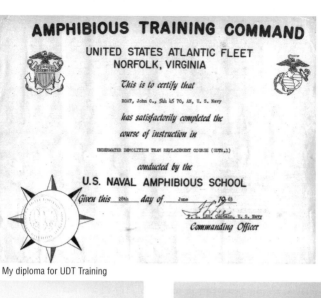

AMPHIBIOUS TRAINING COMMAND

UNITED STATES ATLANTIC FLEET
NORFOLK, VIRGINIA

This is to certify that

ROAT, John C., Slh 45 70, AN, U. S. Navy

has satisfactorily completed the

course of instruction in

UNDERWATER DEMOLITION TEAM REPLACEMENT COURSE (UDTR.1)

conducted by the

U.S. NAVAL AMPHIBIOUS SCHOOL

Given this 28th *day of* June *19 68*

F. L. Lee, Captain, U. S. Navy
Commanding Officer

My diploma for UDT Training

Death Trap during Hell Week

Class-29 at Underwater Swim School, Key West, Florida

Army Jump School, the 250 foot tower

Carl Thomas "Tom" Allen, EM3

Ralph Diebold, SN

Neil G. Dow, AN

Leo Duncan, SN, and me, John Roat

Ronald T. "Shorty" Flockton, BUL3

Richard L. Fradenburgh, RDSN

Thomas L. "Bimbo" Gaston, Ens.

Leroy C. "Gedunk" Geiger, MMFN

George C. "Curt" Gibby, Lt. (jg)

Jessie James Hardy, SFM3

Richard A. "Dick" Hauff, Ens., my swim buddy

James Hawes, Ens.

Forrest Dearborn Hedden Jr., SA

John P. "Killer" Hunt, Ens.

David Janke, Ens.

Ronald E. "Ron" Jarvi, BTFN

Richard G. "Dick" Johnson, Lt. (jg)

Ronald W. "Ron" Lester, IC3

Trailor L. Lewis, SN

John R. "Jack" Lynch Jr., SN

Thomas "Mac" McCutchan, SM3

Gene M. Munson, BM3

Robert A. "Bob" Neidrauer, BMSN

Clarence T. "Ted" Risher III, AMHAN

John Roat

Roat, with feet in bucket. Training for me was about overcoming the *pain* in my feet!

Paul T. "P.T." Smith, SR, at boot camp

Commander P. T. Smith after 36 years and 9 months in the U.S. Navy

Steven W. Swartley, Ens.

Troy E. Vaught, EMFN

James C. Walker, Ens.

Kenneth T. "Tommy" Winter, SN

Gerald Yocum, Ens.

Puerto Rico. Left to right: P.T. Smith, Fast Eddie Leasure, Ron Jarvi, Shorty Flockton, Instructor Fraley, Ron Lester, James Cook

Left to right: George E. Leasure Jr., SN (aliases: Fast Eddie, Chink, Skill, Eddie); John C. Roat, AN; Harry J. Humphries, SN

Our Royal Dutch Marine classmates. Left to right: Coenraad Pauli, Cpl.; Robertus J. Hack, Pvt.; Hendrik J. Ravensburg, Cpl.; Egil O. H. Magnussen, Lt. (Norway); Martinus J. De Beers, Cpl.

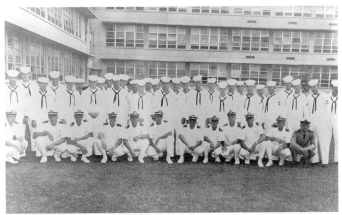
Graduation day for Underwater Demolition Teams

Instructor Tom Blais

Instructors Tom Blais (left) and Chuck Newell

Instructor Bernie Waddell

Left to right: Instructors Hammond, Cook, Clements, and Fraley

Reunion, 1998, after a four-mile run. Top row, left to right: Jim Hawes, John "Jack" Lynch, David Janke, Dick Hauff, Richard "Dick" Johnson, John "Killer" Hunt. Bottom row, left to right: Coenraad Pauli, John Roat, Richard "Dick" Shea, Hendrik Ravensburg

Reunion, 1998. Back row, left to right: Coenraad Pauli, P.T. Smith, Dick Johnson (behind my head), Curt Gibby, Dick Shea, David Janke, John "Killer" Hunt, Dick Hauff, Ron Lester, Hendrik Ravensburg. Front row, left to right: Jack Lynch, Shorty Flockton, me on Shorty's knee, Bob Neidrauer

Reunion, 1998. Back row, left to right: Dick Shea, Harry Humphries, P.T. Smith, Jack Lynch. Front row, left to right: Ron Lester, Shorty Flockton, Bob Neidrauer

Reunion, 1998. Dick Shea entertains his classmates.

Freddy the Frog,
UDT shoulder patch

chief needed help or, worse, had drowned? Our clothes had not been moved from the running board of the Cushman—maybe they didn't have our ID cards? Grab the clothes and run for the water! But what about the chief? If I was going to haul ass, I had to do it *now*. All that crap flowed through my brain before the base police were out of their truck. As soon as I snatched up our shorts and shirts to run, I knew I was had; there was no wallet weight! Stay, and keep your big mouth shut! The first thing out of their mouths was "Where's the chief?"

In those days if someone in the military was captured by an enemy of the United States, under the Code of Conduct he could only give his name, rank, and serial number. If he told the enemy anything else he could go to prison. Well, if I could do that for my country, I could just keep my damn mouth shut and take what was coming now. "Where's the chief?" I gave no answer. "What in the hell are you up to?" I gave no answer. "Is this Shorty Lyons's motor scooter?" With that question, all six foot three of underwater swim school's naked chief master at arms walked out of the dark. Misery surely does love company, and I was glad to see the chief!

This chief was everything a senior petty officer is supposed to be! The first words out of his mouth were, "Roat, here, is a student under my direction at the swim school. I ordered him to race me around the half-mile buoy. I am the only one at fault in this matter." For several reasons, I almost started laughing. First, with nothing more than relief. Second, the chief sounded so damn formal, standing there in all his naked glory. Third, he was telling them a lie; no one ordered me to race him. Last, but not least, I was still a little drunk.

He and the base police knew each other, and the chief asked if they could talk around the back of the truck. He told me to just stay by the scooter and keep my mouth shut. They were behind the truck for about five minutes. When they walked back to the scooter, the chief told me not to sweat it, just get in the back of the truck, they would drop me off at the barracks. I was not going to be put on report, thank God, but I was to stay in the barracks for the rest of the night.

When they dropped me off at the barracks, I found that the chief and I had not been the biggest infraction of military decorum that evening. Not only was I not the worst, I wasn't even first. Ensign Hawes's boat crew had struck hard that night. Troy Vaught had struck at the heart of the Schaible family before they even got off the base. He had gotten the XO's wife and daughter involved in a nasty little brouhaha at the base main gate.

Troy had quick reflexes, very fast hands, and a never-say-die attitude. He was about middleweight size, with that soft South Texas way of talking. His normal demeanor was laid back and polite, but like his fast hands, that could change *now*! Troy did not need liquid courage to fight, but the booze we had consumed that night did come into play; it had removed Troy's normal common sense. I mean, everyone knows not to knock the shit out of the guard on the main gate. Especially while in the company of the executive officer's wife and daughter.

The Schaibles did not live on the base; they had a home in a nice civilian neighborhood. The XO had driven in in his navy car that morning. Mrs. Schaible and their daughter had driven in the family pickup to come to the beach party. If the XO had been driving the truck, the Marine on the gate would have just saluted and waved them through. As it happened, the Marine guard wanted Troy and the Schaibles' daughter out of the back of the pickup truck. Even then there would have been no problem except that the Marine was rude. When Troy jumped down from the bed of the pickup, the Marine felt he had to put a little bad mouth on him. *Big mistake!* Troy hit him hard, one time in the jaw, and the guard's helmet flew about forty feet. The Marine landed on his ass.

Poor Mrs. Schaible had a world of trouble to deal with! Not only had Troy just done a *big* no-no, but her daughter started throwing beer bottles from the back of the pickup at the Marine. Somehow, Mrs. Schaible and the other gate guard got things back to a semblance of order. Of course, the command duty officer was called, and one of two things was going to happen: Troy Vaught was going to the brig or the XO had enough clout to make the affair as if it never happened. Well, I don't quite mean *never* happened, let us say, on paper it never happened. The XO had the clout, but he was not pleased to have to use it. Class-29 was on the top of his ka-ka list, and our class proctor, Shorty Lyons, was right there with us; Shorty was supposed to see that kind of thing didn't happen.

Our class proctor struck back Sunday morning. Shorty Lyons did not enjoy Mr. Schaible's jumping all over him because of our actions. About 0600, he woke all of Class-29 that was still on the base. We were going for a run. Shorty had his motor scooter and the streets of Key West to lead us through.

Shorty was not thinking clearly that morning, as he had obviously been drinking most of the night. Not only did we run through the base and downtown, but Shorty led us through the neighborhoods. He had us doing the airborne shuffle, slamming our left boots down hard and singing. The only people we saw that morning were leaving an early Mass at a Catholic church. Shorty's problem came from the people we didn't see—the ones we woke as we ran through their neighborhoods. Those people were angry, and a lot of them called the base to let the command duty officer hear just how they felt about it.

Thank you, Troy! Monday morning I got a small amount of heat for my actions, but our man Vaught had caused so much trouble that I was just a small blip on the XO's pooh-pooh meter. Troy, on the other hand, was a whole pickup truck full of fertilizer. The XO, being a former enlisted Team member, knew all about hairy-ass Frogman disease. His problem was how to deal with the odd manifestations of the disease without killing the carrier and still become a commanding officer. Not an easy task!

The kind of diving we were learning was about how to get from one place to another without being seen. We practiced what are called dogleg compass swims almost every day. Our main tool was an attack board, a piece of wood one half inch thick, nine inches wide, and twelve inches long. Mounted on the board were a compass and a depth gauge. The board was held in both hands, and the swimmer kept his eyes on the compass and depth gauge. In swim school, we were required to wear a buddy line—six feet of half-inch rope with a snap hook on each end—connecting us so if the swimmer without the attack board did not pay attention and wandered, both swimmers were jerked up short. Each man in the swim pair took turns with the attack board, so half the time he just swam along, having faith in his swim buddy and the swim buddy's abilities with a compass. Oddly enough, the hardest thing about the dogleg compass swims was overcoming the odd feeling we were swimming in circles. At night—during the day if we had no reference points—our minds would be telling us "You are swimming in a circle!" Every swim was a race, but speed was not the most important factor. Accuracy ruled, and the first swim pair to a designated spot won. No matter how fast we got to the wrong place, we lost.

Ensign Hauff and I worked well together in the water. We were first on all the dogleg compass swims but two: one because God was teaching us all a lesson; the other because Mr. Yocum and Ralph Diebold kicked our asses. They were one of the truly odd couples of Class-29. Ralph big, dark, and stoic. Mr. Yocum about half his size, fair skinned, and outgoing. Mr. Yocum told me later that one of his fins had split jumping into the water, so he felt as if Ralph had been dragging him the whole swim. It would be like trying to win a foot race with two legs and only one foot. But that day, they were the first pair to get to the right location, handicap and all. And they let Mr. Hauff and me know that we had been beat.

On a dogleg compass swim, at least two points had to be reached. The first was usually the buoy one-half mile off officers' beach. The instructors would take us out to sea, let us get a compass fix on the buoy, and off we went. Of course, the start and finish points were different for every swim. For each leg of the swim, each set of swim buddies was allowed one time on the surface to check the compass heading. Once the pair reached the buoy, they surfaced and took a compass reading on some preassigned point on the beach. The first pair to reach that point won.

Our only other loss, in any type of swim, I call a message from God. As soon as our class had become qualified on standard scuba, we started using the Emerson closed-circuit, sneak-attack rig, which was so new that we were the first class to train with it. The main feature of the rig was that it did not leave a trail of bubbles. What we exhaled was circulated through a canister full of pellets of a chemical called Baralime. The Baralime's purpose was to remove the CO_2 from the swimmer's exhaled breath. The rig had one small bottle of pure oxygen that was metered out in small amounts, to make up for what the swimmer's lungs had used. There were two surefire ways to die with that rig: Go too deep, and the body would destroy itself with oxygen toxicity. Very unpleasant. The second way was a little more insidious and a whole lot less unpleasant: CO_2 buildup, when the mind's not working too well because the body cannot rid itself of carbon dioxide, the by-product of used oxygen. If the swimmer's not paying attention, CO_2 can just sneak up on him, and he peacefully dies. Well, compared to dying from oxygen toxicity, it's peaceful.

The Emerson was so new that the navy had taken delivery on only twenty-five rigs, so our class was split in two groups because there were not enough rigs for us all to swim at one time. The instructors worked out a system for us to check out the rigs at the start and finish of each dive. The system was pretty good; it had just one small weak spot that God would point out to us. My problem was, I got to be the pointer.

Because Baralime was expensive, it was only replaced when it was no longer able to absorb CO_2. It generally lasted two swims, and its state was easily checked because the pellets changed color as they absorbed CO_2. The weak spot in our checks was when we looked at the Baralime. It was checked at the end of a swim. If it was bad, the Baralime was dumped and the canister was left open for the next swimmer to fill. If it was still good, the canister was closed back up. If the canister was closed when we made our predive check, we were to consider it good; if it was open, we filled it with Baralime and closed it up. Considering the Baralime good without looking was our weak spot.

It was a daylight swim on one of those beautiful south Florida days. All we had to do was read the compass and kick our way through the clear blue Gulf Stream waters. About twenty minutes after starting the swim, I started to feel frustrated; I just couldn't keep up the pace. We had been warned about CO_2 poisoning and its symptoms—two of which are frustration and weakness—but for the last five months, we had been succeeding by exerting extra effort. We had learned to push past frustration and weakness, so I pushed to that point where God was just whispering in my ear, "You are breaking my law of physics." After a few minutes of pushing harder, God gave me a signal I couldn't ignore.

I'd never had headaches, so I figured they must feel like bumping my head on something hard. That was not what I felt at all! Since my first headache was a message from God, it had to be something special. It felt like an explosion had been set off in my head. I swear, I heard the bang and saw the flash. No question, I headed straight for the surface, spit out my mouthpiece, and started gulping air. I had no doubt that something was wrong with my Emerson.

We didn't have to use the signal flares we had taped to our knifes; the safety boat was already headed our way when we started looking for it. By the time the boat reached us, I had explained to Ensign Hauff what had transpired, and both my headache and the feeling of weakness were gone. As soon as the boat eased up to us, Instructor Cahill started giving us a blast of shit about being quitters. He kept up with his, "yeah, right" attitude while we got on the boat, and I tried to explain what had transpired. God bless my swim buddy. Mr. Hauff, in his best prick-officer voice, told Cahill, "If Roat says something is wrong with his rig, there is something wrong. Check it!" When an officer puts on *that* attitude, even an instructor had better make sure he's right before dumping on him. Cahill pulled the backpack cover off the Emerson and started to remove the Baralime canister. He got a funny look on his face as he lifted the canister away from the backpack. I know he could feel the difference in weight, because he said, "Damn." When he pulled the lid off the canister, we could all see why. There was nothing but a small amount of Baralime dust in it. Well, I had just learned what carbon dioxide poisoning felt like. Needless to say, Baralime was inspected on the predive checks from then on. Oh yeah, we didn't win that one either.

Barracuda, a fast fish with lots of teeth, two to three feet long, that's what I thought. But around South Florida, there is a thing called the *giant* barracuda. That one gets up to seven feet long, and it is still fast, with lots of teeth. On most swims since we got to Key West, we had been seeing one or two of them. Swimming with them inspired awe in all of us; they are truly one of God's great predators. On a swim shortly after the no-Baralime incident, I had the attack board. We were on the second part of the dogleg, and I had my eyes tightly glued to the compass and depth gauge when Mr. Hauff gave a couple gentle tugs on our buddy line, the signal for "Look at me!" Just before the tugs, the water got a little darker, as if a cloud had passed in front of the sun. I looked to my left at my swim buddy. He was in an odd position. When I had the attack board, he usually stayed to my left, about two feet higher, with me a head-length in front. But he was about two feet lower than me, and he was pointing up, but not looking up.

I looked up toward the surface and stopped swimming; it *was* a cloud, a cloud of giant barracuda. We were on the second leg of the course and in shallow water, about twenty-five feet. Those damn things took up the first ten feet of water as far as we could see in any direction. There wasn't one of them less then five feet long, and so damn many, I couldn't see the surface. I went into what I think of as my "scared-calm" state, in which all panic is stored up in a tight little ball for later. One thing for sure, we were not going up. I kept thinking, Emerson, do not fail us now.

The only thing I could think to do was stay as close to the bottom as possible and just keep swimming for the beach and out from under that particular cloud. Mr. Hauff seemed to have the same idea, so we hugged the bottom and tried to stay on course. We swam in a very different manner than normal, much slower and shoulder to shoulder, like we were trying to become one. Even scared calm, I could not keep my eyes on the compass, look at the attack board, look up, back and forth.

As we swam and bumped along the bottom, the barracuda had been thinning out for a little while. Finally, my fondest hope was realized in ten feet of water. The big bastards were gone, nothing left but blue water with the sun shining through. We immediately started pushing hard, moving our big duck-feet fins as fast as we could for the beach. I had never been so glad to get out of the water. As it turned out, we were lucky in a couple ways. Several of the swim pairs swam into water waist-deep, with the giant barracuda still surrounding them. They had to take off their fins, stand up, and *walk* to shore through the barracuda. There is an old Team saying that when said politely goes, "Better you than me!" That's exactly how Mr. Hauff and I felt about that bit of luck. Our second bit of luck was that we hit the target dead on. It certainly had nothing to do with my close attention to our compass.

One night I had walked into a bar called the Top Hat, and there sat Jesse James Hardy, drinking a beer, with a monkey sitting on his shoulder. Jesse told me the monkey belonged to the piano player and his wife, the singer, who were up on a small stage doing a set. The monkey was jabbering away and picking through Jesse's hair as if he was looking for lice. As I walked up, Jesse said, "Be careful; this monkey bites if he doesn't like you, and he doesn't like many people." But by the end of that night the monkey and I had become fast friends as it moved back and forth between Jesse and me, jabbering away and picking through our hair. I swear neither Jesse nor I had head lice, but whatever the monkey was finding kept him happy for hours. But in two weeks of dealing with that monkey, I never saw it be friendly with anyone but its owners, Jesse, and me. It did bare its fangs at a lot of people, and it bit one Marine on the finger.

Trailor Lewis, the monkey, and I were going to be the center of a lot of problems for underwater swim school and Class-29. The thing was, Trailor and I were as innocent as newborn babes. I don't know if the monkey was a victim, or just made his escape and left Trailor and me holding the bag. I do know that the XO and our class proctor, Shorty Lyons, thought that I had committed the crime and that Trailor was covering for me. In truth, if I were in their position, that's how I would have figured it, too. You might say I was just a little off the wall.

For the last time, in front of God and everybody, I swear on my grandchildren's heads, "Neither Trailor L. Lewis, nor John Carl Roat, had anything to do with either the disappearance or the demise of that mean-ass little monkey."

Trailor fit in anywhere; like Humphries, Jesse J., and Fast Eddie, he was loved by one and all. If Lewis had any shortcoming at all, it was that he believed everyone. Trailor didn't lie, so he thought everyone else was telling the truth, especially the police. The night of the monkey's disappearance or demise was a Saturday. We were enjoying a well-earned weekend liberty and Class-29 was spread all over South Florida. To move us around the

Keys, Trailor and I had a red Chevy four-door he had rented. We were barhopping, looking for ladies, and not having a lot of luck. There were so few ladies around, we had even driven out to the Boca Cheeca Inn, a drinking bar of the first magnitude: unpainted cinder-block walls, dirt floor, no jukebox, no wine, and no food. Now, I loved the place, but it definitely was not a pickup bar. Trailor was not a hard-core drinker, and since we were looking for women, I was just sipping. We had a couple beers at the Boca Cheeca and decided that of all the places we had reconned, the best chance of our scoring was back in Key West at the Tomato Patch or the Top Hat.

We tried the Top Hat first. Of about ten people in the place, three were women, all married and well past fifty. Trailor was down at the far end of the bar, talking with one of the married couples. I was down by the small bandstand, my buddy the monkey sitting on my shoulder, picking through my hair. The black couple that owned the monkey was entertaining us with some fine blues. If there had been a few single women around, the night would have taken a different turn.

The couple finished their set and took a break. As they were walking out the back door, they asked me to put the monkey up on the piano if I left. I told them that would be no problem, and thanked them for the good music. They were out the door about twenty seconds before a Marine sat down on the stool next to the monkey and me. He was wearing dress greens and had a Marine Corps–issue whitewall haircut and a friendly smile. He bought a beer and asked about the monkey. I told him who it belonged to and that it bit anyone it didn't like. The grunt wanted to try making friends, so I told him the monkey liked the big warm pretzels the bar sold. He promptly bought one and handed it to the monkey. The monkey took it even more promptly, then sat on my shoulder, munching on the pretzel and screeching at the Marine. If the Marine touched the monkey, I was sure he was going to be bitten. Well, I was wrong; the monkey bit him before he was touched. The poor grunt had just stuck his finger up there, and the monkey leaned over and bit the hell out of him. The Marine didn't seem too upset about being bit, he just said, "That monkey sure is an ungrateful bastard." About that time, Trailor walked the length of the bar and we decided to try the Tomato Patch. With a little luck, we might find some ladies yet. I took the monkey up on the bandstand and set him on top of the piano. Soooo looong, monkey! We jumped into the car and headed to the Tomato Patch. Nothing, not a lady in the place. It was as if every single lady in town had split for parts unknown. We had one beer and decided to head back to the Top Hat, which at least had good live music.

We didn't hear any more live music that night; the cops were on us as soon as we stepped out of the car. They put Trailor up against the wall of the bar and me against the car. After we went through a quick pat-down, the black couple came out front, pointed at me, and said, "That's him." Well, our weekend was screwed. The cops went through the car first, under the seats, glove compartment, in the trunk, even under the hood. As soon as they were done with the car, they separated us, one cop with Trailor and one with me. Trailor and I spent the rest of the evening with the cops, trying to convince them we had not committed the dastardly crime of Grand Theft, Monkey.

It seemed that when the entertainers had returned from their break, the monkey and I weren't there. When they had left, he had been sitting on my shoulder, and we were close to the back door. To them, it was obvious; I stole the monkey. They called the police. We were transported to the Key West police station and immediately separated. I didn't see Trailor again for hours, till we were turned over to our slightly drunk class proctor. The police kept asking me questions I had already answered, same shit over and over. They said there hadn't been any Marine, that no one else had seen him. At one point, one of the cops drove me around the bars of Key West, to "point out [my] fictional Marine." Well, I never saw the Marine, so there was no one to point out.

When we got back from our little cruise around the bars of Key West, they left me alone in an interrogation room for about thirty minutes. When the two assholes who had busted us came into the room, they told me a story so dumb that I started laughing: "Lewis has confessed, you might as well make it easy on yourself and tell the truth." Those guys were turkeys: Trailor *never* lied; we had been harassed by experts of every stripe for over five months. With reinforcements, those wimps couldn't crack Trailor Lewis on their best day.

After that, I just thought the whole event was funny, screw 'em! I don't think the cops thought we did it, but I'll be damned if Mr. Schaible and his whole crew of instructors didn't. They had rounded Shorty Lyons up out of some bar to deal with us and our problem with the police. According to Shorty, I was in big trouble and dragging Lewis down with me. If I would tell them where I had hidden the monkey, they would get the civilian charges dropped. All I would have to face was captain's mast at the school.

Report chits were written up—charges—and we were restricted to the barracks and chow hall for the rest of the weekend. The cops had told Trailor that the monkey was worth five hundred dollars, which made our crime a felony, and that we were seen with the little beast *after* leaving the bar so they had enough evidence to convict us. They also told him they knew I was the guilty one, but unless he told them what I had done with the monkey, he would be convicted as well. One of the cops said we would receive bad conduct discharges and brig time from the navy. To top it all off, when we got out of the brig, the state of Florida would put us in prison. Trailor just could not believe the cops would lie about having a witness; he thought someone was lying to the cops.

Monday morning early, Shorty Lyons was on me like stink on skunk. I had to see the XO as soon as Shorty got done with me. He was spouting the same old crap, with one new wrinkle: If I had killed the monkey, I was in a deeper hole than I thought possible! Now I was a monkey murderer. I blew off some steam, and used a bunch of foul words to describe how I felt. Shorty told me I had better get a grip on myself, if I talked to Mr. Schaible like that, I would go to the brig just for my big mouth! Well, Shorty was right about that.

Since I was already on report, I had thought Shorty was telling me I was having an executive officer's mast, the first step on the way to a court-martial. Not so; what I had was a stand-to-attention, reasoned rant and rave. When Shorty and I went into the XO's office, the chief master at arms and Mr. Schaible were waiting. I was called to attention in front of the XO's desk. For the next ten minutes, I was ignored. The three of them talked, I have no memory about what, but none of it had anything to do with me. When the chief and Shorty left, Mr. Schaible sat at his desk doing paperwork, and I stood at attention happy to be ignored. God knows how long that went on, but when he looked up from the paperwork, the ass-chewing was on.

It boiled down to my being a liberty risk. The XO felt that things would be just fine if I was locked up and only let out to work. I could never quote everything the XO said because it ran from reasoned commentary on my strengths and weaknesses to foul-mouthed rant and rave about the problems I had caused the school. He ended with, "Roat, I want the truth, and I want it now!" So, I ran through the whole thing again. He looked at me for a long time, then all the XO had to say was, "Get out of here." I split quick. The odd thing was, those were the last official words I ever heard about the monkey.

One last thing transpired over the monkey's disappearance. The base police and the CID (Criminal Investigation Division) held a surprise shakedown of underwater swim school. I guess they thought the whole class was in cahoots on a kidnap for ransom. They looked in every nook and cranny, including the XO's office. Just another reason for Mr. Schaible to be unhappy with Class-29 and me.

Trailor Lewis and I hadn't had a good weekend. But to balance things out, Harry Humphries, Leo Duncan, and Jessie James Hardy had. Their weekend had made every member of Class-29 drool. Harry's uncle ran some of the family's business interests in Miami. He flew the guys up there, and took them out for dinner, drinks, and a show. But not just anyplace; he took them to what was then every young guy's high-class fantasy, the Playboy Club. They even had pictures of themselves with Bunnies.

We had a sneak attack against a sub-tender and some of the other ships in Key West harbor. A submarine-tender is a huge ship that spends about 90 percent of its time in port. Submarines tie up alongside her to have their every need filled—fuel, food, or fabrication; a sub-tender can handle it all. Think of it as a big fabrication and electrical shop with an endless supply of food to give away. Kind of like Mom.

When we held sneak attacks against our own ships, we had to let them know we were coming within a certain time frame. That always struck me as odd. "Hey, watch out, I'm sneaking up on you," just did not seem too sneaky to me. We were going to assault the ships in every way possible: closed-circuit rebreathers with no bubbles, open-circuit with bubbles, and surface swimmers. Mr. Hauff and I were assigned as surface swimmers against the sub-tender. Everyone in the class was involved, but we all had different assignments, different times, and different jump-off points. There were five swim pairs going in as surface swimmers and our jump-off point was the school. We had to do a sneak and peek across at least half the base just to get to the water. The base police would be on the lookout for us, so there was a chance we would be caught before we even got to the water.

The rest of the navy loved their Frogmen, but they loved catching us on a sneak and peek better. To get a hit on a ship, we had to be on the surface and beside the ship, then pull a night flare. That let everyone know the ship had been blown up. We tried to slide up the side of the ship, with our hands extended above the head. One hand held the flare, the other ready to pull the ring that lit it as soon as our hands broke the surface. If we could get it done with just our hands above the water, we did. Those sailors really got into protecting their ship, and they used some odd weapons against us: garbage bombs, egg hand grenades, etc. They wanted to make us pay. If a ship was alongside a pier, the crew might have their families running all over the place with flashlights, looking for us. Those "sneak" attacks always had an under-the-big-top, three-ring-circus flavor.

Mr. Hauff and I had picked a route that would take us off the base before we entered the water. Our water entry point was an aquarium, just outside the fence on the west end of the base. Military bases are well lit, and usually have plenty of manicured lawns and wide-open spaces. Not at all like sneaking through a forest or a jungle. We crossed the base, and got over the fence onto the aquarium grounds without being seen. That was entirely due to the fact that those who were looking for us had little training in repelling saboteurs. Defense is more difficult then offense, and defensive forces have to watch all the paths to the objective; those on the offensive just have to worry about one, the one they're taking.

We had only one confrontation that night. As we slipped up on the sub-tender, I had the crap scared out of me and made a lot of noise, a big no-no. The pier we were moving along had a sheet-pile face; this had little dark indents just big enough for one man to slip into. Take a breath, slide a couple feet underwater, move across the outer face of two or three sections of sheet pile, slip into an indent, and surface. Mr. Hauff and I moved along about one hundred yards of pier like that without problems. Our plan was to work our way to a position adjacent to the sub-tender's bow, slip under water, then swim the thirty feet or so to the side of the ship. If we had our flares ready, and pulled them as soon as we hit the surface, we might even get away before anyone could throw an egg or drop garbage.

As I surfaced in the indent just opposite the bow, something jumped on my head. I must admit I didn't handle the surprise well. A startled sound escaped my mouth, and I thrashed around trying to knock whatever the hell was on me off. I had disturbed a crab, five or six inches across. The damn thing was unhappy that I had entered its home unannounced. The crab won; I beat a hasty retreat one indent over. But our luck had held; my losing battle with the crab hadn't attracted anyone's attention. We made our hit that night and got out of there without suffering the indignity of eggs or garbage. That crab had injected a little much-needed humility into my over-grown Frogman ego.

For myriad reasons, our next training exercise was right up there with our final demolition problem. It was real Frogman stuff: submarine lock-out, lock-in procedures. That was something I would never grow tired of doing. The submarine we were to use was the *Balao*, a diesel boat stationed in Key West. I had seen the sub in *Operation Petticoat*; for some reason to do with the plot of the movie, they had painted it pink. That first day down at the pier, we could still see traces of pink paint where the current paint job was flaking off.

We had some classroom study, slides, movies, diagrams, and lectures on operating the escape trunk. Then we spent a couple days on the sub, alongside the pier. Submarine sailors are a special breed of human, and they bow to no man, especially when in their own underwater world. In its own way, the test to become a submarine sailor is as difficult as that of the Teams. Most people could not even live on a submarine let alone function at the high level of proficiency necessary.

Submarine sailors were required to attend school at New London, Connecticut, for three months, studying every aspect of the submarine. Still, at graduation, they were not submariners. If they passed that school they were assigned on a sub as trainees. That's when the real test for submariner begins. Each man is required to qualify at every station on the boat; if I remember right, there are around twenty. They take an oral test, a written test, and have to operate that station error free for a predetermined amount of hours. Then they are signed off for that given station.

They have to accomplish this with each station *then* they face the COB. The COB has nothing to do with corn; it's the acronym for chief of the boat. I promise you I would rather wipe my butt with a corncob than have the chief of the boat give me that final test to become a submariner.

During that final test, the only way for a candidate to finally earn his dolphins, the COB goes through the whole submarine with the candidate, asking questions. The candidate has to be able to demonstrate, physically and orally, the operation of every valve, circuit, and switch on the submarine. The problem is they can't just say you open this valve, you have to tell the COB what happens when you open that valve, what position every other valve in the system must be in, and what will transpire if something is wrong. It is the most nerve-racking test I have ever witnessed, but if a man is going to live in a moving metal tube a few hundred feet underwater, he had better not be a screwup. Sub sailors don't have a chip on their shoulder, they just don't accept a man until he has proved himself. A sailor with the submarine dolphins on his chest is a man who can stand up when most would fall.

All submarines are tightly packed; no wasted space allowed. Crewmen even sleep on top of torpedoes. If you are a nonsubmariner, they quickly let you know the rules: where you can be, what you can touch, even when you can shower and how. It is a tightly ordered society, and they brook no deviation; their lives depend on it. Our time at the pier was more a quick course on how to get along on a sub than on operating the escape trunk. One of the truly amazing wonders of submarine life is the food. On the *Balao* the galley was smaller than a good-size bathroom. How the hell a cook could feed so many men four times a day and keep it Mom quality is beyond me, but they do. And the cook, like every man on that submarine, had to qualify as a submariner.

With the *Balao*, all our lock-out, lock-in operations

were done underway in the open ocean. It is an odd feeling, being in the middle of the ocean banging two pieces of pipe together so the sonar man can get a fix on you. I don't think anyone in the class feared what we were going to do; the training was pure excitement. I felt not the slightest reluctance, none of the "what the hell am I doing" I had felt about jumping out of an airplane. As far as Class-29 was concerned, it was Frogman stuff. We would have paid to do it.

Six of us rode out into the deep blue of the Gulf Stream with Shorty Lyons on the safety boat. The rest of the class had boarded the *Balao* at the pier. The cook on the sub played a little submariner trick on our classmates, who were jammed into his galley. As they were leaving Key West, running on the surface, he tied a three-quarter-inch rope from one side of the *Balao* to the other, right through the middle of the galley. He cinched it down so there was no sag in the line. The trainees were just staying out of the way and feeling the excitement of their first dive in a submarine. There were alarms, a lot of commands being passed over the PA, valves were being opened, closed, or checked. As the submarine started to dive, they could hear air escaping the ballast tanks and the sound of rushing water replacing it. A lot of terrible sounds were going on all around them. The worst was the sound of steel being compressed. The cook got a big laugh out of seeing the reaction of my classmates as the tightly tied rope started to sag. It dawned on the guys in the galley; *the submarine was getting smaller!* The inside of a submarine stays at atmospheric pressure; the outside is a different matter. Every time the sub descends another thirty-three feet, one more atmosphere of pressure is added on the outside. That pressure is trying to crumple the hull like a crushed can, and the steel of a submarine lets the passengers hear its pain. The cook had used the rope to let my classmates know they were in *his* world.

The *Balao* and the safety boat rendezvoused far enough from Key West that we could see nothing but deep blue water and light blue sky. The sub was running with about forty feet of water over its main deck. Only the *Balao*'s periscope could be seen, just above the water, leaving a small wake in the Gulf Stream. Three swim pairs had traveled out in the boat. Once in the water, we strung ourselves out in a straight line, with a rope stretched between each man from one end to the other. The men on each end had two 1½-inch diameter pipes 12 inches long that they smacked together. The sonar man on board the submarine would detect the direction from which each of the "beacon" sounds was coming and vector the submarine on a course that would cause the periscope to hit the middle of the rope.

The surface of the sea that day was flat as a millpond, not a ripple or a wave. With our heads above the water, we could see the periscope heading for us from at least a quarter mile out. When we stuck our faces back underwater there was nothing but deep blue beautiful ocean. The *Balao* was only about three hundred feet out and forty feet below us when its bow finally began to materialize out of the sea water as if the big black war machine were growing out of the blue waters of the Gulf Stream. Submarines, viewed in their element, under the water, are magnificent. Like any of the other predators in the sea, as they move through the water, they exude strength and beauty.

When the *Balao*'s periscope hit the middle of our line, it dragged the middle forward, and the two ends together. All we had to do was hang on as the six of us were towed along by the submarine's periscope. We next pulled ourselves down some lines rigged from the periscope to a hatch between the inner and outer hull. As we reached the deck, we were greeted by two safety swimmers. Extra scuba bottles with regulators were lashed to the deck in case we lost air. The submarine had tailing lines rigged just in case we lost our grip on the deck.

The only real danger was losing a hold on the submarine and not getting away from it fast enough. If we got too close to the screws that were pushing the *Balao* faster than we could swim, we were going to be hamburger. I cannot explain what it felt like to hold on to that beautiful murder machine and be pulled through the Gulf Stream. Let me just say we belonged there, every one of us.

The escape trunk on the *Balao*, as on most submarines, was in the centerline, overhead of the forward torpedo room. The trunk has three hatches, top, bottom, and side. The bottom hatch is the only one that opens inside the submarine. Only the side and bottom hatches are used for lock-out, lock-in procedures. The top hatch is only used for mating up an escape bell during a rescue. Operating the trunk is a fairly simple procedure. To get into the sub, the swimmers enter the flooded trunk through the side hatch, secure the hatch, then blow the water out with compressed air. When the trunk is dry, its air pressure is equalized with the forward torpedo room, the lower hatch is opened, and the swimmers climb down the ladder, home free. To lock-out, it is just the reverse, no rocket science in any of it. Just following God's laws of physics.

From the time we left the safety boat till we locked into the *Balao*, we had seen not one of the Gulf Stream's shark population. Of course, we lied through our teeth; there were sharks *all over* the place, big ones, little ones—the damn things were all around the *Balao*. The six of us were on the sub all day, waiting for our turn to lock-out. All day, as the rest of our classmates locked-out and then back in, we heard our lie confirmed by one group after another. At the end of the day, when it came our turn to lock-out and return to Key West on the safety boat, the lie had expanded. "There were eight or nine sharks, from seven to fifteen feet, swimming along with the *Balao*." Yeah, right! We *started* that lie.

Somewhere along the line our lie had turned to truth. Big sharks were swimming along both sides of the sub, like pilot fish. I'm six foot one, and some of those damn things were twice my size. My first thought was I hope those sharks have a full belly. My second thought, *Please, sharks,* stay with the sub when we break off and go up to the safety boat.

We were to leave the submarine on command, two taps on the hull meant five minutes to location. Four taps meant depart the sub; the *Balao* was in the area of the safety boat. Tom Allen pulled himself along the deck to a rope about thirty feet long that was tied to a cleat on the bow. The rest of us were back by the sail, all huddled together in a tight group. Tom seemed to have some perverse need to get closer to those monstrous sharks, but none of us joined him. When he had the free end of the line in his hands, our man Allen put on a show that has always stuck with me. Tom used the rope to swing in the current. By turning his body, he could swing off either side of the *Balao* and insert himself among the sharks. The sharks seemed to pay no attention to Tom, but he had all of mine. I expected one of those big bastards to bite him in two at any second. But those sharks were beautiful!

After ten minutes or so, we got the two knocks on the hull, and still in one piece, Tom returned to the huddled mass by the sail. When four taps sounded on the hull, I got most of my wish. We didn't have to swim hard to get away from the submarine, just steadily fin to one side. If we had tried to go straight up, we would have been hit by the sail, the big towerlike thing that sticks up from the deck of a sub. All of us kept our eyes glued on the *Balao* as we swam up.

The big sharks all stayed with the sub, but one little three- or four-footer broke away and started up with us. Thank you, Lord! The *Balao* just dematerialized, bow and sharks first. It looked as if it were being swallowed by the Gulf Stream. The last to go were the rudders and the big spinning screw. By the time we reached the surface, the *Balao* and its attending sharks could no longer be seen. It was six trainee Frogmen, one four-foot shark, and Shorty Lyons in the safety boat, about fifty yards away.

As the safety boat approached, our little shark started to become very curious. We were in a tight little group, waiting for the class proctor to get us out of the water. McCutchan was dead in the middle, surrounded by Ensign Hawes, Ensign Hauff, Ensign Janke, Tom Allen, and myself. The shark seemed to be falling in love with McCutchan. It kept approaching us from the bottom and putting its snout right up against McCutchan's fin. Mac would kick it in the snout, and it would back off, then move right back to his fin. McCutchan even made a surface dive and chased the little bastard down to twenty feet, but when Mac came back up, so did the shark.

Shorty Lyons thought the whole episode was funny. He had stopped the boat right in front of us but would not lower the ramp. Shorty kept repeating, "Don't you big bad Frogmen hurt the sharks." Now I must admit this one was not a large shark, but we had completed our assigned task. Who the hell wanted to be bitten by even a small shark? I just wanted into the safety boat. But for a while, Shorty just sat in it, laughing at us and repeating his little refrain. When he finally lowered the ramp, I don't think we looked much like mighty web-footed warriors getting out of the water.

We had a nasty final written exam and then graduation

from underwater swim school. I, and several other of the enlisted men who were not academic giants, had been helped by our classmates who were. Physics, diving medicine, and figuring decompression tables were all things we needed to stay alive. Rich Fradenburgh and Ron Lester were enlisted men but academically strong, and both were natural teachers who would work with us till we "got it." Well, I passed those damn tests, just barely. One more missed question on any of them, and I would have failed.

For me, graduations have always been little more than a big pain in the posterior. As they go, the graduation from underwater swim school was pretty laid back. If I remember right, we even wore our old greens. Then it was time to pack up and head back to Little Creek, Virginia, for graduation into the Teams. Now, *that* was a graduation I looked forward to, no matter how big a pain in the butt it might prove to be. True to form, I damn near snatched defeat from the jaws of victory.

GRADUATION, AND
OTHER THINGS!

It's odd, but when you go from full-tilt, long-term effort to *done*, the transition can be hard to handle. To tell the truth, I didn't handle it well at all. I was drunk before we left Key West, and I pretty much stayed that way right up to graduation, the sole exception being a day spent with Ted Risher and his family.

Risher had a really nice family. I had been to their house for dinner two or three times since training started. Like many young guys, me included, Ted had that "Dad can do no right" thing going on. He had joined the navy just to piss off his dad. Ted's dad was a "full bird" colonel (pay grade O-6, the equivalent of a navy captain) in the United States Marine Corps. Risher told me that when his just joining the navy didn't upset his father, he figured becoming a Frogman would. I don't think even Ted believed what he told me. At any rate, he had failed.

I have saved mention of my classmate, BM3 Class Gene M. Munson, for last. Like many of us, Gene was another odd ingredient in the mix of Class-29. One night at Camp Pickett, Munson told me why he was going through training: He figured that with the extra money he would get each month after we graduated and the reenlistment bonus he would receive for shipping over, he could afford a new car! It was not just any old car he wanted, and he had a very specific reason for wanting it: *women*.

The car was to be a red Ford Fairlane 500 convertible.

To Gene's way of thinking, women could not resist that car. Now most of us young guys liked to think of ourselves as pretty good with women, whether we were or not. But no one in Class-29 thought more about or prepared more for women than Munson. Gene turned every discussion I ever had with him to women. He figured that if he were a United States Navy Frogman and had that car, no woman could resist him. For Gene, *women* were the reason for existence. I must admit, I found that not an entirely bad thought. At least Gene knew why he wanted into the Teams. I had no reason I could articulate other than "because." Picture one of those young, East Coast, big-city guys—slicked-back hair, cocky, with a big heart. Kind of a cross between John Travolta and Andrew Dice Clay. That's Gene M. Munson.

I have no idea who set up our graduation party, but I wish it had been scheduled for the night after not the night before graduation. Oh well, my problem was not when the party was; it was my total misuse of alcohol and the strange effect the alcohol had on me. There were two major problems and one minor problem with my drinking. The minor one was that I wasn't old enough. As to the majors, well, I never have had much inhibition, and the little bit I do have is barely enough to keep me within the outer limits of society's bounds; it disappears entirely with booze. And, for some reason, I do not pass out. If I'd passed out, I might still be drinking today. The only two things booze does completely stop are my ability to think things out and to speak clearly.

Gene Munson lent me some fine civilian clothes for our party. His clothes may not have been to everyone's taste, but they were always high quality. I borrowed a brightly colored silk shirt and a pair of drop-dead cowboy boots that had cost Gene a hundred dollars—in the early sixties, a huge sum of money. Gene's only comment when he lent me the clothes was, "Don't fuck up my boots, or you'll have to buy me a new pair."

It was a party, and I wasn't the only drunk there; there was a lot of the usual young-guy party-hardy bullshit. A few beer-guzzling contests and a lot of "Thank God it's over!" We were all slapping each other on the back and just generally enjoying our success. The next day, half of Class-29 would go to Team-21, the rest of the guys to Team-22, all but one. My boat officer, Mr. Hawes, was going to the training unit.

Before we left for the land of warm, Hawes had disappeared for a good part of a day, twice. I never knew what had transpired till well after training, but it was never a good thing when the instructors separated a man from his classmates. Ensign Hawes, being the good poker player type he was, hadn't said what was going on. It turned out that to pass his pretraining physical Hawes had pulled a fast one. He didn't really cheat, he had just used a new and, at the time, not widely known technology to assist him: contact lenses.

Hawes had easily passed the running, swimming, and PT test required for selection to training. He had been highly recommended by his command. But my boat officer knew he would fail the eye test he had to take during the physical. So, he bought a set of contacts. Hawes never spoke a lie, no one asked him why his eyesight had improved so much. Hell, the doctor had looked right in his eyes and never said a word. Anyway, Ensign Hawes had gotten away with his ruse long enough to prove he belonged in training. By the time the brass figured out what he had done, they were faced with following the rules and losing a good man. The days Hawes had disappeared, his career hung in the balance.

In the officer pecking order of the navy, an ensign is as

last as you can get. The first peckers are admirals, number two are captains. Those guys rarely talk to a lowly ensign; they usually just pass orders down the chain, and they damn well better be followed. However Hawes's eye problem was discovered, the word was quickly kicked up to the number-two pecker, a captain in charge of all training in the amphibious navy. My boat officer said his knees had felt weak, but he must have acquitted himself as a Frogman because he was next sent to see the number-one pecker himself. Hawes said his private audience with the admiral had left him with hope in his heart but still no decision on his fate.

A few days later, he was called back to the captain's office. This time the number-two pecker did some serious ass-chewing, after which he told Hawes he had one choice: complete his own training, then become a training officer at the UDT Replacement Unit. Damn, like six months of that place weren't enough. Hawes had the balls to tell the captain that he wanted an operational platoon, not the training unit. Captains are not used to ensigns saying anything other than, "Yes, sir." I would have loved to have seen the look on that captain's face, when a lowly ensign actually said something besides "Yes, sir." Of course, the captain won. For a while, that is. Just remember, you might be able to put a good Frogman down, but he will never stay there!

Sometime during the party, I decided to forget graduation and hitchhike to Michigan. I had a girlfriend there, and it seemed like a good idea to go see her. Now, I know it wasn't too bright, but I headed north. By three o'clock in the morning, I was in jail. And a very angry Instructor Bernie Waddell was out of his bed and on the way to get me. Woe is me! Woe is me!

I actually got about a hundred miles north of Norfolk, Virginia, before I sobered up enough to figure out I was screwing up big time. So I walked across the road and started hitchhiking back. Two rides later, I caught a ride with three young guys headed for Virginia Beach, who were going right by Little Creek and offered to drop me off. They had a 1949 four-door Ford, and two of them were sitting up front drinking beer. The third guy was in the back with me, sitting behind the driver and sucking suds. When they picked me up, they asked if I had any gas money, and I had given them a couple bucks. I just put my head back on the seat and dozed, in and out of sleep. The three of them were talking away while they drank their beer. At first their voices were just background noise. Then five words leaped out of the background and snapped my brain into gear: "I want the cowboy boots." All of a sudden, I was listening real hard. I heard things like, "He's got more money, find a dark place." Those guys were going to try and roll me.

The driver pulled the old Ford into a church parking lot and stopped about forty feet from the road. Those guys were not too bright. If I were going to roll someone, it wouldn't be in plain view of the road. Maybe they thought I would just give them Munson's boots, my money, and get out of the car. Fat chance! As soon as we stopped, I was opening my door. The asshole in the back with me says, "Give me your boots." As I stepped out of the car, he was coming after me, across the seat, and out my side, so I just slammed the door on his head, then opened it, pulled him out, and hit him once. He sat down in the parking lot against the rear tire, one idiot who didn't want any more. With the point of a boot, I kicked his buddy square in the nuts as he got out of the passenger side of the car. He just folded up in the parking lot and spewed all over the place.

By the time I got to the other side of the Ford, the driver had turned into Mr. Chickenshit. He had the windows on his side up and the doors locked. Just to scare him I did a forearm smack to the driver's window and cracked his window. By then he was on the other side of the car rolling up windows and locking doors. I really didn't want much more to do with those guys, but I didn't want them getting themselves together and coming after me either. I walked around the car, doing a good rant-and-rave, froth-at-the-mouth act, hit each of the driver's friends, that he had locked out of the car, just once more for good measure. I used my forearm to crack a couple more passenger windows, and I was done.

As far as I'm concerned, fighting is a load of crap. I didn't like it then, and I don't like it now, but when a man is pushed, it had better be done well. I walked a couple hundred feet down the road and started hitchhiking. I could still see the Ford and the would-be thieves, who were having an argument. Those guys had a problem: With friends like each other, they didn't need any enemies. Unfortunately, the first car past was a cop car with two cops. They turned around, down the street, and drove back to the church parking lot. Damn!

The cops were talking to the bad guys. The bad guys kept waving their arms around and pointing in my direction. One of the cops walked toward me and motioned for me to come to him. Well, all of us ended up in jail. The bad guys told the cops I had beaten them up and taken their money. To me it felt like the monkey incident all over; I had the truth, but I was not being believed. The cops wondered why, if they had been trying to roll me, I didn't have any marks on me. The guy I had hit with the door, and a couple good punches, looked pretty bad. His friend who had gotten Gene's cowboy boot to the nuts was still in bad shape. All the broken windows in the car didn't look too good for me either. Boy, was I having fun now.

By the time Instructor Waddell took custody of my hope-to-be-a-Frogman ass, the cops had decided they pretty much believed me. I found out later those three had been rolling people for a while, and the cops were happy to have them. Not that it did me any good at the time; Instructor Waddell was pissed. On the way back to Little Creek, Waddell let me know what the theme for our early morning evaluation was.

It was a two-part exercise, part one, mental; part two, physical. The mental part had to do with me not being allowed to graduate. They were going to send me back to the fleet. I was reminded that I had been warned when I murdered the instructors' candy machine. I did have fear in my heart. Part two was the only thing that gave me hope. Every time Waddell looked at me, I was given squat jumps, push-ups, and the like. My hope was that if I acted like a good trainee, they might not get rid of me. One of the physical parts I remember well. Bernie was sitting at his desk; it had to be around 0800 as a couple other instructors were in the hut. I was squatted down, duckwalking around the office, quacking like a duck. It was a relief when Waddell had me push Virginia away; I got to straighten out my cramped legs.

About thirty minutes before graduation was to start, Waddell told me, "If you want to graduate, get your ass over there." I was gone! That half mile or so to the Teams' barracks was the fastest I ever ran. Not only did I have to shower and shave, I needed to do some borrowing as well. I had only one white hat, the Dixie cup a sailor wears, and it was dirty. My neckerchief was a wadded ball and absolutely unacceptable. One of my classmates lent me a hat, but no one had an extra neckerchief. My next move must have really impressed my soon-to-be teammates, who had moved us temporarily one floor up from the Teams. I beat feet down the stairs and did what I had to do: I begged.

There were five or six Team guys in their barracks. What they saw was a nut running around, in near panic, saying something like, "Please, I need a neckerchief to graduate." I know I was saying it over and over. Very rarely in my life have I been close to panic; that day I was. I didn't give a damn who thought what, as long as I got a neckerchief and made it to graduation. Someone took pity on me and gave me a rolled and tied neckerchief. With a "Thank you!" I was gone to *graduation*.

It's funny what you learn on what day. I had been in a fight, in jail, had six or so hours of Instructor Waddell's personal attention, and made an ass out of myself. What did I learn that day? A simple thing: to appreciate my dad. Risher and I learned that lesson at graduation. His father was there, and mine was three thousand miles away.

It was a nice graduation. We had two navy captains as speakers, and Rear Admiral Dempsey presented our diplomas and made comments. Harry Humphries was our class Honor Man, and I don't believe anyone in our class disagreed with that choice. The Honor Man's job that day was student speaker. Harry had to get up there with the top of the navy's pecking order and give a speech. To my way of thinking, that day, his was the only one that counted!

There were moms and dads, brothers and sisters, friends, and Team members, at our graduation. But the person who stood prouder that day than anyone was a United States Marine, Colonel Clarence T. Risher II, Ted's dad. A Marine's Marine in his Class-A uniform is a sight to behold. His dad was a Marine's Marine. He had gone from private to colonel, up through the ranks. Colonel Risher had fought in World War II and Korea. He and my dad had only one thing in common, honor. They strove to live as they believed.

One of the things Ted and I had in common was a

thing many teenage boys go through: No matter what, Dad can do nothing right. If he says blue, it had to be red; if he says right, it had to be left. Our graduation from Class-29 into the Teams was the day Ted and I admitted to ourselves that we were proud to be our father's sons. More than anything I wanted to see my dad that day. Ted shared his with me, and I couldn't think of a better stand-in.

At last, we were what we had been thinking of ourselves as since training started, United States Navy Frogmen. After graduation there were class pictures and a little get-together, kind of a briefing, with a picnic, get-to-know-your-new-teammates thing. Well, that was when we found out why the hell our training class was so big: The navy had formed a new top-secret Team, called SEAL. The name was an acronym formed from the words sea, air, and land, and SEAL Teams were the navy's way of expanding its special warfare responsibilities. The rumor was that the CIA had asked for a new small military group that it could use for clandestine operations. Kennedy was our president, and a former naval officer, so when he gave the go-ahead, it was sailors who got the job. I don't know if the story we were told was true, but a lot of us believed it.

It was explained that no one in Underwater Demolition Teams was required to go to SEAL Team. A Frogman could volunteer and his name would be placed on a list. When the Team needed someone with his skills, he would be brought over.

We were Frogmen.

THIRTY-FIVE YEARS LATER

It was Saturday morning, July 18, 1998. Fifteen of us from Class-29 were at a big round table up front by the speakers' rostrum. We would have breakfast, a briefing on the Teams that day from the big kahuna himself, four star Gen. Peter J. Schoomaker, the commander in chief of the United States Special Operations Command. It sounds like a big deal, and it is. Then there'd be a short UDT-SEAL Association business meeting, and on to the best dog and pony show in the world. The United States Navy SEAL Teams under the command of an *army* general?

It was the second day of the annual UDT-SEAL Association reunion. There were two large rooms full of guys just like us, all Scouts and Raiders, Underwater Demolition Units, Underwater Demolition Teams, and SEALs. Men my father's age, my age, and my sons' age. Members from the start of the Teams in World War II to today's Team members. I believe there is no tougher group of men on earth—a group not mean, nor vicious, but just plain tough!

There are a lot of things that go on during a reunion weekend. A few people do a lot of hard work so the rest of us can kick back and enjoy each other's company. The men's breakfast is one of the few times we are all on the same page in the same place.

Class-29's own Jack Lynch had become one of the small group that busts ass to put the reunion on. Jack sits on the board of directors, which means he gets to help plan the reunion then do the physical labor of setting everything up and taking it down. Jack would not get to join us at our table until all hands were fed.

He is actually the man who came up with the idea of getting our training class together. Seven years before, in Panama City, Florida, he and I had met up with two other old Team guys, Hoss Kazinkski and Dusty Roads. The four of us rode to the UDT SEAL Museum at Fort Pierce in Dusty's motor home. Every November, on Veterans Day weekend, a muster is held at the museum. It is built on the ground where those first Scouts and Raiders and Underwater Demolition Units suffered their training, and I damn well mean *suffered*!

At the time, I hadn't cared about the museum, I had really just wanted to see Jack. I had never been big on the past, museums, high school reunions, and the like. It had been Jack's idea for us to attend the museum muster, and God bless him, it had been a good one. I had never really thought about the Teams' history. I had a general idea, of course—hell, some of the World War II veterans had been my teammates. Guys like C. B. Thomas, Red Hunter, Sam Bailey, Rudy Bauch, were all still good operators when Class-29 joined the Teams. Visiting the museum brought home to me just how tough it was for those World War II guys. Just give a moment's thought to swimming into a well-fortified enemy-held beach—Normandy on D day for instance—not just once but twice, your only weapon a knife. Your first swim, to gather intelligence; your second swim, to drag in explosives and blow up obstacles that might impede the landing.

Damn, they had done a good job with the museum, and they had done it like everything else Frogmen do—the hard way. Several World War II Frogs had retired in the Fort Pierce area. They got the idea to have a reunion and, hell, nothing was going on out there where they had trained so why not put up a museum? They were able to generate some interest from local officials but ran up against state and federal red tape and general disinterest. Hell, that's no hill for a climber!

One of the truly great things about the guys from the Teams is that our big egos rarely get in the way of what needs to be done. Among our team members, former and present, are farmers to senators, bikers to ministers, men from every walk of life. All we have to do is look around, find the right teammate, and he'll carry the load to the top of the hill. In this case, they picked a just-retired Frogman, Norm Olson. What set him apart from most of his teammates, in and out of the navy, was that he had attained the rank of captain, just one grade below admiral. The politics of the United States Navy were such that officers who chose to stay operational Frogmen were forced to forgo advancement. So damn few officers retired from the Teams as captain. Capt. Norm Olson had two important talents— he was infected with hairy-ass Frogman disease, and he had the political acumen to know when to bull his way through obstacles and when to do a little stroking. But I'm going to let Captain Olson say it in his own words. His speech on Veterans Day, 1985, for the opening of the UDT SEAL Museum, tells the story much better than I can!

Commodore Flynn, Mr. Bush, Mr. Ward, Ms. Rights, distinguished guests, and most importantly, past members of the naval combat demolition units and underwater demolition teams, and present members of the Navy's sea, air, land teams. It is my pleasure to welcome many of you back, and all of you, to the birthplace of the Navy Frogman.

First and foremost, I want to convey my appreciation to the official party: to Lucille Rights for her full and unconditional support over these past (9) months; to Dick Ward for being the primary provider of funds, artifacts, and personnel assistance during this embryo stage; to Father Mac, whose close ties with the SEALs in Vietnam will never be forgotten; to Prescott Bush for providing the personal interface with our founder, Rear Admiral Draper L. Kauffman, the "father of demolition"; and to Commodore "Irish" Flynn, a close personal friend for over (20) years, who is not only the senior naval special warfare officer on active duty, but the first and only naval officer to ever attain flag rank from within the UDT-SEAL community. It's a sincere pleasure to have all of you aboard.

One year ago today, I visited Fort Pierce for the first time to attend the groundbreaking ceremony for this museum. Following the event and for the next (3) months, I was courted, led down a primrose path, and finally seduced into becoming the museum's director. Ladies and gentlemen, I want you to know that it's been a long, lonely, difficult pregnancy.

As with any prospective blessed event, there were mixed emotions: elation on one hand; grave doubt on the other. Also, there was an immediate craving for support, but all I got was smiles.

In month two, morning sickness reared its ugly head. Although we all know it's in the mind, anxiety and tension did in fact set in, causing a great deal of heartburn. At this juncture, there appeared to be no relief in sight, and I began to ask myself, "Do I really want this pregnancy?"

As I came into April, I realized there was no turning back, and I began to accept my fate; however, morning sickness still prevailed, and I now began to feel physically and psychologically uncomfortable. I even started to act a bit crazy, but it received virtually no attention.

In month four, I began to feel unloved, and I became grouchy, paranoid, and downright ugly. I even lashed out at the few friends that I had locally.

When June rolled around, serious doubt set in, and I began to wonder how I got into this jam in the first place. Intense work was followed by questions, such as, "Will it be on time?" and "How will it turn out?"

The following month, I began to feel better, so I took a trip to Norfolk, Virginia, to see if this unwed mother-to-be could obtain a handout. It apparently worked. The trip also cured my nausea, but my heartburn continued, and added to my dilemma was a severe backache from the load I was carrying.

In August, it became candidly clear that there would be a birth, whether I liked it or not, so I began organizing the nursery, buying a few essentials, and enlisting some volunteer help.

In the eighth month, I really began to feel physically uncomfortable and started to have false labor pains, but this was somewhat compensated for by the baby shower, which brought forth gifts and enough money to take care of expenses.

As the final month came into full view, there were more false labor pains, insomnia set in, my feet began to swell, and I was having great difficulty just sitting.

And, as the final hours drew near, and the pain became more excruciating, I still could not help but wonder if it would be on time, or, for that matter, whether it would be healthy.

Ladies and gentlemen, it was a close call, but as you can see, the blessed event took place without serious complications. Although there are a few rough spots, both within and without, I anticipate that in very short order, these wounds will be healed.

Oh yes—I almost forgot, this beautiful baby does

have a name, and a new play toy. [unveil the sign] Furthermore, its birth is in honor of those who made the ultimate sacrifice for God, country, and the United States Navy. [unveil the memorial statue]

Jack and I had each known where the other was, and pretty much what the other was up to. Not too hard since we were both divers, Jack in the navy, me a commercial diver, mainly oilfield related. The museum had a strange effect on Jack and me. Our tough old Frogman hearts were touched; laid out before us was the history of the Teams and those willing to put everything on the line for God and Country. While we were walking through the museum, toward the end of that very good weekend, Jack put his arm around my shoulder and said, "You know, next July it will be thirty years since we graduated from training. We ought to find our classmates and get together at Little Creek." When he said it, it just sounded right. My first thought: What a good idea!

Lynch had handled the mailings and general organizing of our effort. It had been my job to find the guys we had no address on, over half our classmates. A little over a year later, Class-29 had gotten together as a training class. We had picked the annual UDT-SEAL Association reunion at Little Creek, Virginia, for our get-together. As it turned out, Jack's idea had been a damn good one! We had enjoyed it so much that some of the men came to Little Creek every year, and we tried to have the whole training class every five years. In a way, you could pin this book on Jack. Yeah, that's a good idea; it's all Lynch's fault!

Later in the day, Jack would share some of his pride with us; his son Brett would give the members of Class-29 a personal tour of a SEAL's operational locker. Since our last reunion, Brett had joined the navy and gone through training as a graduate of Class-212. He'd become a member of SEAL Team 2. Today, Brett would open his locker and show us all the little things that only a Team guy could love—boots, webbing, side arms, holsters, hot-line gloves, body armor, all the small but important things in a SEAL's life.

Breakfast was a lot of laughter, a lot of movement between tables, and just comfortable guy patter. Over the previous two days, Class-29 had again easily fit together. After thirty-five years, the strands in our net were still strong. Lynch and I had a pleasant surprise for the rest of our classmates: Three of our Royal Dutch Marines, and their wives, had come to the reunion. Ravensburg, Pauli, and Hack were with us again. In some strange ways, we are still the same not-so-young bucks who graduated into the Teams all those years ago. Of course, I had to get one over on my classmates and the whole UDT-SEAL Association.

There were so many of us that the organizers had to set up the breakfast serving line in another room normally used as the bar, which was split level, a half floor higher than the large meeting room. The ladies setting up the line had to push the trays of food up an inclined hallway to the bar. At the bottom of the inclined hall to the bar was an area where the wheels of the heavy food carts were getting stuck. I just stationed myself at the bottom of the hall, lifted the front wheels over the bad area, and helped push the carts up the hall. As far as the serving ladies were concerned, I could do no wrong. Mom would have been proud. My next move would have had Mom shaking her head and wondering where she had gone wrong.

I had an inspired thought. If I could get my food before the line opened, I could stir a little ka-ka. The ladies allowed me to heap up two plates full of food. Arms extended over my head, I then carried my two trophies into the room full of very hungry web-foot warriors. My appearance had the desired effect; many of my team-mates made their move to get food. Darn! The serving line would not be open for another thirty minutes. There is just something special about sitting in a room full of hungry old Frogmen and being the only one with food.

The UDT-SEAL Association reunion was the culmination of a strange year in my life. I had written *Class-29: UDT SEAL*. It had started as a chapter in a novel called *The Terrorist*, in which the main character had attended UDT training. I had thought I would just write about our training class, make copies for the guys, change the names, and use that material in my novel. It didn't work like that; thanks to the generosity of several of my class-mates, it became a limited-edition hardback of five hundred copies, and each class member had received one. The rest were being sold at fifty dollars a copy, with all profits being split between the UDT-SEAL Association Scholarship Fund and the UDT-SEAL Museum in Fort Pierce, Florida, in the name of Class-29.

When I was writing the pages on Hell Week and So Solly Day, I had wished I could see a film of our class that day and had written, "We must have been a pitiful-looking bunch!" Lynch made my wish come true, he found an old training film that had part of CLASS-29's So Solly Day from Hell Week all those years ago. The first night of the reunion, Jack gathered us around one of those huge projection televisions and showed us just how *pitiful* we had been. He had had the film duplicated on video and gave each of us a copy. We probably watched the cassette twenty times that night—and laughed uproari-ously each time, for there is no doubt that *we were a pitiful-looking bunch*!

The strangest thing of all, thirty-five years later, I was

going back to training. My efforts to write about our training class had come to the attention of Darryl Young, another former SEAL, and a well-regarded author. He read some things I had posted on the Internet and sent me an E-mail asking if I wanted an editor and publisher. I promise, I did not say no. The publisher liked what I had written, but felt the original book wasn't long enough, so I proposed to supplement it by writing about training today, from the instructors' point of view. My editor accepted that idea because the new material would demonstrate the validity of the Teams' training concepts. Since I had never been an instructor and left the navy in 1969, I had a problem.

After floundering around trying to figure out how the hell I was going to write about something I knew little about, I sent a request to Rear Adm. Thomas R. Richards, the big kahuna of naval special warfare. I enclosed what I had written for my classmates and explained my needs— to observe as much of a training class as possible and to interview the instructors. Two days before our reunion, I received word that Admiral Richards had approved my request. I would be going back to training, now called BUD/S, for Basic Underwater Demolition and SEAL. I planned to pay very close attention to General Schoomaker's briefing.

All meetings of the UDT-SEAL Association start with the pledge of allegiance to the United States of America. In our group, the pledge is not taken lightly; with us in the room were the spirits of teammates who had lost their lives for their country, men who carried the scars of battle and wore the Purple Heart, bearers of the Congressional Medal of Honor and every other honor our country can bestow on its fighting men. At Class-29's table the men had tears in their eyes during the pledge, and I had a lump in my throat and huge goose bumps on my arms.

For me, all that emotion is not about my country right or wrong, it is about those who went before; those who put everything on the line for a few thoughts on a piece of paper, the Declaration of Independence. The people with the courage to struggle to do what's right; those who had built, piece by piece, what I was born to. When I say that pledge, I am saying, "God bless you for what I was given; I will do my best to pass more on!"

But, an *army* general in charge of the Teams? From what the men involved had to say, that arrangement not only worked, it worked damn well. Somebody had finally gotten smart and removed the worst of interservice rivalry, the fight for a buck. We all fought the same wars, on the same damn side. One good thing had come out of Vietnam; a bunch of very pissed-off young officers who stuck around, worked their way up through the ranks, and made some damn good changes. In the sixties, the military had been full of cover-your-ass, just-make-it-look-good officers. I am not talking about the Teams' officers; they were exceptions. They did their job and then some; a good part of the time, their skinny officer asses were hanging out in the wind.

I'll give it to you straight from the Special Operation Forces "Posture Statement," then I'll do it in English. SEAL Teams belong to what is called a SOC, the acronym for Special Operation Command, "A subordinate unified or other joint command established by a joint force commander to plan, coordinate, conduct, and support joint special operations within the joint forces commander's assigned area of operation."

In English, that means that each of the three services has its own SOC (as always, the Marine Corp comes under the navy). The navy being a little different, its SOC is called Naval Special Warfare Command, and it is head-quartered at Coronado, California. The army has its Special Operation Command at Fort Bragg, North Carolina, and the Air Force Special Operation Command is at Hurlburt Field, Florida. Now if that was how things were left, they would not be much different from when I left the navy in 1969, when our senior officers had to fight for every damn penny just to operate. In the early days of the Teams, there was a lot of, *take* what you need to operate. Don't ask; they won't give it to you. Do not let the assholes catch you! We didn't steal to line our own pockets; we took what the Teams needed to operate. Besides, it was good practice for covert operations.

But something called a *Joint* Special Operations Command, JSOC, is what makes the world of military special operations a new and wonderful world. The JSOC is in charge of everything; all three service SOCs come under the command of the JSOC. In simple language, four-star general Peter J. Schoomaker, the guy that was about to brief us on special operations, is the big kahuna, the man with the fuzzy nuts. His full big kahuna title is Commander in Chief, United States Special Operation Command. All money for military special operations comes from the Congress of the United States to the JSOC. Special operations operators are no longer second-class citizens; they get their own money, a separate appropriation from that of the Departments of the Army, Navy, and Air Force.

Let's see how clear I can make this; the job of our military is to be so good that nobody wants to fight, but if there is a fight, then it is to fight to *win*. In a big war, SEAL Teams' "job," read Special Operations, is to do whatever it takes to help the troops on the ground, the sailors at sea, or the airmen in flight, to *win* with as few of our troops dying as possible. In today's world, with no superpower opposition, what really sets Special Operations apart, and why they get their own money, is a thing called a low-intensity conflict. That just means the military is to recognize a problem early, then take care of it before it gets out of hand and becomes a bigger problem, that is, a full-blown war. SEAL Teams, along with the rest of the Special Operation community, is kept busy, staying on top of small hot spots all over the world.

If General Schoomaker was not the man to command Special Operations, it would show in this room. His audience was full of proud old Frogmen who loved their outfit. Roy Boehm, the first SEAL, and many of the men who made up those first two SEAL Teams, sat in the general's audience. There were retired officers in that room, men whose careers had been limited by their effort to build SEAL Teams into an effective fighting force, Roy Boehm included. If those men thought General Schoomaker was not the man to lead what they had built, everyone would know.

The general fit, and every old Frogman in the room was at ease. We received a no-nonsense briefing on the state of Special Operations. All the knickknack shit that makes good ideas work. The part of his briefing that hit home with me, what got to the heart of everything, was a short little sentence: "Everything but our *core values* are on the table; we have to be ready to change anything but those *values* to get the job done." *The* core value for a SEAL Team is the people, that basic World War II webfoot warrior. That core has nothing to do with all the high-tech weapons the Teams were about to show off at the dog and pony show. It has everything to do with Hell Week and its final day, So Solly Day. That's how trainees prove their core, what allows them to take their place as Team members. On August 24, I would be afforded the opportunity to observe a training class, interview the instructors, and see for myself if those core values were still intact.

After General Schoomaker's briefing, all us old Frogs were jacked up, ready to do whatever necessary for truth, justice, and the American way. Hell, we were all ready for combat. God bless John "Fly" Fallon; it took him all of fifteen seconds and maybe ten words to get the whole room back to reality. Fly is a legend. He is also the man who takes care of the UDT-SEAL Association scholarship fund. I have never been able to figure out how he does it, just a few words, spaced with little pauses, and he has everyone's attention. He can cut through the bullshit quickly, and raise a laugh while he does it. A couple things you have to know about Fly Fallon: He always wears red socks, I have no idea why, and he enjoys presenting the scholarship winners at the men's breakfast.

Fly loves to stand up there and remind us what truth, justice, and the American way are all about. In the Association, as in the Teams, there is a strong belief in hard work, so the Association's way is to award a lot of partial scholarships; no full scholarships are given. In a way, the money the kids receive is like the hand Neidrauer gave me at the top of the cargo net during Hell Week: If I hadn't been an ass-buster, Bob wouldn't have wasted his energy. The money the kids are being given is just a hand-up to ass-busters near the top of the net. That helping hand will likely be the most far-reaching thing the UDT-SEAL Association does.

I am sure the Teams have been doing dog and pony shows since the beginning. I know we were doing them in the sixties, and I hated the damn things. It seemed I was always the guy who had to stand around wearing a full wet suit in ninety-degree heat. Dog and pony shows have a long history in the military and serve an important but simple purpose. Like a dress rehearsal for a big Broadway show, the directors/senior officers, and the investors/we the taxpayers can see how ready the Teams are for the big show, *the bad business of war*. War is not a thing you want to lose, practice makes perfect. The show that is put on during the UDT-SEAL reunion is open to the public, and it's a dynamite show, the best of the year.

There is one reason it's the best: Sitting in the stands are guys from the first Teams of World War II. Those original webfoot warriors are tough old bastards, and would be the first to let today's Team members know if they were not living up to the standards established during World War II. Today's Team members have egos just as big as us old guys, and they love the challenge. In our day, there was no UDT-SEAL Association but if we'd had one show a year for the old farts, I would have loved it. We always wanted the old guys to respect us as Team members.

There is no other way to say it; today's Teams have weapons that *kick ass*! Their tools of war make us old Frogmen drool: personal weapons, delivery systems, worldwide communication systems, and high-tech gadgets we didn't dream of having in my day. The Teams now have a wide range of weapons, ships, submarines (big and little), aircraft, and boats, with trained crews, whose main purpose is to support the Teams. Under simulated combat conditions, the dog and pony show would show off most of those weapons systems, and the skill of those who operate them.

Order of Events

- National anthem (navy jump team fly in with U.S. Flag)
- Traditional beach clearance/naval guns mission (6 swimmers)
- C-130 RIB drop (6 jumpers)
- C-130 rubber-duck drop (4 jumpers)

- Softduck insert by CH-46 (4 persons)
- RIB, MK5, and Patrol Coastal conduct drive-by gunshoot
- Rappel insert (4 persons)
- McGuire extract (2 persons)
- Fastrope insert (4 persons)
- SPIE Extraction (6 persons)
- Military free-fall jumpers insert CAS mission (8 persons)
- Sniper demonstration (1 person)
- F-14 flyby
- Freddy the Frog jump (ISC Blackwell with navy jump team)

The show was kicked off with presentation of "the colors," our American flag, performed in a most spectacular way by the Leapfrogs, SEAL Teams' parachute demonstration team. Three men depart the aircraft as a group at 3,500 feet. As soon as their parachutes open, they build a "three-stack," each jumper standing on the parachute below him, in this case three high. The jumpers had damn well better know what they're doing; it would be easy to ruin everyone's day. If a jumper comes in too fast, he could easily collapse the parachute below. Three guys all tangled in each other's canopies and risers would fall like a rock. The parachute the Leapfrogs use is called a ram-air square. It looks like a big wing and is highly maneuverable, much more maneuverable than the paracommander, the top chute in use when I left the navy in 1969. Maneuverable or not, what the Leapfrogs did next impressed the hell out of this hairy-ass old Frogman. They dropped out of the stack and lined themselves up in tight formation, a straight line, wingtip to wingtip. Using nylon webbing with built in quick-releases, the outside jumpers each attached an inner leg to a leg of the center jumper. Then the center jumper deployed the American flag, which, streaming out in the wind, hung below him from a six-foot weighted line while smoke trailed from the outboard jumpers' heels. The three of them flew their parachutes as one, making tight banking turns, Old Glory streaming below.

As they came flying in over the spectator stands from the sea, the Leapfrogs made a tight turn over the sand dunes behind the stands and popped the quick releases. The center jumper then flew the flag to a waiting member of the ground crew, who gathered it before it hit the ground. They had made two tight turns, broken their connection, and retrieved the flag so it didn't touch the ground, all within thirty to forty feet of touching down. Of course those guys made it look easy. It had damn well better; they are SEALs!

After our flag came the basics, the hard-learned World War II techniques of clearing obstacles from an enemy-held beach. A lot of Frogs had died developing those techniques during war. As the Frogmen were cast and swimming in to set their charges on the obstacles, they were given gunfire support from special boat squadrons. (More on special boat squadrons, how, what, and why, a little farther on.) The fire is meant to keep the bad guys' heads down so they can't take easy shots at the guys swimming in. It is damn effective and very impressive to see.

There was one Cyclone-class ship, the USS *Shamal*. It has a crew of four officers and twenty-four enlisted men; it is 170 feet long, with a beam of 25 feet, and a draft of 8 feet. It has a listed speed of thirty-five knots, and a range of two thousand nautical miles. The *Shamal* carries a wide range of weapons, including nine SEALs and all their personal weapons, one Stinger missile station, one MK-38 25mm rapid-fire gun (unstabilized), one MK-96

25mm rapid-fire gun (stabilized), four pintiles (gun supports) supporting twin .50-caliber machine guns, M-60 machine guns, and a MK-19 grenade launcher.

There was one MK V special operations craft with a crew of five. That thing looked mean just sitting at the pier; on a firing run it kicked ass. It is eighty-two feet long, has a beam of seventeen feet, and a draft of five feet. Its top speed is listed as fifty plus knots, with a range of six hundred nautical miles. The MK V weapons include sixteen SEALs and their personal weapons, one MK-38 Mod 1 25mm rapid-fire gun, one MK-44 GUA-17 7.62mm minigun, one MK 95 Mod 1 twin .50-caliber gun, one MK 93 mount with M60E 7.62 machine gun, and one MK 19 Mod 3 40mm (grenade) machine gun. As a side note, this thing can be put inside a C-5 transport and flown wherever the hell it's needed.

The third vessel giving gun cover for our World War II Frogman operation was a "NSW RIB," which stands for Naval Special Warfare rigid inflatable boat, and it is my personal favorite. The RIB has a crew of three, and is 35 feet 11 inches long, with a beam of 10 feet 7 inches, a draft of 2 feet 11 inches, and a top speed listed at forty plus knots. Its weapons include eight SEALs with personal weapons, two gun mounts, one fore and one aft, capable of holding .50-caliber machine guns, M-60 machine guns, or the MK-19 MOD 3 40mm (grenade) machine gun. I like it best because it's versatile, a small fast target that can haul ass in three feet of water. The RIB can be dropped from a C-130, flown in or out under a helicopter, or be launched and retrieved from ships.

Those were the three vessels running parallel to the beach, pounding the back shore area with their weapons. The scouts and raiders and the naval combat demolition units that cleared the obstacles from the beaches of Normandy would have loved that kind of gun support. When the bad guys have the high ground and you have to swim in and work right under their guns, anything that keeps their heads down makes you feel good. Tongue firmly in cheek, the Teams call that type of operation "a drive-by shooting." While all the shooting was going on, the charges had been set and the SEALs had swum out and got in a recovery line. As soon as they had been snatched from the water, *Bam!* the obstacles on the beach were blown.

The whole show had the look of smooth uninterrupted power, as if it took no effort, as if it were as natural as breathing. As each part of the demonstration flowed into the next, it was easy to forget just what it takes to bind all those diverse people and weapons together. There were fifty-five military personnel from SEAL Teams and supporting units. One ship, ten assorted medium to small high-speed boats, seven aircraft (ranging from a CH-46 helicopter to an F-14 Tomcat). On the nonmilitary side, everything had to be coordinated with the appropriate civilian authorities: Virginia Beach police and fire departments, Federal Aviation Administration, Environmental Protection Agency, and every hospital and medevac outfit in the area. The dog and pony show was planned by one SEAL Team lieutenant and seven senior enlisted SEALs. Anywhere else in the military, that size operation would be in the hands of more senior personal. *So you want to be a SEAL?* Well, big boy, you damn well better perform!

To all those outside the Teams, it all looks like a bunch of fun and games. I mean hell; lock-out of submarines, leap out of airplanes, and blow things up. I'll not dispute that hairy-ass Frogmen/SEALs think it's fun, but even in practice, it can be very deadly fun. Outsiders never see the hours of preparation: planning sessions, briefings, equipment maintenance, and practice sessions. The six Ps apply: *p*rior *p*lanning *p*revents *p*iss *p*oor *p*erformance! In the old days, we had all kinds of people trying to stick their hands in the pie and do the planning. If things went wrong, it was usually someone else's fault. Today, most of the planning rests squarely on the shoulders of SEALs, and proper planning is almost as important as being a good operator.

To my way of thinking, the most important component in being a good *operator*, and what made UDT then and SEAL Team now stand apart is the ability to overcome the unexpected. The unexpected, when *the whole world turns to shit*, those days when there's a twelve-thousand-foot peak where yesterday was a valley. That's when the Teams really shine; that's when the operators prove themselves. People can look at UDT training then or BUD/S training now as a brutal test to prove a person's right to be there when *the whole world turns to shit*. Not a place most people want to be, or should be.

Other than women, the most common topic of past and present Team members is the state of training. Every training class is told by the instructors that it is a *pussy* class, the worst damn class ever! "If it was up to me, you pack of shitheads would all go back to the fleet!" And, one way or another, after a new class graduates from training, the former trainees are informed that the test is not over! Bob "Eagle" Gallager made the point to me shortly after our graduation.

Eagle Gallager is an operator's operator! I don't care what kind of operation you're on, from a dog and pony show to the worst firefight imaginable, if Eagle is there, you feel better. Gallager is one of those people who, looked at piece by piece, seems nothing out of the ordinary; not too big or small, neither too handsome nor too ugly. All his parts seem to fit together in the normal way, that is until you get to his eyes. Eagle has eyes that tell you everything you need to know: *Do not fuck with this person!* I don't remember where we were, just a bunch of Team guys having a beer and bullshitting about training. I do remember those damn eyes looking straight at me and every word Eagle said: "Aha, you're all a bunch of pussies! Two weeks preconditioning? We didn't have any preconditioning. I reported to training, and Hell Week started at midnight, that day! Only pussy classes had preconditioning!"

This year at the reunion, I sat with Bob in the old chiefs' club bar and talked with him about training in general and his class in particular. He had half the bar laughing when he told us about his Hell Week. Bob was just seventeen when the chief he worked for on his ship told him he should sign for the program. Gallager had no idea what underwater demolition training was, but if the chief said it was for him, that's what he would do. Bob had filled out the paperwork requesting orders to training, taken the tests, and promptly forgotten about it. Gallager's ship was home-ported in Little Creek, Virginia, so on the day he was to report for training, he just had a mile or so to go. Training in those days was held right where we were drinking; the chiefs' club had been built over the old UDT training area. Eagle said they just took his orders and assigned him a bunk in one of the old World War II Quonset huts. No one told him anything or asked him anything.

Bob "Eagle" Gallager's next action surprised me; he got agitated talking about his training class's Hell Week. His eyes got big, he was waving his arms around, and he said, *"It was the damnedest show I've ever seen in my life."* Now Gallager is one of the toughest of the tough, a plank holder in SEAL Team 2.* Eagle has been shot at, has killed people, leaped out of airplanes, been locked out of submarines, and blown things up all over the world. The damnedest show he ever saw in his life was Hell Week. His story just brought home to me that for most Team guys, no matter what you do in the rest of your life, training will always rate right at the top.

* In the navy, a plank holder is a member of the unit who has been there since the day it was commissioned. In plain English, from the git-go.

TRAINING TODAY:
CLASS-221

One hundred and ninety-two training classes ago, the 134 young men of Class-29 stood poised to start training. But now it was Class-221's turn. They started their training with one hundred young men, officers and enlisted, and one old Frogman standing in the background, watching. The truth is, if BUD/S training was not up to par, I would not demean my classmates and our instructors' efforts by finishing this book with a section called "Training Today"!

Today's Teams have a saying, "Good to go." Well, the Training Command is doing its part in keeping SEAL Teams good to go. Getting through training today, I would have different problems; more demands are placed on the trainee's military bearing, academics rear their ugly head from the git-go, and the impossible physical demands are still there. The military bearing and the added academics just raise the stress level. In truth, the whole training program is still just a stress test.

There are many differences between then and now, starting with the fact that all training is run at the Naval Special Warfare Center at Coronado, California. More important, training is under the complete control of SEALs. The instructors no longer answer to ship drivers who have no understanding of what training for the Teams is about. The Training Command has its own four-striper, Capt. Joseph Maquire. He answers to Rear Adm.

Thomas R. Richards, who is the commander, Naval Special Warfare Command. These two men proudly wear the Budweiser on their chest. Budweiser? Why would they pin a beer on their chest? Well, the official naval term is Naval Special Warfare insignia. I promise you, Team members, from the admiral to the newest guy who has earned the right to pin it on, call it a Budweiser. As young officers, both the admiral and the captain completed training and earned that right. They know what all the pain and sweat are about.

There is another big difference: Well before arrival at the Training Command, each man is completely informed of what is required to complete BUD/S. It is called the "BUD/S Warning Order." Of course, the trainee will not understand what he is being told until after he has completed Hell Week. Tell them everything or tell them nothing, I don't think it makes a damn bit of difference to who gets through training. It is my strong personal opinion that it is impossible even to watch training and *understand* what it takes from the trainee. But I think the warning order causes those who are timid never to make the effort. It clears away those who may have a want but don't have the courage to fail. The next few pages are excerpts from the official BUD/S Warning Order, with a few notes from me. The entire text, including suggested student preparation, is found in Appendix Two.

BUD/S
WARNING ORDER
NAVAL SPECIAL WARFARE

Prior to every mission in SEAL Teams, a Warning Order is given explaining everything that is needed for the upcoming mission. This is your Warning Order! It will give you a guideline of how to prepare your next mission—Basic Underwater Demolition/SEAL (BUD/S) Training. The key to success at BUD/S is proper preparation prior to arrival.

BUD/S WARNING ORDER

I. Introduction
BUD/S is a challenging and rewarding training program which requires the individual to be self-motivated and physically fit. There is some very valuable information in this booklet on subjects such as a course description of all three phases of BUD/S, workouts to get you prepared for the physical stress of BUD/S, and helpful hints on nutrition.

II. History
Sea-Air-Land (SEAL) Teams trace their history back to the first group of volunteers selected from the Naval Construction Battalions in the Spring of 1943.* Their mission was clearing obstacles from beaches chosen for amphibious landings, which began the first formal training of the Naval Combat Demolition Units (NCDUs). The NCDUs distinguished themselves at Utah and Omaha beaches in Normandy and in Southern France. In the Pacific, the NCDUs were consolidated into Underwater Demolition Teams (UDTs).

* Author's note: Now to a little history: In the official SEAL Team warning order history section, there is no mention of the Office of Strategic Service (OSS) or Scouts and Raiders. OSS was a joint organization formed in February 1942 at Camp Pendleton, California. It had a maritime unit (MU) that was composed of three separate operational swimmer groups (OSGs). OSG #1 formed the nucleus of UDT-10. These men were formally trained as combat swimmers. UDT-10 men conducted the first submarine-launched reconnaissance ever conduced by American commandos during World War II.

The newly formed UDTs saw action in every corner of the Pacific during World War II. In September 1950, the UDTs participated in the Korean War at Inchon, Wonsan, Iwon and Chinnampo. The redeployment of the United Nations Forces featured the UDTs conducting delaying operations using guerilla warfare.

In January 1962, the first SEAL Teams were commissioned to conduct unconventional warfare, counter-guerilla warfare and clandestine operations in maritime and riverine environments. These Teams were SEAL Team One on the West Coast and SEAL Team Two on the East Coast. During Vietnam, the SEALs compiled an impressive record of combat success.

Since the close of the Vietnam conflict, the ever-changing world situation and increased operational tasking have prompted the expansion of SEAL Teams in number, size and capabilities. To effectively respond to this evolutionary process, Underwater Demolition Teams have been re-designated as SEAL or SEAL Delivery Vehicle (SDV) Teams. The newly designated

---

Scouts and Raiders were formed in August 1942. Many men from Scouts and Raiders later served in the Teams. In front of the Naval Special Warfare Center, where all SEALs are trained today, is the name Phil H. Bucklew; the center is named after the most famous Scout and Raider of them all. On the quarterdeck of the building, where all SEALs start their training, is a big, fat, brass bullfrog, which has the names of the longest serving members in the Teams mounted below it on brass nameplates. No one has served longer then BMCM Rudy Boesch, a member of the last Scouts and Raiders training class. Command Master Chief Boesch served his country from April 1945 to August 1990! Rudy is one of the most respected men in all of Special Warfare!

The navy has no paper trail that leads straight from the Office of Strategic Services or Scouts and Raiders to SEAL Team, but there is no doubt they are the SEALs' spiritual forefathers. They came first, and they did it well!

SEAL Teams acquired the SEAL mission and retained the amphibious support mission inherited from their UDT forefathers.

SEAL and SEAL Delivery Vehicle Teams and Special Boat Units comprise the elite combat units of Naval Special Warfare. These units are organized, trained and equipped to conduct special operations, unconventional warfare, foreign internal defense and clandestine operations in maritime and riverine environments. These highly trained specialists are deployed worldwide in support of fleet and national operations. The wide range of tasks performed by Naval Special Warfare and their outstanding combat records have earned an enduring and highly respected reputation.

Naval Special Warfare extends a personal challenge to those interested individuals like yourself. This program will push you to your physical and mental limits, again and again, until you are hard and strong, both physically and mentally, and ready for the adventure of a lifetime in SEAL Teams. Free fall parachuting at 10,000 feet, traveling by small rubber boat for 100 miles, conducting a mission, then traveling 30 miles out to sea to rendezvous with a submarine, is a typical mission for the SEALs and an adventure most people can experience only reading a book. If you are ready for both a challenge and an adventure, the Navy has just the training to test your mettle. BE SOMEONE SPECIAL!!!

As a BUD/S student, you will participate in challenging training and encounter opportunities to develop and test your stamina and leadership. BUD/S training is extremely thorough both physically and mentally; but through adequate preparation and a positive attitude, you can meet its challenges with confidence. The workout schedules in this booklet are designed to prepare you physically for BUD/S. You are the one who has to prepare to give all you have every day. At BUD/S it is essential to live, eat, and sleep BUD/S. 110% is required of you every day. BUD/S is a challenge, but if you meet it head-on with determination not to fail or quit, it will be the most rewarding time of your life. Good Luck!!!

COURSE DESCRIPTION

I. First Phase (Basic Conditioning)

First Phase is eight weeks in length. Continued physical conditioning in the areas of running, swimming, and calisthenics grow harder as the weeks progress. Students will participate in weekly four mile timed runs in boots, timed obstacle course, swim distances up to two miles wearing fins in the ocean and learn small boat seamanship.

The first four weeks of First Phase prepare you for the fifth week, better known as "HELL WEEK." During this week, students participate in five and one half days of continuous training, with a maximum of four hours sleep. This week is designed as the ultimate test of one's physical and mental motivation while in First Phase. HELL WEEK proves to those who make it that the human body can do ten times the amount of work the average man thinks possible. During HELL WEEK you will learn the value of the mainstay of the SEAL Teams: *TEAMWORK!* The remaining three weeks are devoted to teaching various methods of conducting hydrographic surveys and how to prepare a hydrographic chart.

II. Second Phase (Diving)

After you have completed First Phase, you have proven to the instructor staff that you are motivated to continue more in-depth training. The diving Phase is seven weeks in length. During this period, physical training continues, but the times are lowered for the four mile runs, two mile swims and the obstacle course. Second Phase concentrates on combat SCUBA (Self Contained Underwater Breathing Apparatus). Students are taught two types of SCUBA: open circuit (compressed air) and closed circuit (100% oxygen). Emphasis is placed on a progressive dive schedule which emphasizes basic combat swimmer skills that will qualify you as a com-bat diver. These skills will enable you to tactically insert and complete your combat objective. This is a skill that separates SEALs from all other Special Operations forces.

III. Third Phase (Land Warfare)

The demolition, reconnaissance, weapons and tactics is ten weeks in length. Physical training continues to become more strenuous as the run distances increase and the minimum passing times are lowered for the runs, swims and the obstacle course. Third Phase concentrates on teaching land navigation, small-unit tactics, rappelling, military land and underwater explosive and weapons training. The final four weeks of Third Phase are spent on San Clemente Island, where students apply techniques acquired throughout training in a practical environment.*

---

* Author's note: If a man is injured in training he can be rehabilitated in what is called Physical Training Rehabilitation Redemption (PTRR), and allowed to begin a new training class, in the last Phase he successfully completed. If a man has successfully completed HELL WEEK, but not all of Phase One, he may be allowed to rejoin a new Phase One class after HELL WEEK.

IV. Pre-BUD/S School

The Naval Special Warfare BUD/S selection course is designed to provide an overview of SEAL Training and the Naval Special Warfare Community. The five day course, held at the Naval Training Command, Great Lakes, is offered to all active duty Navy enlisted personnel from the Fleet, Service Schools and Boot Camp. Applicants will be temporarily assigned (TAD) from their parent command to the Selection Course. TAD funds are provided by Naval Special Warfare Center, more specifically, outlined in NAVADMIN 062/96 (15180ZMAR96). Requirements for the course are the same as those for attending BUD/S training. For further information contact the Physical Training Rehabilitation Remediation (PTRR) office at 619-437-0861 (DSN 577-0861). For a quota contact student control at 619-437-2578 (DSN 577-2578).

V. Post-BUD/S Schools

BUD/S graduates receive three weeks basic parachute training at the Army Airborne School, Fort Benning, Georgia, prior to reporting to their first Naval Special Warfare Command. Navy corpsmen who complete BUD/S and Basic Airborne Training also attend two weeks of Special Operations Technicians Training at the Naval Special Warfare Center, Coronado. They also participate in an intense course of instruction in diving medicine and medical skills called 18-D (Special Operations Medical Course). This is a 30-week course where students receive training in burns, gunshot wounds and trauma.

After assignment to a Team and successfully completing a six-month probationary period, quali-fied personnel are awarded a SEAL Naval Enlisted Classification (NEC) Code and Naval Special Warfare

Insignia. New combat swimmers serve the remainder of their first enlistment ($2\frac{1}{2}$–3 years) in either an SDV or SEAL Team. Upon reenlistment, members may be ordered to additional training and another SDV or SEAL Command, where they will complete the remainder of a five-year sea tour. Advanced courses include Sniper, Diving Supervisor, language training and SEAL Tactical Communication. Shore duty opportunities are available in research and development, instructor duty and overseas assignment.

In addition to normal pay and allowances, Naval Special Warfare personnel currently receive $175/month dive pay, $300/month SDV pay, $225/month HALO (jump pay) and $110/month special duty assignment pay.

You will find the physical fitness standards and the rest of the Training Command's warning order in Appendix Two.

One damn thing that's the same today as it was when we were in training is that the warning order sounds as if it were written by the same guy who wrote the instructors' synopsis for Class-29 that I used to introduce each phase of training. Could it be?

The most obvious difference, and maybe the least important, is the facilities. Training at Little Creek and at Roosevelt Roads was housed in old worn buildings, stuck away in far corners of the bases. In Coronado, they are right in the middle of the Teams. In the old days, the instructors had good reason to stay as far out of the way as possible; it decreased interference from people who had no clue about what was going on or why. From the outside, basic training for the Teams, UDT-RT then and BUD/S now, appears to be senseless brutality. Nothing could be farther from the truth.

First, the trainee can still quit anytime he wants without punishment. If a man decides he does not want to complete training, he can go. Second, but foremost, today's instructors have some things to work with that ours didn't. In the old days, an instructor had no place to put an injured trainee; today they do. I'm not talking bruises, blisters, strained muscles, or light abrasions; you treat those and keep going. I'm talking broken bones, torn muscles, deep cuts, or concussion. Many of the men who get through training will do whatever it takes to hide serious injury. Our instructors were reluctant to drop a man for physical injury who didn't want to go; they knew how hard it was just to get to training and, for the injured, how hard to get back. Today, the Teams have their own medical facility with excellent rehabilitation capability. Trainees who are seriously injured can go through rehabilitation at the command. If the trainee chooses, he can rejoin another class at the start of the phase he was injured in.

Class-29's own Two-Time Tom McCutchan had been saved from returning to the fleet, because a tough old Frogman asked him, "Why did you quit?" Tom quickly let him know he hadn't, that he'd broken his leg with two weeks to go. That Frogman had a need, and a lot of power—it was Lt. Roy Boehm. His next question to Tom was, "Can you type?"

When Tom replied, "No, sir," Lieutenant Boehm replied, "You will learn." With that, Roy Boehm got orders for Tom McCutchan to the just-formed SEAL Team Two. It would be years before the Teams had their own rehabilitation unit, but Tom had the plank holders of SEAL Team Two to rehabilitate his young ass.

I asked Roy Boehm, the first SEAL, for a short history of how SEAL Team came to be. No one could tell it better than the man himself. So here is a letter Roy was kind enough to send me, answering some of my questions.

John,

Initially, on the East Coast we had just UDT-21 to take from. I had trained about 80 percent of team 21 for the special unit later named SEALS. Cdr. Bob Terry was the skipper of UDT-21, and we negotiated the people to become a part of the SEAL unit, without stripping the team of its essential personnel. I was too much a sailor to kill one outfit to create another. There have been some controversies over who was and who was not a plank owner because many that we earmarked had to complete their operational commitments. Remember, I was also Operations Officer of 21 when we got the word. I received that word on Sunday, January 7, 1962—A friend in the Bureau called from his home to let me know. I quote him: "Roy, what in the hell is a SEAL? I am calling from my house as it is so secret I was afraid to call from the office. In any event, you have a license to steal and I know you are going to jail. I just want to say I don't know you!" That John is pretty close. Cdr. Terry and I fought it out on the 8th, a Monday. At the time I wanted all volunteers from the enlisted, and officers to be assigned. I appeared before my selected group in bloused boots and starched greens, and informed them that dressing like Joe Shit the Rag Man was over!

No matter what you read about 37 plank owners or that the team went into commission on 1 January 1962, they don't know what they are talking about. We went into commission on 9 January retroactive to 1 January 1962. I had been training a special group for a year. The only other person that was privy to our state of readiness at the time, 1961, was LCD Bill Hamilton (LCD Terry relieved him). When we found out that there would be a team on each coast, we were elated. As it was, we were overburdened with operations and the demands for UDT-21 special operations were straining our capabilities. As far as personnel were concerned, with three teams to choose from, the West Coast was in better shape. I turned over all my training contacts, Jump School, Jungle Warfare, Survival, Ranger, Martial Arts, Sailing, and Correctional facilities (Jail), and a host of others to the West Coast teams. At that time DelGuidice asked me to do for Team One whatever I was doing for SEAL Team Two—I complied by ordering a duplicate of all equipment.

There is a lot more that went on. Too much to describe, and too controversial for rehashing by a bunch of second guessers who weren't there and didn't lay their careers on the line. In a navy that was reluctant to go unconventional, many, like Hoot Andrews and others, bent a good many rules in order to provide our Commander in Chief with his commandos.

Roy Boehm

The Teams are about the *people*; they are full of smart, tough, funny people. Remove every piece of equipment from the Teams, impede them from doing their job in every way possible, they will still get it done, and have a damn good time doing it. The only indispensable tool in the Teams is its people. Lt. Roy Boehm knew that and formed SEAL Team Two in just that way.

What is the single biggest difference between training then and now? *Good boots* on trainees' feet! I'm just talking personal here; I mean the single biggest difference for the individual trainee. There are many who will argue that what I have just written is a load of crap. So let me lay out my, admittedly personal, point of view. From our first week of preconditioning, till the four months of Underwater Demolition Team Replacement Training was over, we wore surveyed boondockers, ankle-high work shoes that someone else had worn out before they were issued to us. It was not that our instructors were trying to destroy our feet or were cheap. They just didn't have the money to spend on boots and didn't know how important taking care of your feet is. I do not remember clearly many pains from my early life, but, for me, getting through that four months meant *getting past the pain of my feet*.

The navy has learned. As I watched Class-221 fall in that first morning of training, my eyes went to their feet. *Yes,* no not just *yes*, but *hell yes*, everyone had a good pair of high-top boots and thick socks on. I will state flatly that if we had good high-top boots and thick socks on our feet during the Kennedy Bridge raid, Ens. Charley Rand would not have lost his toes. Somewhere along the line, between Class-29 and -221, they had figured out how important good boots and healthy feet are.

The biggest structural difference in training and, among us old farts the most controversial, is rolling a trainee back. I'm not talking about those injured; most everyone likes that. I am talking about a trainee who does not pass a physical or academic test. Officers and senior petty officers can pass everything in a given phase but leadership, and be rolled back. I am not talking about a written test, but the act of leading as graded by the instructors. In the old days, you passed or you went back to the fleet. Most of us old Frogs have no idea how heavy the academic load is for today's trainee. I didn't until I had the opportunity to observe today's training program. I have come to accept rollback as a necessary part of today's training.

Another big difference, much subtler than boots or being rolled back, is communication—well, at least half the art of communicating, called listening. As near I can tell, it is mainly a function of how we raise and educate our children today. I can sum up the problem fairly quickly: Children raised in the forties and fifties were raised to listen to everyone. Children who came along in the sixties, seventies, and eighties were raised to listen to no one. There seems to be a general proposition adrift in society today that anyone's opinion is just as important as what the next guy thinks. Unlike most of American society, BUD/S instructors will not put up with that silly esoteric shit. In the bad business of war, not listening can get you and your teammates dead, quick. If you're dead you *cannot fucking win*! The whole dynamic of right and wrong has changed, now this might work all right while you are taking a society slowly down the tubes, but in war it does not work. If you can't listen, you can't figure out what is right or, worse, wrong.

The instructors use that common trait of today's young guy not to listen as a teaching tool; if the trainee does not listen, he gets to make his body stronger, lean and rest, push-ups, eight-count body builders, etc. A normal training day is still full of big-time physical exertion; burn-out physical training, obstacle course, long runs in the sand, surf penetration, long swims at sea, and the ever-loved log PT. Every time one of those young guys gets dropped for push-ups because he can't listen, he is just giving himself a little extra physical exercise.

I had arrived at the Training Command at 0600 the morning of August 24, 1998. I missed the start of Class-221, first day in Phase I. They had mustered at 0500, for a lovely little prebreakfast run in the sand, then had departed for their morning meal just as I arrived at the Training Command. After clearing security, I was escorted to the Phase I office. Lo and behold! There stood Class-221's first quitter, waiting to ring the bell. The test had begun. The Training Command used the West Coast method for quitting; on the East Coast you just removed your red helmet, and you were gone. The West Coast method for quitting entails a little more ritual.

The bell is mounted outside the instructors' offices, still the last place a trainee wants to find himself. It is a standard navy bell, made of brass that is kept highly polished. The bell is about eleven inches high and nine-plus inches across the lip. There's one just like it on any ship or naval station. Anytime a trainee has business at the instructors' office, he must come to attention by the bell in front of the office and ring it. When an instructor decides he has the time to deal with the trainee, he will acknowledge the trainee. Until he is acknowledged, the trainee must stand at attention.

If a trainee wants to quit, that has its own special ring—three rapid strikes on the bell—so anyone within hearing knows what is going on. He is then afforded the opportunity to think about what he is doing while he waits for the instructor's attention. Until he speaks the words, "I quit," a trainee can change his mind. If the instructor thinks he might work out, he may let the trainee stand and think about his decision awhile. The trainee who was already waiting to quit before I got there that first morning was gotten rid of quick.

Now, as in the old days, if a trainee goes to the instructors' office, he is going to suffer. If you've read this far, you know that anytime a trainee comes to the personal attention of an instructor, there is a good possibility he will pay the price. Push-ups now, as then, are the main currency of pain. Another thing that's the same today is that the instructors make sure the trainees' muscles are always in the condition of pain. The object is still to find the people who do not take the easy way out. I don't care how good a trainee is, the instructors will make him pay. You might say they are truly "equal-opportunity employers."

At 0700, that first morning of training for Class-221, they mustered on the grinder, in the middle of the training area. The grinder is asphalt, about seventy-five yards by a hundred, surrounded by the training unit offices, classrooms, and equipment storage areas. Grinder is the perfect name, and that morning Class-221 got its first taste of what happens there. We called it burn-out PT; the instructors just called it physical training. Its object was and is to make the muscles so sore the trainee couldn't do a proper exercise if his life depended on it.

There are only two differences between burn-out and a regular PT session, quantity and quality. A normal session is well beyond what most people would ever attempt, but most trainees come to training in superior physical condition. A good number are in such excellent condition that they find the screening test for BUD/S training easy. A burn-out PT will take care of that! The instructors simply pile on such a large quantity of a given exercise that no trainee could possibly do it correctly. Quality goes out the window; burn-outs are meant to make the body hurt. Class-221 would feel every muscle in its collective bodies for the next twenty-five weeks!

On the north end of the grinder is a raised platform for the instructor that leads the PT. Behind the platform, chin-up bars cross the north end of the grinder. On the northwest corner, long sets of dip bars, between the dip bars and the platform, a fully inflated "inflatable boat, small," sits on the grinder. One odd thing about the boat, it was full of water. It didn't take long to find out its purpose. As that first burn-out PT wore on and the trainees started to heat up, it was used for cool-down. An overheated trainee was told to stop whatever exercise he was doing and crawl through the water in the boat. Not a bad idea, but that boat was also a trainee trap.

Anytime you are hot, getting cool feels good. If a

trainee thinks he is near heat prostration, he can stop whatever exercise he is doing and crawl through the boat. The trainee does not need an instructor's permission. Hell, that makes sense to me, where's the trap? It's subtle but, if you understand the kind of guys the Teams are *not* looking for, easy to understand: They don't want a man who cuts corners to make things easy for himself, the kind of guy who would stop an exercise not because he is over-heated but just to give himself a little break. Those guys were easy to spot; they hit the boat more than anyone else.

Water and the consumption thereof was one more sur-prise. Each trainee wore a standard military-issue web belt with two canteens attached. For the PT session, they had taken the belt and canteens off and laid them on the grinder beside their workout spot. Several times during the PT session, the instructor on the platform had stopped the exercise and told the trainees to "Hydrate." Each trainee then grabbed a canteen and took a couple of big slugs of water. In our training class, we were never allowed to drink water when heated up. We had been trained to take a mouthful, rinse our mouths, and spit it out. I must admit, I always cheated and swallowed some. The medical opinion of the day had been that drinking water when you were heated up would make you sick. Medical opinion is different today, and not only are trainees kept in the water but water is kept in them as well. If a trainee is found without his canteens, or they're not full after he has had the opportunity to fill them, he will pay dearly.

Another big surprise for me, and one of the bigger dif-ferences between training then and now, was the number of instructors involved in every evolution. When we had been in training, on things like PT there was one, or at most two, instructors. Our whole instructor staff con-sisted of ten enlisted and one officer. That first morning of Class-221's PT, seven instructors met the trainees, one on the platform, the rest out on the grinder, all of them watching the trainees closely. It took me a while to figure out why there were so many instructors.

In today's navy there is only one training unit; in my day there had been two. One at Little Creek, Virginia, the other on the Strand in Coronado, California. Between both coasts, there had been four training classes a year. Today the Naval Special Warfare Center runs eight BUD/S classes a year. Not only that, but the center teaches twenty-four other scheduled classes: Basic Underwater Demolition/SEAL Indoctrination, Special Warfare Craft Crewman (SWCC), SEAL Weapons System Operator, Marine Operations, MK-16 Underwater Breathing Apparatus (UBA), MK-16 UBA Maintenance, SEAL Delivery Vehicle (SDV) Operator, SDV Maintenance, SDV Electronic Maintenance, SEAL SCUBA Diving Supervisor, Diving Equipment Maintenance & Repair, Draeger LAR V Closed Circuit UBA, Closed Circuit Diving Procedures, Open Circuit Diving Procedures, Free Swimming Ascent (FSA) Techniques, Submarine Lock-in/Lockout, Combat Fighting Course (CFC) Basic, CFC Advanced, Static Line Jump Master, Midshipman Cadet Orientation, Special Operations Technician (SOT), SOT Refresher, Chief Petty Officer & Lead Petty Officer Training Course, Junior Officer Training Course, Prospective Commanding Officer/Prospective Executive Officer Course.

Special Boat Units are the other leg of Naval Special Warfare and combat sailors of the first order. They all attend Special Warfare Craft Crewman (SWCC) class and have a career path in Naval Special Warfare. In my day, we had Boat Support Unit. It was a duty station, not a career path, there were some damn good men, but they came, did their tour of duty, and moved on. Here is how the navy describes Special Boat Unit's history and SWCC Class.

Special Warfare Craft Crewmember (SWCC)

Today's Special Boat Units (SBU) trace their origin to
Boat Support Unit One (BSU) which was commissioned in 1963 as a component of the Naval Operations Support Group commanded by Captain Phil H.
Bucklew, a pioneer of Naval Special Warfare. The
members of BSU-1 deployed to the Republic of Vietnam as members of the Mobile Support Teams tasked
with the operation and maintenance of the light SEAL
support craft (LSSC) and Medium SEAL support
craft (MSSC). Although other units supported SEALs
during the war, only BSUs were specifically created
to support Underwater Demolition Teams (UDTs) and
SEALs.

SWCC Training is comprised of three core areas:
Physical Fitness/Water Safety Skills, Basic Crewmember Skills and Basic SWCC Warfare Skills. The
first two weeks involve running, swimming and calisthenics, all of which become increasingly difficult
as the weeks progress. The second four weeks teach
combat craft principles of engineering, seamanship,
navigation and communication. Emphasis is placed
on teamwork with the goal of training the students to
become basic combat crewmembers. The next three
weeks concentrate on teaching basic tactics, patrolling and individual and combat craft weapons. The final
week culminates with students applying the skills acquired throughout training in a practical environment
during a demanding 3-day Field Training Exercise.

It boils down to this: They are looking for some special
kind of men, men who will take a small boat full of
SEALs into very bad places. More important to the peace
of mind of those SEALs on the ground, when the world

has turned to shit and everyone is trying to make those SEALs dead, men who will come back and get their ass. The kind of men who love their boat and every damn weapon on it. The United States Navy has an abundance of sailors who love small boats. The best of those boats, and the guys who run them, belong to the Special Boat Unit. Initial training for BUD/S and SBU are separate, very demanding, but different. Once a man has passed his respective basic training and been assigned to a SEAL Team, SEAL Delivery Vehicle Team, or Special Boat Unit, they then train together.

I think you get the idea, but just to drive the point home. The courses listed above are public knowledge; I promise you there are classes we know nothing about, and should know nothing about. To top it all off, other branches of the service run a legion of schools that many SEALs attend. Knowledge is the way through, over, or around an obstacle. SEALs, SEAL Delivery Vehicle Teams, and Special Boat Units are required to gather as much knowledge as possible.

As I looked around the grinder that first morning, I was surprised how much Class-221 was surrounded by history. From Captain Bucklew's name on the training center, the big fat bullfrog on the quarterdeck, to the grinder where a large plaque bears the name of each training-class honor man. Harry Humphries's name is up there, from all those years ago. Many graduating training classes had left marks of their own—paintings, plaques, and statues. Most of them have a likeness of the cocky bullfrog we called Freddy, and a Budweiser, alongside their class number. One graduating class even purchased a huge brass bullfrog over four feet tall. It stands near the door to the instructors' office and overlooks the grinder, an old Freddy Frog keeping an eye on training.

Day one for this class of wanna-be SEALs will set the

tone for the rest of their basic training. Their classroom sessions start on day one and are very different from what Class-29 faced: academics, academics, and more academics. Indoor classes are held in a cement room with wooden school desks and no heat or air-conditioning. The instructor teaches the class from a small raised stage up front. They speak in a soft voice, not monotone, nor amplified. When the inevitable happens and a student nods off, that is used as a lesson. From the rear of the class, one of the instructors will throw a bucket of water in the general direction of the offender. He and those around him will then find themselves in the lean and rest, their notes soaking wet on their desks. They quickly learn that it is damn hard to dry their notes or add to them from the lean and rest.

Now, many may wonder what kind of lesson that bucket of water teaches. Well, it's what I would call a multilevel teaching tool. In a way, it teaches the prospective SEAL everything he needs to know about *teamwork*. If anyone lets a classmate nod off, everyone sitting near the sleeping guy will get his notes wet, and he may very well find himself, along with his sleepy pal, in the lean and rest. Teamwork is about self-preservation, not some esoteric nice-guy stuff. After the first few classroom sessions, rarely will a bucket fly. Trainees who find themselves getting a little drowsy get up and stand in the back of the class.

That first day started with an introduction to the hydrographic survey, one of the technical things that we in Class-29 didn't get till our last five weeks of training. First phase has just one interruption to its academic endeavors, Hell Week, which now comes in the fifth week of training. By the end of first phase, most of Class-221 will be gone. But those who are left will be able to gather the information and prepare a hydrographic chart like the one we prepared for our final demolition problem.

Each training class still learns the same things during Hell Week: You can go farther than you ever thought possible, but you can't do it alone, and everyone left standing belongs there. Hell Week has changed less than any part of training, for one simple reason: The instructors cannot find a better way. You can't pick the ones who can hack it by their looks. No written test will find out if a man is a Team player. If it was possible to get good operators by letting some shrink interview trainees and say yea or nay, the navy would love it. The big problem is, the psychologists can't predict who will survive five-plus days of no sleep, with constant harassment, and impossible physical demands with an easy way out. That's still the test.

Those who reach second phase, in the ninth week, will begin a much more extensive diving program than we received at underwater swim school. And many of the young men will receive a terrible shock, no calculators are allowed! Dive phase is heavy in mathematical formulas all worked out by mental calculation or by pencil and paper. For many, it will be the first time in their young lives that they have not been able to use calculators on an exam. So classroom sessions in phase two of training are full of trainees who are paying attention. I wonder why? Meanwhile, all the usual heavy physical demands are still being piled on the would-be SEALs. Their times must be improving on the obstacle course, runs, and swims. Of course, swim and run distances have been increased, and all exercise repetition has been jacked up. By this time, the trainees now know what is meant by the old Team saying, "The only easy day was yesterday!"

One of the things new trainees learn that we didn't is "drown proofing." By the time they have that technique down pat, a whole class of trainees bound hand and foot will be bobbing up and down in ten feet of water. Given trainees' excellent condition and swim skills, many people might think that training tool is way over the edge. Well, SEALs have drowned by leaping off a boat with sixty to eighty pounds of full combat gear strapped to their ass. Second phase is not just about learning to dive; like all of training, it is about how to *win* and *live* in the *bad business of war*.

With third phase, success is just ten very tough weeks away, and every trainee can taste it. But even if they survive ten more weeks, the trainees won't be full-fledged SEALs; they will just have completed the hardest part, Basic Underwater Demolition/SEAL training. Each of them will have, at least, jump school, then six months of probation before he can pin on his Budweiser. But to the men in third phase, none of that matters; the only things that count are land navigation, small-unit tactics, rappelling, land and underwater explosives, and weapons training. And, of course, the heavy physical demands grow more intense—longer swims, runs, and PT sessions.

I observed third phase during a week spent in the mountains a little northeast of San Diego, up around six or seven thousand feet. Most of that week was spent on land navigation, with a little small-unit tactics, reconnaissance, and good old sneak and peek thrown in. I said six *or* seven thousand feet because the trainees spent every day, and a good part of each night, going up and down those mountains on compass courses and gathering intelligence. None of the trainees seemed to be affected by the altitude change. All their previous training had been at sea level, but by that phase of training, they were physical animals. The class had overcome every obstacle, mental or physical, that was placed in its way. By that time, the trainees are truly a *team*, and they damn well know it.

One of the first things that became apparent was instructors still have a problem judging the distance of a run. Due to mechanical problems, I had arrived a little later in the morning than I expected. Thank you, God, for small favors; I missed the run! It had been my plan to run with the class on what was billed as a seven-mile run. How quickly we forget. It must have something to do with the genetic makeup of men who become BUD/S instructors; they never err on the short side. No seven-mile run ever was five miles long, nor were any ever seven! All the instructor said when they returned to the base camp was, "I must've taken the wrong deer trail out of that meadow in the bottom of the valley." Damn, that took me back thirty-five years, it sounded like something Chief Cool Breeze Spiegel would tell us after we had run farther than advertised.

Since arriving at BUD/S, I had had little direct conversation with trainees, not because it wasn't allowed, but because I didn't need to know what a trainee thinks. Not only had I been a trainee, but many of my classmates had written, called, and E-mailed to help me with this book. I needed to talk with, and observe, instructors. I needed to see training from their side of all the *sweat* and *pain*. The instructors at BUD/S made clear to me something I had missed about CLASS-29's instructors. Something that leaped out like a huge flashing sign, something that is exactly the same today as it was thirty-five years ago: They teach teamwork by their example.

Our instructors had never said, "Watch us, this is what teamwork is," they did just what today's instructors do, kept the unspoken example in front of the trainees at all times. Until I had watched those guys work, I had thought just the grueling facts of training had forged us into a team. Not so; we had the same thing today's trainees have, the best teaching tool there is, unwavering example. I had been dead on when I had written, "Core value for SEAL Team is the people." Training is where SEAL Team gets its people, and core value for training is the instructors.

While I was at the training center, three training classes were in progress: First phase was Class-221, second phase was Class-220, and third phase was Class-219. I found the same thing with each phase's instructors—men who worry about the quality of their product—team members—and how they are doing their job. I am not trying to say that the instructors, training, or SEAL Teams are perfect. What I will flatly state is, no group of men is closer to perfection in their chosen field. No group works harder to improve the quality of its work.

After the seven-mile run that was ten-plus miles long, the trainees and instructors were hard at it till well after midnight. If I remember right, I had driven into camp just after 0600, when they had departed on their run. All day, instructors were out setting up compass courses, and the trainees were running them. Every time trainees finished one course, the instructors would retrieve the markers and set out a different one. The trainees, in teams of two or as a fire team of eight to ten, would be given a set of grid coordinates and a team number. The grid coordinates represented a point on a map. They were to take their compass and a map and go to that point. When they reached that point, in an ammo can, they would find another set of grid coordinates written on a small piece of paper with their number on it. They would then take the paper with their number and go to the next point. All of the courses ended at the starting point, a table in the middle of base camp.

Each team leader was briefed and debriefed at that table, and of course, many paid the price for small infractions. Whether a two-man team or a full fire team, a team leader was selected by the instructors, and only the leader was briefed. He was told everything, from what gear to carry to what type of information to return with. It was each team leader's responsibility to pass all information on to the rest of his team. Each of the compass courses was timed and graded. If the team didn't pass, the men would repeat phase three. And *nobody* wants to be rolled back.

"Full ruck," that's everything our wannabe SEALs have in the field, seventy plus pounds of military gear. Ruck is short for rucksack and refers to the backpack each trainee carries his gear in. The last compass course was with full ruck, fire-team-size, and would be a little kiss good-night from the instructors. All day, as trainees had been briefed and debriefed, they had been paying the price for anything less than perfection. All day, the instructors had been using their soft and reasonable classroom voices. Each briefing had ended with "Any questions?"

During every briefing, the trainees had been told to turn in all grid coordinates and notes at the end of each compass course. At the debrief, they had been asked if they had turned in all grid coordinates and notes. All day, the instructors had never checked the small notepad each trainee was required to carry. Well, shakedown time came at the last briefing, and it was more than just checking notepads; the trainees had to empty their pockets, open their rucksacks, and show the instructors their notepads. It was pay-the-price time, advanced education BUD/S style.

Each fire team had at least one man who had notes or grid coordinates or was missing a piece of equipment. Of course, all day guys had been paying the price, one trainee to a fire team at a time. But the shakedown was a training-class thing, and everybody paid. The compass course was being run as a combat situation; stay off the roads, sneak and peek, good platoon movements, etc. So the officers and senior enlisted men had their asses chewed big time, everyone was paying the price in push-ups, and the instructors were no longer speaking in their classroom voices. It was serious business: *"Never go into combat without carrying all required equipment. Never carry unnecessary information, notes from previous operations, grid coordinates that lead to your base camp. The enemy could pick them off your dead body!"*

It's just a different form of the bucketful of water lesson. Check each other out, watch each other's back; it will do nice things for you. Things like keeping your notes dry and you alive! They all did at least fifty push-ups and were kept in the lean and rest till their arms could no longer hold them straight, and then a while longer. Of course, the trainees who caused the rest of their class to receive a little advanced education would hear about it from their classmates. In combat, "little things" can make you hurt, even dead!

A little after 2400, midnight, most of the trainees were crawling into their sleeping bags. Till 0500, when reveille was held, trainees stood watch, a lovely way to end a long day or start the next. After reveille, an hour was spent eating and generally getting ready for the day. At 0600, quarters were held, and the training day started with an hour-long PT session. So, you want to be a SEAL?

Phase three ends with four weeks on San Clemente Island, where the trainees sharpen and put to the practical test everything they have been taught. Like those of us who came before, they will have paid the price to be a SEAL. There is just one coin the price can be paid in— stamina, mental and physical stamina! Some men in every training class will never see one another again, but they will carry their training class with them for the rest of their lives. Ask any of them, thirty-five years later, about their training class, and the one thing all of them will be clearest about is their *instructors*. It's the instructors that make training work!

I am going to leave the last words in this book to three others, Tom Blais and Sam Orr writing about the instructor who affected them the most, and Jim Hawes on being a training officer.

John,

A bit of prehistory to aid the understanding process: During the fall of 1948 I was still attached to the U.S. Navy Bureau of Personnel; I was a seaman and new to the Navy. I received orders to serve at BuPers only because I had high General Classification and Mathematics Test scores. Accordingly, it had been decided, by the navy, that I would be a good yeoman. I did not like it at all, and requested Underwater Demolition Team training. I reported to UDT 2 in December of 1948, and started as a member of class 4 in January 1949. Should you check the records, you will find it was a historically cold winter that year.

I was young and a blessed, gifted athlete in good shape; still I found the training extraordinarily difficult. There was no preconditioning and many fell away quickly. Our instructors were World War Two veterans and were sharply focused. Many were lean and running fools! But you know, they were always fair. There was no impunity, no freedom from punishment, and we all got it stuck in our ears.

One instructor stands out in my mind, Lt. Anderson, a quiet determined person of muscle and sinew. No fooling, he could run up soft, steep, high sand dunes, with absolute apparent ease, backward quicker than a jack rabbit might do it forward. His chiseled granite looking legs pumped like powerful pistons in the soft relenting sand. Because of his unique ability and staying power, he alone caused many of us to fall short of keeping up, and at times to drop to our knees retching and puking into the sand. He would wait as other instructors rounded us up and then head for the surf. He was barelegged with boondockers, shoes just like ours. He would run swiftly in the freezing cold surf smiling all the time, masochistically, I thought. We were taunted to keep up, inevitably that was impossible and so we were allowed to rest lying and rolling in the frigid surf. It actually was such a nice relief until we would start to become numbed. He seemed to know when that was and would lead our water-logged bodies back into the high sand dunes. Oh, the pain! *The terrible frequent pain.*

I came to know him later well, after I successfully completed training. He was a very kind, thoughtful, considerate gentleman, combat seasoned, tough as a stone, very intelligent, and quite humble. He was a highly ranked black belt in judo and taught us how to use combative and countercombative measures, as he called them. He really taught us how to protect ourselves, and how to kill the enemy with ease. He and I became running partners long after training was over. I wanted to learn how to run up those tall sand dunes backward as he had done. He taught me. All it took I found, was continual trying, more pain, and more puking in the sand. It became a great simple success lesson, focus and never quit! He taught me how to stretch and do some yoga. He showed me how to lay any man low and made me practice, practice, and practice more—another success lesson. I didn't realize it then, but Mr. Anderson became one of my role models.

In 1952, my Father became ill with heart ailments, and I went on humanitarian shore duty. During the time I was away from the Underwater Demolition Teams, a change in code numbers occurred and my 5321 ceased to exist within my naval service record, I was told. Further, in 1952, I married the love of my life, Florence Del Rosso, who was a remarkably beautiful and multitalented young woman. She was also a recent honor graduate from a fine all girls Catholic college, and had been trained as an English major with multilanguage disciplines.

She saw to it that I became more cerebral and less physical. She was an outstanding cook, and I became even more rotund accordingly. Although we were ecstatically happy, I missed the underwater demolition team occupation desperately and especially my *teammates*. I knew firsthand now, that in Underwater Demolition Teams, the morale and comradeship was unique; and that I must be a U.S. Navy Frogman once again!

Prior to requesting transfer back to the Teams, I visited UDT Team 2 still located at the USNAB, Little Creek, Virginia, and spoke with the executive officer, Lt. Drum. He was shocked at my self-imposed physical deterioration, and told me so in no uncertain terms: "Petty Officer Blais, you are fat and out of shape! If you expect to become a UDT man again you will have to go through training. I will arrange for orders to be issued to you, for UDT Training, not directly to the Teams." So I did it again, with Class-16.

Later, during my career, I broadened my academic prowess, smoothed a rough personality, learned some humility, practiced more yoga and a beneficial mixture of the martial arts, and stayed with Naval Unconventional Warfare many years, nearly twenty-four. I loved every minute of it and miss it all!

Your friend and former teammate,
Tom Blais

John,

Our class was as miserable as all those that preceded and followed it. It also left me memories I will never forget, both the good and the very painful, and brought me closer to my classmates than anyone else in my life.

There were many instructors who made Class-17 highly meaningful. I remember them all, and have a soft spot in my heart for most of them. Among them, Paul McNally stands out as a giant spirit who typified what UDT was all about. We had instructors bigger than Paul, smarter than Paul, more friendly and helpful than Paul, but none more determined or honest with us than Paul.

It is the job of BUD/S instructors to find out just how much stamina, strength, resolve, self-control, self-discipline, and spirit lies within each trainee. They determine these traits differently. Some of them set trainees in motion and simply watched, adding calisthenics as physical punishment to drain each man. Others came barefoot and wore swim trunks to run trainees who were dressed in greens and boots. Some would direct us into the surf, get us wet and sandy, then run us miles with our greens sandpapering each crotch raw. Paul McNally did none of that.

Paul would show up dressed just the way we were. When we started the run, he was in the lead, and there was no nonsense about making us miserable to increase the pain. Paul just ran us into the ground. When those to the rear got too far behind, he circled around to pick them up again. Anyone immediately behind him went farther than the slow runners, but no one complained. If you were able to stay reasonably close, he might smile and say you were trying a little harder than usual. When he led calisthenics, which was often, we knew we were in for it. It was all smooth, deliberate. He did it all better than any of us, and he smiled all the way. I would rather get a curt nod of approval from McNally than lavish praise from anyone else, because you had to earn it. He was hard, but he was fair. Paul had to win at everything, and was willing to pay the price to do it. He could swim farther underwater than any of us, mostly because he had more will. I once thought to myself that if someone jumped out of a fifteen-story window, McNally would bail out after him just to beat him to the ground. He was the essence of a competitor, and that earned something no one could buy from me, my respect.

Chief McNally is gone now, and I hope others like him came to take his place. But no one else will ever occupy the spot he has in my memory. He was a man with no pretense, who neither gave nor accepted excuses, had great pride, and always got the most from us by sheer example and his desire. Paul McNally had more leadership qualities than anyone I have ever known, and I have thought of him often throughout the rest of my life.

Sam Orr
Class-17, July–November 1956, Coronado, California
World Traveler and Philanthropist
Whereabouts unknown

John,

Thirty-five years after training, my image of the instructors staff has been enhanced by my life experience. As you wrote earlier in the book, to get the Captain of the Naval Amphibious School to approve a waiver for my nearsightedness, I had to agree to return to the training unit as assistant training officer/ instructor. I reported to the Training Unit immediately after our graduation ceremony, instead of reporting to an operational Team which was my strong preference. Normally, a training officer/instructor would rotate into the training unit after serving on the Teams. The opportunity I was unwillingly given, gave me a different perspective on the instructor staff.

Before we finished training in Puerto Rico, it became known to the instructors Blais, Waddell, Sulinski, Spiegel, Cook, Parrish, Newell, Hammond, and Clements that I would become their boss as soon as we completed training. I will never forget Instructor Chief Blais taking me aside during one training day, after my future became known, and in his quiet, most intimidating way, saying something like, "Mr. Hawes, I am going to make it my personal challenge and responsibility to see to it that you earn the right to be our boss." That meant that I received Blais's personal attention on virtually every swim, run, or training exercise for the remainder of training. Blais's personal attention meant a great deal of pain, and a great deal of learning.

When I completed training, I had the same impression as all our class: the instructors were hard, demanding, incapable of being satisfied, but fair. When I reported to the training unit as the assistant training officer/instructor, I was immediately accepted and treated with the respect and camaraderie of a veteran, despite my inexperience. My admiration for these men increased daily. I learned how seriously they took their roles as "keepers of the flame," the spirit of the Frogmen; how fair-minded they were in evaluating trainees; how they agonized over the prospect of screening a trainee, who might be one of those rare exceptions—a candidate who had the will, but not the ability; how heatedly they would argue and debate over the best ways to train and prepare the new trainees for the Teams; how much mutual respect was exhibited every day.

Leadership, leadership-by-example, the demand of higher expectations and accountability, acceptance of the understanding that someone with greater abilities does not diminish one's own abilities, teamwork, sacrifice, patriotism, honor. These were fundamentals perpetuated by the instructors, and inculcated into the spirit of the trainees. To have been instructor was the greatest learning experience of my life.

Jim Hawes
Member Class-29 and Instructor Classes-30 and 31

To: John Carl Roat
From: Admiral Cathal Flynn (Retired)
Subject: UDTRT Class-24

From the Navy's viewpoint, Underwater Demolition Replacement Training Class-24, Little Creek, June to October 1960, met its objective. Its fourteen U.S. graduates, combined with the product of a concurrent course in Coronado, filled the vacancies caused by separations and retirements from the three teams then operating.

In quality, we graduates were as good as the men we replaced. All had developed self-confidence, ruggedness, stamina, and unusual ability to endure pain and withstand claustrophobia. We officers had gained great respect for the men we would be privileged to lead in our Teams. The foreigners—Spaniards, Pakistanis, and a Norwegian—had done everything as we had, in some cases better, despite being several years older; they too became men to respect for life.

The training in tactics prepared us well to conduct the amphibious operations of 1945. It was as if the development of tactics had ended with Kauffman and Hanlon, as if cast and recovery still made operational sense. But if the tactics were mostly worthless, the training still managed to impart much that was valuable. Explosive demolition was taught with great expertise and thoroughness, as was beach hydrographics.

Our instructors were a mixed lot. Of the three officers, two were excellent: self-controlled, physically fit, quietly competent, observant, in charge. The third rarely appeared (we wondered if he was UA), but when he did, his participation in the training activities seemed to be for his own amusement rather than for any instructional benefit. Neither the assigned officers, nor their superiors in the Amphibious Training Command, appeared to give much attention to the unnecessarily high rate of attrition in the class. Too many good men, not quitters, were permanently disqualified by avoidable injuries such as heatstroke.

A couple of Petty Officer "instructors" were there, one suspected, because they had been dumped from Team-21. Overweight, out of shape, or alcoholic, they were best ignored, particularly because they were in marked contrast to the other members of the cadre. To a man, these others were inspirational leaders and very capable instructors, smart, tough, good-humored men one would remember for life. Above all was Bernie Waddell; he brought out the best in everyone, did everything with enthusiasm and flair, and somehow could encourage trainees—even make us laugh— while demanding the last ounces of our endurance. But if Waddell was unique, Spiegel, Parrish, Casey, Waugh, and Gallagher were also highly capable. So with only a couple of exceptions, the instructors were what they should have been: professionals representative of the many great sailors who made service in the Teams of the 1960s so rewarding.

Sincerely,
Cathal Flynn

A FEW THOUGHTS

For me the word "Instructor" is like the words "Mom" and "Dad"; all three should always be capitalized. I have heard comments to the effect that the Teams' instructors are sadistic. *Bullshit!* I never had an instructor use violence on me, nor did I see it used on other trainees. The instructors are men among men, the ones needed when things go bad. War is the most ruthless of man's endeavors, and the Teams' instructors are charged with finding men who will win it for us!

Two of my instructors are right up there with my dad and grandpa, chiefs Bernie Waddell and Tom Blais; when I am challenged, if I get a little weak, they help me through. All those years ago, they taught me a hard lesson: The most important battle is the one you have with yourself.

A lot is said about SEAL Team today, some good, some bad, some true, some not. To the men who were Frogmen and SEALs, and the ones who still are, it is simply the *Teams*. Everyone who makes it through training knows he would have never made it alone. It is a rare thing, being a part of a Team! Teamwork is talked to death by people who have no clue what a Team is, the kind of people who would never take responsibility for one damn thing in their own lives. People who want everyone else to be responsible. Well, step up, asshole, and carry your share of the boat. If you don't find a way to contribute, you don't belong on a Team.

Is training the same today as it was then? No; things *have* changed, small little knickknack shit. At the heart, it is what it has always been, a brutal test of mind and body. Each training class is tested by those who came before, the instructors. The instructors have all taken the test, and have no interest in letting the standards slip. I think that Comdr. P. T. Smith (Class-29's longest serving member: thirty-six years, nine months on active duty) says it best:

Everyone who has remained close to the community has been asked to compare training then and now. In many bars around the globe, I have stated adamantly that we went through the last hard class. The truth is that training is just as hard today as it was back then and in many ways it is far better. Even though training is still hard, it is safer. Exercises like duckwalk and squat jumps that tore up our knees so badly have been taken out of the program. Boondockers are gone and have been replaced by quality running shoes. The result is that they no longer lose excellent candidates because of unnecessary stress fractures. Instructors do a better job of monitoring students today, and medical care is more readily available. I don't think a Kennedy Bridge fiasco would occur in today's training program, and good guys like Charlie Rand would complete today's training.

Today's training program is longer by a total of about four weeks, and the trainees learn a great deal more. By comparison, we learned what was available to be taught at the time: demolition, a few small-caliber weapons, reconnaissance, the basics of patrolling and tactics, and how to work as a team. Today's classes learn what we did plus more sophisticated techniques in closed-circuit diving, combat swimming, details of small-unit tactics, communications, mission planning, and how to work as a team. I had the privilege of working closely with "new guys" right up to the very end of my career. My observation is that when a BUD/S graduate arrives at one of the teams today, he knows at least as much as we knew after two or three years in a team. What today's graduates don't know any better than we did, is how these newfound skills fit into large-scale military operations. That takes many years of experience and is only a learning requirement for more senior team members.

My feeling that training is just as hard now as it was for us is based on personal observation. From 1991 to 1993, I had an unaccompanied tour of duty in Coronado, and I lived in a BOQ that was across the street from the BUD/S training compound. On a daily basis, for two years, I'd see those classes marching, jogging, crawling, and carrying boats from one end of the base to the other. When trainees and I would pass close aboard, we'd be eyeing each other. They'd see a middle-aged commander who was still proudly wearing a highly polished brass SEAL insignia. I'm not sure what they thought of me, but I'd look at their faces and in every class I'd see a Roat, or a Lynch, or a Diebold, or a Yocum, etc., etc. I'd see the combination of strain and determination on their faces. As time went on, I'd see the same classes many times over, and I could literally see the group of individuals transforming into a cohesive unit. They seemed to march with a smoother rhythm. It seemed that the officers and petty officers could give fewer instructions to get the class to do something as a unit. Each man seemed to know what was expected of him. What those observations told me was that the basic elements of training remain intact. Training is hard, to the point of being brutal, and team players succeed.

THOUGHTS FROM FORMER CLASSMATES

UDT/SEAL training has been the only experience of my entire life, where a man was judged solely on his merits and performance with no concern for pedigree, net worth, education, race, or religion. Although life has been very good, nothing has been as exhilarating or fair. I never had an instructor at any university or at Harvard Business School, who matched Sulinski, Waddell, Blais, Spiegel, and Cook. The experience has had a profound impact on my life and how I live it.

Jim Hawes, Member, Class-29

Out of hard times come hard men. This was never more evident to me than in training and Vietnam.

Harry Humphries, Member and Honor Man, Class-29

Being a navy Frogman, and later an instructor, are accomplishments I'll take to my grave.

Bernard Waddell, Instructor, Class-29

I couldn't quit; I would have let my classmates down. I just couldn't do that.

Jesse James Hardy, Member, Class-29

What I learned in training are the three most important words, *attitude*, *attitude*, *attitude*.

Jack Lynch, Member, Class-29

More blood in peace, less in war.

Seriously, John, I was pleased to receive this communiqué. Further, delighted to know that an authentic, tough former U.S. Navy Frogman was actually writing about the making of Frogmen.

Reading the few excerpts you provided leads me to

believe you have the ability to "tell it how it was" honestly, spin the yarn effectively, and hold the reader's attention accordingly. Oh, the pain, and the snot!

I hope, for the Navy, the Teams, and you, that the book is seriously authentic, carefully documented, and holds historical significance. I understand you are already a successful businessman in the field of commercial diving. Congratulations.

Perhaps, this book will depict the true picture of the UDT/SEAL trainee and his magnificent struggle to survive and successfully complete what has been said to be the most arduous training program of its kind in the world.

Some time after Class-29 graduated, I was privileged to relieve Ben Sulinski when he retired, a model Navy Chief and consummate Navy Frogman. John, with the great support, daily, from a superlative UDT instructor staff, we were able to maintain and sometimes intensify the training program.

One last thing, John, for your information, and edification, I successfully completed two UDT training classes, one in 1949 and one in 1956, both in the winter, at Little Creek. I thought you would be pleased to know this since I provided you with so much pain in training. I am proud of you and your effort, John! Drive the spike deeper, daily, while continuing to charge with finesse!

Your friend and former teammate,
Tom Blais, Instructor, Class-29

Training reinforced some of the things my father taught me—don't give up, and "can't" didn't accomplish anything. "Can't" says you are beaten before you start. The above has more meaning, knowing Dad had only one hand. I do not ever recall Dad saying he couldn't do something. He always found a way! UDT-R Training, to me, reinforced those concepts. Training inserted into this attitude, that teamwork by motivated people always could find a way.

Now to the worst part of training, for me it was running—running in the damn sand. I quickly learned to *hate sand.* Wet, dry, in piles, spread out, covered with grass—*I just hate sand.* Thirty-five years later, I still do not go to the beach. *I hate the damn sand!*

Dick Johnson, Member, Class-29

Throughout training I kept having the thought—Well, all they can do is kill me. It seemed to help.

Forrest Dearborn Hedden, Member, Class-29

The experience I had in training and later in UDT-21 has helped me become the kind of person I am today. Hopefully, that means a good husband to my wife and a loving father to my three children. "Quit" never entered my mind going through training.

Trailor L. Lewis, Member, Class-29

I have always been proud that there was only one difference between officers and enlisted men during training. Enlisted men were called low-life worthless scumbags; officers were called low-life worthless scumbags, sir! The group of people I went through training with made me a better officer and man.

Jim C. Walker, Member, Class-29

When I think back on "The Teams," an experience I am forever proud of, which continues to influence me throughout my life, I recall our classmates came from diverse backgrounds and all parts of the country. This group of men, "fired in the hell" of training, created an unequaled bond that has lasted a lifetime. To me, no better words capture the meaning of my feelings for my teammates than:

> "We few, we happy few, we band of brothers; / For he today that sheds his blood with me / Shall be my brother. . . . / And gentlemen . . . now abed / Shall think themselves accursed they were not here / And hold their manhoods cheap whiles any speaks / That fought with us. . . ."
> —Shakespeare, *Henry the Fifth*

David Janke, Member, Class-29

APPENDIX ONE

CLASS-29

HONORS

A. Class record for the mile ocean swim was set by Ens. R. A. Hauff. Time: 29 min., 56 sec.

B. Class record for the obstacle course was set by IC3 R. W. Lester. Time: 12 min., 10 sec.

C. Class record for the timed mile run was set by Ens. J. P. Hunt. Time: 5 min., 9 sec.

D. Class record for the Navy endurance test was set by Ens. J. Hawes with a score of 86.

E. Class average for the ocean mile swim was 35 min., 23 sec.

F. Class average for the timed mile run was 5 min., 50 sec.

Eleven U.S. Naval officers, one officer of the Pakistan Army, one officer of the Royal Dutch Marines, one officer of the Norwegian Navy, and one officer of the Royal Hellenic Navy, four Royal Dutch Marines, and thirty U.S. Navy enlisted men graduated. This comprises 36.57 percent of the total personnel starting the course six months ago; 63.43 percent of those who reported for training last January failed to complete the course.

The outstanding student, class "honor man," based on physical performance, academic marks, proficiency in

UDT techniques, leadership, contribution to class morale, and development of team spirit is Harry J. Humphries.

Author's Note: The navy's percentages on completing training neglect to figure in the over one thousand three hundred sailors who tested for selection to training. Only the top 10 percent of that one thousand three hundred started training. If you run the numbers on one thousand three hundred attempting to start training and forty-nine completing, you get a different picture of what it takes. If you're interested, run the numbers; it will give you something to think about.

GRADUATES OF CLASS-29

Gaston, Thomas L.	Ens.	USN
Gibby, George C.	Lt. (jg)	USN
Hauff, Richard A.	Ens.	USN
Hawes, James M.	Ens.	USN
Hunt, John P.	Ens.	USN
Janke, David C.	Ens.	USN
Johnson, Richard G.	Lt. (jg)	USN
Shea, Richard H.	Lt. (jg)	USN
Swartley, Steven W.	Ens.	USN
Walker, James C.	Ens.	USN
Yocum, Gerald R.	Ens.	USN
Doumouras, A.	Ens.	Greece
Magnussen, Egil O. H.	Lt.	Norway
Qureshi, Hakeem A.	Maj.	Pakistan
Tiel, Alexander E. R.	Lt.	Netherlands
Allen, Carl T.	EM3	USN
Camp, Joseph H.	RM3	USN
Cook, James H.	AA	USN
Coligan, Ralph D.	ADR3	USN

Diebold, Ralph	SN	USN
Dow, Neil G.	AN	USN
Duncan, Leo	SN	USN
Fauls, Raymond A., Jr.	SN	USN
Flockton, Ronald T.	BUL3	USN
Fradenburgh, Richard L.	RDSN	USN
Geiger, Leroy C.	MMFN	USN
Hardy, Jessie J.	SFM3	USN
Hedden, Forrest D., Jr.	SA	USN
Humphries, Harry J.	SN	USN
Jarvi, Ronald E.	BTFN	USN
Kopetski, John C.	RDSN	USN
Leasure, George E., Jr.	SN	USN
Lester, Ronald W.	IC3	USN
Lewis, Trailor L.	SN	USN
Lynch, John R., Jr.	SN	USN
McCutchan, Thomas C.	SM3	USN
Munson, Gene M.	BM3	USN
Neidrauer, Robert A.	BMSN	USN
Risher, Clarence T., III	AMHAN	USN
Roat, John C.	AN	USN
Smith, Paul T.	ETN3	USN
Vaught, Troy E.	EMFN	USN
Winter, Kenneth T.	SN	USN
Woodsworth, Raymond K.	SK3	USN
Youngs, Robert J.	SN	USN
De Beer, Martinus J.	Cpl.	Netherlands
Pauli, Coenraad	Cpl.	Netherlands
Ravensburg, Hendrik J.	Cpl.	Netherlands
Hack, Robertus J.	Pvt.	Netherlands

INSTRUCTORS OF CLASS-29

Tyrie, J. C. Lt. (jg)
Sulinski, B. J. GMGC
Waddell, B. ENC
Blais, T. E. DMC
Parrish, J. H. BMC
Spiegel, H. A. GMGC
Cook, J. F. SMC
Clements, H. C. MN1
Hammond, A. G. MN1
Newell, C. A. AO1
Painter, J. M. HM1
Fraley, E. T. ADR2

These men were our *instructors*. All of them had been trainees themselves. In the case of Tom Blais, he went through training twice. Without the dedication of the instructors, there would be no SEAL Team.

They cared enough for every mother's son to train us hard in peace so we might live if it came to the bad business of war. As Tom Blais said, "More blood in peace, less in war!"

APPENDIX TWO

WARNING ORDER

Prior to every mission in the SEAL Teams, a warning order is given explaining everything that is needed for the upcoming mission. This is your Warning Order! It will give you a guideline of how to prepare for your next mission—Basic Underwater Demolition/SEALS (BUD/S). The key to success at BUD/S is proper preparation prior to arrival.

BUD/S Warning Order

I. Introduction

BUD/S is a challenging and rewarding training program which requires the individual to be self-motivated and physically fit. There is very valuable information in this booklet on subjects such as a course description of all three phases of BUD/S, workouts to get you prepared for the physical stress of BUD/S, and helpful hints on nutrition.

II. History

Sea-Air-Land (SEAL) Teams trace their history back to the first group of volunteers selected

from the Naval Construction Battalions in the
Spring of 1943. Their mission was clearing
obstacles from beaches chosen for amphibious
landings which began the first formal training of
the Naval Combat Demolition Units (NCDUs). The
NCDUs distinguished themselves at Utah and
Omaha beaches in Normandy and in Southern
France. In the Pacific, the NCDUs were consolidated into Underwater Demolition Teams (UDTs).

The newly formed UDTs saw action in every
corner of the Pacific during World War II. In
September 1950, the UDTs participated in the
Korean War at Inchon, Wonsan, Iwon, and
Chinnampo. The redeployment of the United
Nations Forces featured the UDTs conducting
delaying operations using guerilla warfare.

In January 1962, the first SEAL Teams were
commissioned to conduct unconventional
warfare, counter-guerilla warfare and clandestine operations in maritime and riverine environments. These Teams were SEAL Team ONE on
the West Coast and SEAL Team TWO on the East
Coast. During Vietnam, the SEALs compiled an
impressive record of combat success.

Since the close of the Vietnam conflict, the
ever-changing world situation and increased
operational tasking have prompted the
expansion of SEAL Teams in numbers, size, and
capabilities. To effectively respond to this
evolutionary process, Underwater Demolition
Teams have been re-designated as SEAL or SEAL
Delivery Vehicle (SDV) Teams. The newly
designated SEAL Teams acquired the SEAL

mission and retained the amphibious support mission inherited from their UDT forefathers.

SEAL, SEAL Delivery Vehicle (SDV) Teams and Special Boat Units comprise the elite combat units of Naval Special Warfare. These units are organized, trained and equipped to conduct special operations, clandestine maritime and riverine operations, foreign internal defense and unconventional warfare. These highly trained specialists are deployed worldwide in support of fleet and national operations. The wide range of tasks performed by Naval Special Warfare and their outstanding combat records have earned an enduring and highly respected reputation.

Naval Special Warfare extends a personal challenge to those interested individuals like yourself. This program will push you to your physical and mental limits, again and again, until you are hard and strong, both physically and mentally, and ready for the adventure of a life-time in the SEAL Teams. Free fall parachuting at 10,000 feet, traveling by small rubber boat for 100 miles, conducting a mission, then traveling 30 miles out to sea to rendezvous with a submarine is a typical mission for the SEALs and an adven-ture most people can experience only reading books. If you are ready for both a challenge and an adventure, the Navy has just the training to test your mettle. Be Someone Special!!!

As a BUD/S student, you will participate in challenging training and encounter opportunities to develop and test your stamina and leadership. BUD/S training is extremely thorough both physically and mentally; but through adequate preparation and a positive attitude, you can meet its challenges with confidence. The workout schedule in this booklet is designed to prepare you physically for BUD/S. You are the one who has to prepare to give all you have every day. At BUD/S it is essential to live, eat, and sleep BUD/S. 110% is required of you every day. BUD/S is a challenge, but if you meet it head-on with determination not to fail or quit, it will be the most rewarding time of your life. Good Luck!!!

Course Description

I. BUD/S Indoctrination

BUD/S indoctrination is two weeks in length. This is a mandatory course and it is designed to give students an understanding of the technique and performance required of them. The first obstacle is faced when the student must pass the BUD/S Physical Screen Test in order to class up and start training. For further information contact the Physical Training Rehabilitation Remediation (PTRR) office at (619) 437-0861 or (DSN) 577-0861.

II. First Phase (Basic Conditioning)

First Phase is eight weeks in length. Continued physical conditioning in the areas of running, swimming and calisthenics grow harder and harder as the weeks progress. Students will participate in weekly four mile timed runs in boots, timed obstacle courses, swim distances up to two miles wearing fins in the ocean and learn small boat seamanship.

The first four weeks of First Phase prepare you for the fifth week, better known as "Hell Week." During this week, students participate in five and one half days of continuous training, with a maximum of four hours of sleep for the entire week. This week is designed as the ultimate test of one's physical and mental motivation while in First Phase. Hell Week proves to those who make it that the human body can do ten times the amount of work the average man thinks possible. During Hell Week you will learn the value of the mainstay of the SEAL Teams: TEAMWORK! The remaining three weeks are devoted to teaching various methods of conducting hydrographic surveys and how to prepare a hydrographic chart.

III. Second Phase (Diving)

After you have completed First Phase, you have proven to the instructor staff that you are motivated to continue more in-depth training. The diving phase is seven weeks in length. During this period, physical training continues, but the times are lowered for the four mile run, two mile swims, and obstacle course. Second Phase concentrates on combat SCUBA (Self Contained Underwater Breathing Apparatus). Students are taught two types of SCUBA: open circuit (compressed air) and closed circuit (100% oxygen). Emphasis is placed on a progressive dive schedule emphasizing basic combat

swimmer skills that will qualify you as a combat
diver. These skills will enable you to tactically
operate and complete your combat objective. This
is a skill that separates SEALs from all other
Special Operations Forces.

IV. Third Phase (Land Warfare)

The demolitions, reconnaissance, weapons and
tactics phase is ten weeks in length. Physical
training continues to become more strenuous as
the run distances increase and the minimum
passing times are lowered for the runs, swims
and obstacle course. Third Phase concentrates on
teaching land navigation, small-unit tactics,
rappelling, military land and underwater
explosives and weapons training. The final four
weeks of Third Phase are spent on San Clemente
island, where students apply techniques acquired
throughout training in a practical environment.

V. Post-BUD/S Schools

BUD/S graduates receive three weeks basic
parachute training at Army Airborne School,
Fort Benning, Georgia, prior to reporting to their
first Naval Special Warfare Command. Navy
corpsmen who complete BUD/S and Basic
Airborne Training also attend two weeks of
Special Operations Technicians training at the
Naval Special Warfare Center, Coronado. They
also participate in an intense course of
instruction in diving medicine and medical skills
called 18-D (Special Operations Medical Sergeant
Course). This is a 30-week course where

students receive training in burns, gunshot wounds and trauma.

After assignment to a Team and successfully completing a six-month probationary period, qualified personnel are awarded a SEAL Naval Special Warfare Classification (NEC) Code and Naval Special Warfare Insignia. New combat swimmers serve the remainder of their first enlistment (2½ to 3 years) in either an SDV or a SEAL Team. Upon reenlistment, members may be ordered to remainder of a five-year sea tour. Advanced courses include: Sniper School, Dive Supervisor, Language training, SEAL tactical communication and many others. Shore duty opportunities are available in research and development, instructor duty and overseas assignments.

In addition to normal pay and allowances, Naval Special Warfare personnel currently receive $175/month dive pay, $300/month SDV pay, $225/month HALO (jump pay), $110/month special duty assignment pay and $50 to $100/month language proficiency pay for speaking a second language.

Physical Fitness Standards

First Phase

PHYSICAL EVOLUTION	REQUIRED TIME
50 meter underwater swim	PASS/FAIL
Underwater knot tying	PASS/FAIL
Drown Proofing test	PASS/FAIL
Basic Lifesaving test	PASS/FAIL

PHYSICAL EVOLUTION	REQUIRED TIME
1,200 meter pool swim with fins	45 min.
1 mile bay swim with fins	50 min.
1 mile ocean swim with fins	50 min.
1½ mile ocean swim with fins	70 min.
2 mile ocean swim with fins	95 min.
Obstacle course	15 min.
4 mile timed run	32 min.

(Post Hell Week)

PHYSICAL EVOLUTION	REQUIRED TIME
2,000 meter condition pool swim without fins	Completion
1½ mile night bay swim with fins	Completion
2 mile ocean swim with fins	85 min.
4 mile timed run (in boots)	32 min.
Obstacle course	13 min.

Second Phase

PHYSICAL EVOLUTION	REQUIRED TIME
2 mile ocean swim with fins	80 min.
4 mile timed run (in boots)	31 min.
Obstacle course	10:30
3½ mile ocean swim with fins	Completion
5½ mile ocean swim with fins	Completion

Third Phase

PHYSICAL EVOLUTION	REQUIRED TIME
Obstacle course	10 min.
4 mile timed run (in boots)	30 min.
14 mile run	Completion
2 mile ocean swim with fins	75 min.

Academic standards required on written tests
before graduation from BUD/S are:

80% or above for officers	70% or above for enlisted

Suggested Student Preparation

The following workouts are designed for two
categories of people: Category I are those future
BUD/S students that have never or have not
recently been on a routine PT program. Category
II is designed for high school and college athletes
that have had a routine PT program. Usually
athletes that require a high level of
cardiovascular activity are in Category II.

Swimming, running and wrestling are good
examples of such sports that work out your
cardiovascular system.

Workout for Category I

Running: The majority of the physical
activities you will be required to perform during
your six months of training at BUD/S will
involve running. The intense amount of running

can lead to overstress injuries of the lower
extremities in trainees who arrive not physically
prepared to handle the activities. Swimming,
bicycling, and lifting weights will prepare you for
some of the activities at BUD/S, but ONLY
running can prepare your lower extremities for
the majority of the activities. You should also
run in boots to prepare your legs for the
everyday running in boots at BUD/S (Boots
should be of a lightweight varity, i.e., Bates
Lights, Hi-Tec, etc.).

The goal of the category I student is to work
up to 16 miles per week of running. After you
have achieved that goal then and only then
should you continue on to the category II goal of
30 miles per week. Let me remind you that
category I is a nine week build up program.
Follow the workout as best you can and you will
be amazed at the progress you will make.

Running Schedule I

Running Schedule

Weeks	Exercise	Amount
Weeks #1, 2:	2 miles/day, 8:30 pace	M/W/F (6 miles/week)
Week #3:	No running. High risk of stress fractures	
Week #4:	3 miles/day	M/W/F (9 miles/wk)
Weeks #5, 6:	2/3/4/2 miles	M/Tu/Th/F (11 miles/wk)

Weeks	Exercise	Amount
Weeks #7, 8:	4/4/5/3 miles	M/Tu/Th/F (16 miles/wk)
Week #9:	same as #7, 8	M/Tu/Th/F (16 miles/wk)

Physical Training Schedule I
(Monday/Wednesday/Friday)

Week Number	Sets of Repetitions	Week Number	Sets of Repetitions
	4×15 push-ups		6×25 push-ups
Week #1:	4×20 sit-ups	Weeks #5, 6:	6×25 sit-ups
	3×3 pull-ups		2×8 pull-ups
	5×20 push-ups		6×30 push-ups
Week #2:	5×20 sit-ups	Weeks #7, 8:	6×30 sit-ups
	3×3 pull-ups		2×10 pull-ups
	5×25 push-ups		6×30 push-ups
Weeks #3, 4:	5×25 sit-ups	Week #9:	6×30 sit-ups
	3×4 pull-ups		3×10 pull-ups

*Note: For best results, alternate exercise. Do a set of push-ups, then a set of sit-ups, followed by a set of pull-ups, immediately with no rest.

Swimming Schedule I
(sidestroke with no fins 4–5 days a week)

Weeks #1, 2:   Swim continuously for 15 min.

Weeks #3, 4:   Swim continuously for 20 min.

Weeks #5, 6:   Swim continuously for 25 min.

Weeks #7, 8:   Swim continuously for 30 min.

Week #9:   Swim continuously for 35 min.

*Note: If you have no access to a pool, ride
a bicycle for twice as long as you would
swim. If you do have access to a pool, swim
every day available. Four to five days a week
and 200 meters in one session is your initial
workup goal.

Also, you want to develop your sidestroke
on both the left and right side. Try to swim
50 meters in one minute or less.

Workout for Category II

Category II is a more intense workout
designed for those who have been involved
with a routine PT schedule or those who have
completed the requirements for category I. Do
not attempt this workout schedule unless you
can complete the Week 9 level of Category I
workouts.

Running Schedule II

Weeks	Days M/Tu/Th/F/Sa	Total Distance
Weeks #1, 2:	3/5/4/5/2 miles	19 miles/week
Weeks #3, 4:	4/5/6/4/3 miles	22 miles/week
Week #5:	5/5/6/4/4 miles	24 miles/week
Week #6:	5/6/6/6/4 miles	27 miles/week
Week #7:	6/6/6/6/6 miles	30 miles/week

*Note: For Weeks #8–9 and beyond, it is not necessary to increase the distance of the runs; work on the speed of your 6 mile runs and try to get them down to 7:30 per mile or lower. If you wish to increase the distance of your runs, do it gradually: no more than one mile per day increase for every Week beyond Week #9.

Physical Training Schedule II
(Monday/Wednesday/Friday)

Week Number	Sets of Repetitions
	6×30 push-ups

Weeks #1, 2:	6×35 sit-ups
	3×10 pull-ups
	3×20 dips

Weeks #3, 4:	10×20 push-ups
	10×25 sit-ups
	4×10 pull-ups
	10×15 dips

Week #5:	15×20 push-ups
	15×25 sit-ups
	4×12 pull-ups
	15×15 dips

Week #6:	20×20 push-ups
	20×25 sit-ups
	5×12 pull-ups
	20×15 dips

These workouts are designed for long-distance muscle endurance. Muscle fatigue will gradually take a longer and longer time to develop doing high repetition workouts. For best results, alternate exercises each set, in order to rest that muscle group for a short time. The below listed workouts are provided for varying your workouts once you have met the category I and II standards.

Pyramid Workouts

You can do this with any exercise. The object is to slowly build up to a goal, then build back down to the beginning of the workout. For

instance, pull-ups, sit-ups, push-ups, and dips
can be alternated as in the above workouts, but
this time choose a number to be your goal and
build up to that number. Each number counts as
a set. Work your way up and down the pyramid.
For example, say your goal is "5":

Exercise	# of Repetitions
pull-ups:	1, 2, 3, 4, 5, 4, 3, 2, 1
push-ups:	2, 4, 6, 8, 10, 8, 6, 4, 2 (2×#pull-ups)
sit-ups:	3, 6, 9, 12, 15, 12, 9, 6, 3 (3×#pull-ups)
dips:	same as push-ups

Swimming Workout II
(4–5 days/week)

Weeks #1, 2:	Swim continuously for 35 min.
Weeks #3, 4:	Swim continuously for 45 min. with fins.
Week #5:	Swim continuously for 60 min. with fins.
Week #6:	Swim continuously for 75 min. with fins.

*Note: At first, to reduce initial stress on your
foot muscles when starting with fins, alternate

swimming 1,000 meters with fins and
1,000 meters without them. Your goal
should be to swim 50 meters in 45 seconds
or less.

Stretch PT

Since Mon/Wed/Fri are devoted to PT, it is
wise to devote at least 20 minutes on
Tue/Thu/Sat to stretching. You should always
stretch for at least 15 minutes before any
workout; however, just stretching the previously
worked muscles will make you more flexible and
less likely to get injured. A good way to start
stretching is to start at the top and go to the
bottom. Stretch to tightness, not to pain; hold for
10–15 seconds. Do not bounce. Stretch every
muscle in your body from the neck to the calves,
concentrating on your thighs, hamstrings, chest,
back, and shoulders.

Nutrition

Proper nutrition is extremely important now
and especially when you arrive at BUD/S. You
must make sure you receive the necessary
nutrients to obtain maximum performance
output during exercise and to promote
muscle/tissue growth and repair. The proper diet
provides all the nutrients for the body's needs
and supplies energy for exercise. It also
promotes growth and repair of tissue and
regulates the body processes. The best source of
complex carbohydrates are potatoes, pasta, rice,

fruits, vegetables. These types of foods are your best sources of energy.

Carbohydrates, protein, and fat are the three energy nutrients. All three can provide energy, but carbohydrates are the preferred source of energy for physical activity. It takes at least 20 hours after exhaustive exercise to completely restore muscle energy, provided 600 grams of carbohydrates are consumed per day. During successive days of heavy training, like you will experience at BUD/S, energy stores prior to each training session become progressively lower. This is a situation in which a high carbohydrate diet can help maintain your energy.

The majority of carbohydrates should come from complex carbohydrate foods that include bread, crackers, cereal, beans, peas, starchy vegetables, and other whole grain or enriched grain products. Fruits are also loaded with carbohydrates. During training, more than four servings of these food groups should be consumed daily.

Water intake is vital; stay hydrated. You should be consuming up to four quarts of water daily. Drink water before you get thirsty!!! Substances such as alcohol, caffeine, and tobacco increase your body's need for water. Too much of these substances will definitely harm your body and hinder your performance. Supplemental intake of vitamins, as well, has not been proven to be beneficial. If you are eating a well balanced diet, there is no need to take vitamins.

Training Table Concept

Nutrient	Intake
Carbohydrates	50–70% of calories
Protein	10–15% of calories
Fats	20–30% of calories

Applying for BUD/S Training

In-Service Candidates

Requirements and procedures for BUD/S training application.

Package Requirements:

1. Meet ASVAB test score requirement

2. Meet age, EAOS, and rating requirement (page 13 may be required)

3. Pass physical screening test

4. Pass diving physical

Procedures:

1. Put in a "Special Request Chit" through your chain of command requesting BUD/S Training.

2. Submit a "Personnel Action Request" (Form 1306/7) to SPECWAR/Diver

assignment. Submit the following with your request:

- A certified copy of your ASVAB test scores
- Your physical screening test results
- Pressure and oxygen tolerance test results (if completed)
- Your completed diving physical (Form SF88-SF93)
- Certified copy of your last performance evaluation report

3. Mail your package to:

SPECWAR/Diver Assignment
BUPERS PERS401D1
5720 Integrity Drive
Millington, TN 38055-0000
Phone Number:
Com. (901) 874-3622 • DSN 882-3622

All Candidates

Requirements

Physical/Mental

1. Pass a diving physical exam
2. Eyesight cannot be worse than 20/40 in one eye and 20/70 in the other eye and must be correctable to 20/20 with no color blindness
3. Minimum ASVAB score: VE + AR = 104, MC = 50
4. Must be 28 years old or less
5. Only men are eligible
6. Must be a U.S. citizen

Physical Screen Test

1. 500 yard swim using breast and/or side stroke in 12:30—Ten minute rest
2. Perform Minimum of 42 push-ups in 2 minutes—Two minute rest
3. Perform minimum of 50 sit-ups in 2 minutes—Two minute rest
4. Perform at least 6 pull-ups, no time limit—Ten minute rest
5. Run 1.5 miles, wearing boots and pants, in 11:30

*Note: As a reminder, there are no maximums on these physical tests. The prospective trainee should provide the best scores possible, i.e., give his best effort.

Points of Contact

SEAL Recruiter West Coast	SEAL Recruiter East Coast	Officer Detailer Bureau of Naval
Naval Special Warfare	NSWC DET Little Creek	Personnel
2446 Trident Way	1340 Helicopter Road	Pers 416, BLDG 791
San Diego, CA 92155-5494	Norfolk, VA 23521-2945	Millington, TN 38054-2014
Com. (619) 437-2049/ 437-5009	Com. (757) 363-4128	Com. (901) 874-3911
DSN 577-2049/5009	DSN 864-4128	DSN 882-3911
FAX: Com. (619) 437-2018		
DSN 577-2018		

SEAL Detailer   Dive Motivators (SEAL)
SPECWAR/Diver Assignment   BLDG 1405
BUPERS PERS401D1   Recruit Training
5720 Integrity Drive   Command
Millington, TN 38055-0000   Great Lakes, IL 60088
Com. (901) 874-3622   Com. (847) 688-4643
DSN 882-3622   DSN 792-4643

E-mail: recruiting@navspecwarcen.navy.mil
Toll-free Info Line: 1-888-USN-SEAL

For more detailed information about the Navy
SEALs contact:

Public Affairs Office
Naval Special Warfare Command
Naval Amphibious Base Coronado
San Diego, CA 92155-5037
(619) 437-3920

APPENDIX THREE

TWO CLASS-29S?

Yes, two groups of men suffered under the class number of 29, and mine wasn't the first. Today there is one training unit in Coronado, California; in our day there was a training unit on each coast. Our Class-29 was the East Coast class, at Little Creek, Virginia. The West Coast Class-29 took place in Coronado, California. It commenced 23 August 1962 and graduated 10 December 1962. East Coast Class-29 commenced training 2 January 1963 and graduated 28 June 1963.

Why was our class longer? Because the West Coast guys still had Jump School to do. That was accomplished after they graduated into the Teams. Most of the West Coast guys became jump qualified at army jump school, Fort Benning, Georgia; the rest took jump school in Okinawa. They also had completed their dive training in the main body of UDT-RT (Underwater Demolition Team Replacement Training), as it is done today in BUD/S (Basic Underwater Demolition and SEAL Training).

One little funny side note, the guys on the West Coast called us "East Coast Pukes," and we called them "Hollywood Frogmen." The funny part is with all BUD/S training done in Coronado, California, the guys stationed on either coast still claim they are better SEALs than those on the other. God bless strong competition!

After Vietnam kicked off, many of both classes of 29 would serve together. Like our class, many of the West

Coast guys have kept track of each other. After I got out of the navy, I worked with three West Coast 29s as a commercial diver—John Phillip House (the artist Barney Steel), George Falk Layton, and Billy Ray Ledford, all topflight hands.

Another member of Class-29 West was Kenneth Craig Marley. He and Billy Ray Ledford were selected for training from boot camp, a vary rare thing. Craig and our own David Janke operated together in Vietnam. A couple of years before I started this book, Craig wrote several pages about his Class 29. With his permission, I'm going to quote one of the paragraphs:

> Class 29 has many stories to tell. Each one of us has his own special view of what it took to overcome the stress test, the physical and mental torment, the cold, the obstacle course, the ocean swims, night problems, and Hell Week. Each of us dealt with our fear, pain, and sheer exhaustion in our own silent way. When one of the trainees broke, they were immediately removed from the ranks. Those remaining looked around to the left and right, mentally calculating the number still in the program, and shared a brief moment of victory over the elements with their teammates.

R. D. Russell, another graduate of 29 West, has invited us East Coast Puke 29ers to join the Hollywood Frogmen 29ers at the graduation of BUD/S Class 229 on June 23, 2000. What a good idea! For you computer guys interested in the Teams, R.D. and his wife Pam run the best Team Web site on the Internet, U.S. Naval Special Warfare Archives. Their mission statement: "To record the history and build and maintain the archives of special warfare in the U.S. Navy, to authenticate the credentials of the members of the special warfare community in the

U.S. Navy, and to act as a communication clearinghouse for the special warfare community in the U.S. Navy. A collection of the military records, photographs, and written works of the men of the Scouts & Raiders, NCDU, UDT, and SEALs." You can find their Web site at www.navyfrogmen.com.

GRADUATES OF CLASS-29 WEST COAST

Arsenault, Donald E. IC3
Boyd, John Theodore Ens.
Brown, William Morel FN
Cannon, James Anthony SA
Clark, Bobby Lee SN
Coates, Richard J. SA
Devine, David Eugene SA
Dorfi, Michael Norman SA
Dulin, Duane R. SA
Edmiston, Edgar Bartly SA
Eskotter, Anthony W. SA
Hicks, Michael Randolph FTG3
House, John Phillip SN
Howard, Calvin M. FN
Jones, Luther Glen SA
Kelley, Robert Edward ADJ1
Kibler, Robert Louis SA
Kruger, Gary A. SA
Layton, George Falk SA
Ledford, Billy Ray SA
Lee, Henry K. SN
Malak, Thomas J. SN
Marley, Kenneth Craig SA
Matherne, Albert R. SA
McNair, Martin Bennett Ens.

Rand, Brian Thomas SA
Russell, Bruce Thomas BM3
Russell, Robert Doyle SA
Sawyer, Willits Herbert Lt. (jg)
Sheridan, Robert Randall SHSN
Tune, Harold Noble SA
Vonalvensleben, Michael J. SMSN
Wardrobe, James Eugene YN3
White, William Thornton, III Ens.
Wilber, Robert Charles SA
Withers, Ronald Maurice SN
Witter, Peter Cox Ens.
Wonneman, Carl C. SA
Wooten, James Perry Ens.
Wrightnour, George Brooks Lt. (jg)
Yoakum, Howard Kenneth SA

Do you know where
your swim buddy is?

There is no winning for those who won't dare the loss. There is no winning for those who won't lose and get back up. God made it so!

—John Carl Roat